# Prosody and Poetics
# in the Early Middle Ages

*Essays in Honour of*
*C.B. Hieatt*

C.B. Hieatt

# Prosody and Poetics
# in the Early Middle Ages
*Essays in Honour of*
*C.B. Hieatt*

Edited by M.J. Toswell

UNIVERSITY OF TORONTO PRESS
Toronto Buffalo London

© University of Toronto Press Incorporated 1995
Toronto Buffalo London
Printed in Canada

ISBN 0-8020-0653-1

Printed on acid-free paper

**Canadian Cataloguing in Publication Data**

Main entry under title:

Prosody and poetics in the early Middle Ages :
essays in honour of C.B. Hieatt

Based on a conference held at the University of
Western Ontario, Mar. 4–6, 1993.
Includes bibliography.
ISBN 0-8020-0653-1

1. English poetry – Old English, ca. 450–1100 –
History and criticism – Congresses.    2. English
poetry – Middle English, 1100–1500 – History and
criticism – Congresses.    3. English language –
Versification – Congresses.    4. Epic poetry, English
(Old) – History and criticism – Congresses.
I. Toswell, M. J.    II. Hieatt, Constance B., 1928–

PR205.P76 1995        829'.1        C94-932538-4

University of Toronto Press acknowledges the financial assistance to its
publishing program of the Canada Council and the Ontario Arts Council.

# Contents

# Foreword

JAMES M. GOOD

Having, as a student, left the University of Western Ontario for New York's Columbia University in 1965, I returned as faculty four years later to find Western changed. A major alteration was the presence of the Hieatts, Kent and Connie, who in the interim had departed that American metropolis to seek sanctuary in southwestern Ontario. It was a time of protest in the United States, with graduate students facing the military draft and occupying university presidents' offices to register dissatisfaction.

Yet I doubt if Constance Hieatt was – or would be – fleeing anything. Canadian universities, with strong academic traditions and good students coming out of rigorous secondary school programs, were healthy and growing. Western's English Department, under the new leadership of the late Professor Paul Fleck, was vital and energetic, a mixture of the young idealism of recent junior appointments and the more experienced presence of those well schooled in the cultures of the University of Toronto and beyond. With her Yale thesis defended in 1957 and almost a decade behind her of teaching at the City University of New York and St John's University, Professor Hieatt recognized opportunity. Western had the foresight to realize the contributions she and her husband Kent could make.

The scholarly achievement is a matter of record, well documented in bibliographies and citations. Less easily captured, perhaps, is that cosmopolitan presence that offered leadership and guidance. Connie is a gracious and accomplished hostess who did more than her share of bringing this academic community together in relaxed and convivial settings. She showed a real and sympathetic interest in the work of younger colleagues. She also held a no-nonsense view of the commitment necessary to scholarly pursuits, and expected of others the high standards she set for herself.

This volume is the product of much work by many people who know and understand Professor Constance Hieatt's place in her profession. It is a tribute to what could be termed 'the Hieatt Years' at the University of Western Ontario, an era already viewed with nostalgia and one not likely soon to return.

Dean, Faculty of Arts, University of Western Ontario

# Preface

M.J. TOSWELL

It is an old axiom that how you say something is as important as what is being said, an axiom which is arguably the overriding principle of the scholarly career of Constance B. Hieatt. Since she defended her Ph.D. thesis at Yale in 1957, and went on to teach first at St John's University in New York and for the past twenty-five years as a member of the Department of English at the University of Western Ontario, Constance Hieatt has been concerned with communication. She has communicated her interest in matters medieval with the broadest possible range of people. Her audience has included the children who enjoyed her series of translations of medieval romances, the teenagers who studied (as I did in high school) the facing-page translation and edition she and her husband, A.K. Hieatt, produced of Chaucer's *Canterbury Tales* – an edition which incidentally has recently been translated into Japanese – as well as scholars in a wide variety of medieval disciplines. In the last decade she has turned her attention (or at least part of her attention, since Connie normally has more major projects in progress than any other three scholars) to another mode of communication: that of the production of food. She has edited, alone and jointly with Sharon Butler, several cookbooks, including the very popular *Pleyn Delit*, which has brought medieval cookery out of the manuscripts and back into the kitchens of the world. For an academic audience she has written important articles and books on such diverse topics as medieval falconry, Old and Middle English dream visions, structural and lexical patterns in *Beowulf*, the Old Norse saga of Charlemagne (*Karlamagnus saga*), hypermetric lines in Old English poetry, Middle English debate poetry, and Old French romances. Furthermore, she is a dedicated teacher, having produced not only texts but also computer programs for the teaching of Old English to undergraduate and graduate students at Western. Finally, as a member of the Royal Society of Canada since the early 1980s, she has communicated the concerns of scholars to the community at large. In all of these endeavours Connie's concern has been to speak and write clearly and succinctly, to take apart, as it were, the bones of her material and reveal its hidden interests.

It was not difficult, as a result, to organize a conference in honour of Connie Hieatt, and the one held from 4 to 6 March 1993 at Western attracted more than sixty participants, despite a major snowstorm. Co-organized by Peter Auksi and me, the conference included twenty-four papers and a splendid medieval banquet whose recipes were all drawn from the honorand's books. Because we had to concentrate on one aspect of Connie's scholarship as a focus for the conference, we chose heroic poetry, and encouraged participants to focus on the prosody of early medieval poetry if possible. Most of the papers in this volume were delivered at that conference, which received support from a number of sources: funding from the Department of English, the Seminar for Medieval and Renaissance Studies, and the Faculty of Arts at UWO, and also a grant in aid of the conference and this publication from the Social Sciences and Humanities Research Council of Canada. In addition to providing tangible aid, Alan Somerset and Paul Gaudet (Chairs of the Department of English the year before and the year of the conference, respectively) and Tom Lennon and Jim Good (Deans of Arts the year of and the year following the conference) all helped with arrangements for the conference and for this book. I am also grateful to those speakers who so graciously withdrew their papers when it became clear that a volume focused on matters prosodic and poetic was emerging; they include Karen Arthur, D.M.R. Bentley, George Clark, Rosalind Clark, Patrick Deane, Robert E. Finnegan, Richard Firth Green, Richard Harris, Brenda Hosington, Joyce Lionarons, and Paul Szarmach. John Leyerle delivered the banquet address. Among the graduate students who helped with the arrangements for the conference were Brock Eayrs, Angela Kelly, Peter Roccia, and Susan Terry. Many other colleagues and friends deserve notice, but the exigencies of time and space require that I stop here with the hope that Constance Hieatt will enjoy reading these papers as much as their authors have enjoyed learning from her.

University of Western Ontario
Trinity 1994

Prosody and Poetics
in the Early Middle Ages

*Essays in Honour of*
*C.B. Hieatt*

# Introduction

M.J. TOSWELL

This collection of articles on the prosody and poetics of medieval verse consists mostly of papers delivered at a March 1993 conference in honour of C.B. Hieatt and subsequently revised for publication. Two former graduate students and one current one present papers in this volume. Douglas Moffat brings together modern linguistics and early Middle English prosody to produce a convincing new model for Laȝamon's approach to metre, and Brian Shaw undertakes a close analysis of the Old English *Andreas* to determine the power which the words of the hero wield in that poem. James Keddie, in a preview of his thesis on comparative Old English and Old Norse metre, presents a new approach to the analysis of resolution, using *Beowulf* as the test case for his theory. David Megginson also attended the conference as a former student of the honorand, having been attracted to medieval literature by her undergraduate Old English course at Western. His paper considers the myth of the general Old English poetic dialect, documenting its origin, rise to prominence, and subsequent fall in order to point out the importance of precision and accurate terminology when we consider this material, and the need for careful historiography of the assumptions made by other scholars – if only to remind us of the need constantly to examine our own first principles.

Other papers in the volume come from long-standing friends, colleagues, and admirers of C.B. Hieatt. Eric Stanley considers the heroic vocabulary and ethos of a number of Old English riddles. Robert Creed and Mark Griffith both turn their attention to *The Battle of Maldon*, Creed to consider the metre as a manifestation of the poem's performance, and Griffith to consider the thematic and stylistic effects of the proper names in the poem. From widely divergent points of view, they come to the same conclusion: *The Battle of*

*Maldon* poet was a sophisticated practitioner of the art. Two papers, those of T.A. Shippey and John Miles Foley, concern themselves with speeches in early medieval poetry. Shippey, in a paper making use of modern linguistics in a manner analogous to that employed by Doug Moffat, considers the speeches of *Hamðismal* and the ways in which they are integral to the meaning and purpose of that Old Norse poem. Foley parallels Brian Shaw's paper in that he also considers *Andreas*, but his focus is a particular passage of what he felicitously terms 'performance anxiety' on the part of the poet. Geoffrey Russom similarly parallels James Keddie in approaching the problem of resolution in *Beowulf*, but his paper reaches a different conclusion, and by a different route. Duncan Macrae-Gibson, who has collaborated with the honorand in the production of computer teaching programs, turns his expertise to the development of a computer program for the analysis of Old English metre and makes a provisional report, with his co-author J.D. Lishman, of the results of this research. And, to take the first paper last, Tom Cable considers the Middle English alliterating long line in some detail, revisiting the vexed question of final *-e* and its implications for the metrical analysis of Middle English verse.

A second link among these papers is, however, also present. What all of these papers have in common is a concern with the style of the poetry. Style is a word which has been strangely absent from recent criticism of Old English and early Middle English poetry, partly because it is difficult to define, partly because other concerns such as the typological, historical, political, and social backgrounds of the poems have been at the forefront of recent scholarship, and partly because to discuss style is to engage in evaluation – which is a procedure generally kept implicit. That is, the texts studied and analysed are considered as much for their excellence, or their uniqueness, in connecting meaning with form, but the pretence that has recently held sway suggests that a particular poem bears reading rather for its cultural construction than for its intrinsic merits. The notion that texts are entirely social constructs, however, intersects rather too neatly with the 'New Critical' analysis of texts for their literary excellence when both approaches continue to be applied to the same collection of texts. The papers in this volume suggest both implicitly and explicitly that whatever cultural constructions are relevant to the poetry of Anglo-Saxon and Anglo-Norman England, the poems remain worthy of study in and of themselves. The intrinsic merits of these texts are, however, rarely elucidated in such a way as to create an even-handed approach to the wide range of early medieval poems. Such an approach might help to situate the stylistic analysis of medieval verse in the eddying cross-currents of 'modern (or 'postmodern') and 'traditional,' 'theoretical' and 'humanistic' approaches to the surviving texts of the period.

The study of style could establish a set of criteria and a series of ways to approach individual poems and passages from poems which would permit more coherent analysis of these works. The first requirement of such an approach is the establishment of some general definition of what style constitutes for these poems. That general definition of what the study of style in early medieval verse includes is, however, more difficult than might be expected. As with many other apparent abstractions, style is constituted differently in the approach and analysis of every student of the poetry. Style is not at all a transparent and eternal given. Because my own field is Old English, I am going to concentrate in the next few pages on consideration of these issues in the standard critical commentaries on Old English literature in order to suggest some of the ways in which style has been defined and elucidated. Similar results can be obtained through consultation of the frequently read works on early Middle English verse.

The well-known reference works and analyses of Old English literature evince little agreement about the definition and exemplification of style in the poetry. In her book, Barbara Raw includes a chapter titled 'Rhythm and Style,' in which she analyses the rhythmical and alliterative patterns of the verse, pointing out the *Beowulf* poet's skill in varying his rhythmic patterns so that heavily stressed verses occur at crucial points in the action.[1] The style of discourse in the speeches of different characters varies according to the content and purpose of the speech, not according to the individual speaking. The high style – which is not clearly defined – corresponds to lofty subjects and is marked by its distance from prose in rhythm, syntax, and vocabulary. Milton McC. Gatch, in his introduction to the subject, refers not to style *per se*, but defines the 'method the singer used in performing his task' as depending on three things: the use of formulas and other mnemonic devices, the prosody of Germanic poetry, and the use of accompaniment.[2] In C.L. Wrenn's study, the third chapter in the section labelled 'General Features,' titled 'Form and Style in Anglo-Saxon Literature,' includes a discussion of the basic pattern of the verse with a detailed analysis of the metre, and points out that 'the poetic vocabulary and style were exceptionally remote from those of ordinary speech.'[3] The diction abounds in 'oral-formulaic' inherited phrases, synonyms or near-synonyms, other descriptive and figurative periphrases, and an abundance of figurative words and phrases. At the end of the chapter he argues: 'It will be appropriate to conclude this exposition of metre with some references to the development of prose generally, especially in its relations with verse in matters of style, rhythm, and the employment of alliteration.'[4] To Wrenn, therefore, style is a mixture of diction and metre, with some acknowledgment of an oral-formulaic tradition of composition.

For T.A. Shippey the matter is somewhat more complex. The principles of poetic production are unity, relevance, ambiguity, and individuality. However, he says, 'in Old English, style is not the man.'[5] The verse is a learnt technique with almost a separate poetic language, and we must consider the originality of Old English poetry based on the interrelation of language and subject-matter. In his fourth chapter, entitled 'Language and Style,' Shippey therefore considers the manuscript context, the historical phonology, and the parallels of phraseology which suggest an oral-formulaic theory of poetic composition rather than creation, only then turning to a description of metre.[6] He argues that four types of intangible pressure contribute to the form of Old English verse: compounding, metre, rank, and alliterative collocations of particular words. Finally, there is a limited set of syntactic patterns, and what gives a poem its individual voice is the remarkable variation which can exist within a strongly homogeneous form. Shippey's work is perhaps the most systematic approach to style in Old English poetry so far available. Even he, however, is unable to determine a clear set of categories and subheadings for the analysis of style in this verse.

More recently, the revised version of Stanley Greenfield's history begins with the remarkable claim that 'Anglo-Saxon prose and poetry are the major literary achievement of the early Middle Ages' and argues on the next page that 'Old English poetry presents stylistically a unique body of material in which oral poetic techniques fuse with literary or rhetorical methods.'[7] In his fifth chapter, he provides, in only eight pages, what he euphemistically entitles 'Some Remarks on the Nature and Quality of Old English Poetry,' and suggests that scholars have examined the rhythmic and phonemic principles and practices of Old English poetry, and have devoted considerable attention to the nature of its diction and to aspects of its style. Quite what 'style' is remains a bit uncertain here, but it seems to include variation as defined by Brodeur, sound patterns, paronomasia and etymological word-play, interlace patterns, and the linguistic and semantic 'facts' that permit us to edit and emend Old English texts, or that restrict us from doing so. This is a useful collection of stylistic aspects, but hardly represents a coherent framework within which to approach the style of an individual work.

Unfortunately, in the most recent introductory text on Old English literature, style seems hardly to exist. The *Cambridge Companion to Old English Literature* is a text which seems virtually to have ignored the existence of style as a feature of Old English poetry.[8] In the index to this volume there are nine references to metre, four to the kenning, and three to oral tradition – but none for style. Variation appears on occasion in the text, but does not receive an entry in the index.[9] The only chapter to concern itself with what the material so far surveyed would suggest is style is Donald G. Scragg's 'The

Nature of Old English Verse,' which discusses the metre, use of variation, synonyms and poetic compounds, and kennings with epithets.[10] The next mention of style in the volume is F.C. Robinson's statement that 'The style and metre of *Beowulf* is essentially that of other early Germanic poems.'[11] Robinson mentions style explicitly on two more occasions, suggesting on one of them that 'in few poems is style so important, a fact which makes *Beowulf* a notoriously difficult challenge for the translator.'[12] After this, the contributors to the volume confine themselves exclusively to analyses of themes, allusions, ideas, and sources. Only in the last paper of the volume is metre again discussed, when Patrizia Lendinara points out the Anglo-Saxon fascination with Latin metre, as proven by the treatises and examples of both Bede and Aldhelm.[13] Other than Lendinara's and Robinson's comments, then, this introduction to the world of Old English literature does not acknowledge, either explicitly or implicitly, the issues surrounding the definition and study of style in this material.

It seems, then, that the study of style has lost its charm. Of late, Anglo-Saxonists have involved themselves in large projects, in establishing all the sources of early medieval writings in Britain, in defining all the words used (insofar as we can determine them from the written record), and in reorganizing and reproducing all the manuscripts of the period. This, perhaps, is an answer to the uncertainty about knowledge and to the theoretical sophistication which characterizes the study of literature of more recent periods. Having always been aware of the profound uncertainty of knowledge and the ambiguity inherent in any interpretation of the surviving texts, students of Old and early Middle English literature have reacted by choosing to establish whatever facts are clearly available.[14] The result has been avoidance, perhaps unknowingly, of some of the elements which draw readers to this material in the first place. The poetry, and particularly its style, is something that we all describe as 'complex,' 'sophisticated,' 'extraordinarily compressed,' or simply 'dense and difficult.' Further, we teach specific poems to undergraduates on the grounds that they are somehow more worthy of study than others.[15] Any coherent justification of the canon of literature studied by undergraduate and graduate students must involve some relatively formal consideration of the evaluative techniques used and the criteria for evaluation established in the search for suitable texts. Perhaps the most appropriate way to approach these issues is by making use of the recently developed approach of that branch of linguistics known as stylistics.

The study of stylistics concentrates on variation in the use of language, often, but not exclusively, with special attention to the most conscious and complex uses of language in literature.[16] Literary language itself uses linguistic elements to build new schemes of its own, adding new rules of metre and line length, of word order and the choice of vocabulary to the existing rules of ordinary language. The first problem here for consideration of Old English literature in general is that of the distinction drawn between literary and non-literary language. It is not entirely safe to assume that the surviving poetry all falls into the category of 'literature.' Furthermore, every word written in Old English shows a conscious choice of the vernacular, a choice which, in these unilingual and supposedly non-hierarchical days, we find progressively more difficult to comprehend. Finally, that Old English poetry was recorded in the manuscripts in such a way as to render completely obscure its taut metrical structure and sophisticated syntax is one of the truisms of the subject. Nevertheless, the schemes of language which appear in Old English poems easily lend themselves to the kind of stylistic analysis that relates them to their contexts and observes the intricate patterns that emerge from the interference of one scheme with another. Particularly interesting for stylistics would be the lack of a single scheme, and the presence in a single text of dual or multiple schemes, a kind of interaction that would complicate the possibilities of choice and subtlety of effect. Rather than drawing from the complexities that result from this interplay, stylistics prefers to consider what parameters have affected the individual choices in question.

The study of style, then, is a consideration of five elements of linguistic interaction: sounds, syntax, vocabulary, context, and register. The sounds involve not just the phonemics of particular alliterative effects but also the metrical structure of the poem, its use of rhythm and pause, and the coincidence or lack thereof of grammatical pause with the end of a poetic line. The basis of Old English verse is stress, and the metrical scheme depends on a norm of four stresses. The syllabic flow of these stresses is such that verses (half-lines) with one or two words generally are preferable to those with a series of monosyllabic words. Finally, sounds involve intonation, something which in the absence of a native speaker is well-nigh impossible to consider. Remarkably, however, Douglas Moffat here illuminates the versifying of Laȝamon's *Brut* precisely by applying the linguistics of intonation to the verse line of that poet.

Although the issues of prosody raised in many of the papers in this volume are also connected with the other categories of stylistic analysis, the first stop for matters prosodic remains the sounds and rhythms of the language. Both James Keddie and Duncan Macrae-Gibson are concerned in their papers with the prediction of prosodic rhythm in Old English poetry. Both wish, after such prediction, to analyse the results in terms of the diction, context, register, and syntax of the poetry, and both attempt to approach this material from the standpoint of the objective listener. The signal difference in their work is that Keddie posits the response of a native speaker somewhat acquainted with the rhythms of Old English speech, while Macrae-Gibson (aided by John Lishman) feeds the prosodic parameters into a modern-day computer, the ultimate example of the disinterested observer. Geoffrey Russom works the other way around, from inside *Beowulf*, to determine what rules for resolution are generated by close attention to the phonological and syntactical structures of Old English poetry, and produces a set of principles based on those observations. He concludes that Old English poetic structure is a series of persistent structures in the linguistic sense, and that the Old English poetic system is a coherent and comprehensible one. His careful analysis points out precisely where the schemes of Old English poetry interact to produce a subtle and complex series of effects. Starting with the Laȝamon poet, Thomas Cable points out that the most important phonological change for the structure of later Middle English verse was the silencing of final -*e*; he argues for the metrical implications of that spelling. This discussion of the implications of orthography for the analysis of sounds thus combines an analysis of the graphology of phonemes with the metrical grammar of the text. Finally, Robert P. Creed uses metrical evidence as a guide to performance, extrapolating from the surviving text of *The Battle of Maldon* to a set of principles guiding the metrical and syntactic structure of Old English verse. His paper, like that of Cable, overlaps the analysis of sounds with the syntax to consider both stylistic entities as affecting the production of the complicated schemes used in the poem.

The syntax of Old English verse embodies a kind of paradox. It is, as Bruce Mitchell puts it, 'made up of a selection of ordinary prose patterns,'[17] and also has, rather more frequently than these prose patterns would lead us to expect, such stylistic ornaments as the *apo koinu* construction, paronomasia or word-play, and variation. Even the question of the apparent stanzaic structure of *Deor*, and possibly of *Wulf and Eadwacer*, is a feature of syntax. However, except for incidental references, the papers in this volume do not concern themselves with the syntactic side of stylistics.

The study of vocabulary in this material involves consideration of such disparate, and overlapping, terms as the epithet, the kenning, the *kend heiti*, word compounding, and *hapax legomena*. It also includes the debunking of the myth of the Old English poetic dialect, as far as spelling is concerned, a contribution provided here by David Megginson. Finally, it overlaps with syntax for studies of Old and early Middle English prosody because it so often includes discussion of variation and other felicities of early medieval verse which involve the juxtaposition or apposition of language and image. Thus, E.G. Stanley's paper considers the heroic vocabulary of the Old English riddles, pointing out the extent to which the vocabulary of these texts suggests that they were bookish and learned productions.

The context is the area where we are most likely to speculate about the relationships between speaker, hearer, and the linguistic code itself. We conclude, therefore, that part of the excellence of *The Wanderer* and *The Seafarer* is a result of the interplay between the frame and the reflections of the personae within those elegies. Only rarely have we seriously considered what an elegy is, and the extent to which a particular kind of frame structure seems to suggest this genre. Such a structure is a standard one elsewhere than in the elegies proper; for instance, the Kentish Psalm, or Psalm 50, has a nicely developed frame for the translation. This structure appears to have been a popular one for various purposes and in various contexts. That the element of context in stylistic analysis is becoming a matter of great interest to specialists in early medieval verse is clear, in that three of the papers in this volume are specifically concerned with context, and others use a number of stylistic aspects to cast light on issues of context and register. Thus, John Miles Foley considers the linguistic schemes involved in the production of *Andreas* as a performance (a study which also has implications, as Foley notes, for register), and, in particular, analyses the metanarrative which results from the poet's self-interruption during lines 1488–91. T.A. Shippey is also interested in the use of linguistics to establish the context of the literature, using Grice's analysis of conversations and those speech-acts known as 'Face Threatening Acts' in order to establish the linguistic codes at work in the Old Norse *Hamðismál*. Brian Shaw works from a more traditional point of view, analysing the way in which the source text for the Old English poem *Andreas* is remade by the translator so that the target text has a very self-conscious narrator. Shaw argues that Andrew ascertains the meaning of God's words and brings that meaning to life by linking in his own words the temporal with the eternal.

Register, the last of the elements involved in the study of style, is something we are only just beginning to acknowledge as an explicit feature of Old English poetic technique, though its existence is implicit in the relatively standard – if not always acknowledged – distinction between 'classical' and 'other' Old English poetry. Future analysis may hold a consideration of the register differences between close translation, loose translation, and paraphrase, or even between the lyric, the lay, and the epic – if those categories exist for this literature.

Finally, several of the papers in this volume consider some combination of the features of stylistic analysis enumerated above. Eric Stanley's paper I have already discussed here under vocabulary, but in fact the analysis ranges through the national and supposedly heroic features of the poetic art and the manuscript context of the Riddles, passes by a number of solutions of these works (which are based on the clash of several linguistic schemes), and concludes with some remarks touching on the register of these short poems.

Similarly, Mark Griffith's paper begins with a consideration of the alliterative and metrical features of the proper names in *The Battle of Maldon* (which combines sounds with vocabulary); looks at various syntactic parallels in the poem; considers various kinds of licence in the poem including anomalies of phrasing, syntax, and vocabulary; examines the onomastic and etymological features of the proper names used in the poem and in other Old English poems; and concludes that many of the warriors – particularly Byrhtnoþ and Byrhtwold – reflect their names in their words and actions. The paper serves as a salutary reminder that there is a lot of overlap in these categories, and that distinguishing among them is a project fraught with uncertainty.

All of the papers in this volume certainly bear in mind one principal difficulty, which is that the study of style, like any other study of Old English poetry, requires a careful distinction between what one wishes to find, and what is there in the material to be found. They consider formal features of the poetry in order to determine what conclusions the material itself permits. Stylistics offers, perhaps, a way to organize the somewhat amorphous statements we make about matters prosodic and poetic. The authors of these papers choose to consider some stylistic features in a new light, but they also acknowledge the following caveat from a well-known article on some stylistic features of *Beowulf*: 'I find it is all too easy to be guided by what one thinks is important rather than by the formal features I have been examining.' Published in the first volume of *English Studies in Canada*, and arguing for a more comprehensive and at the same time more cautious approach to the study of Old English poems, this article was written, not surprisingly, by Constance Hieatt.[18]

University of Western Ontario

## NOTES

1 Barbara C. Raw, *The Art and Background of Old English Poetry* (London: Edward Arnold 1978), 97–122.
2 Milton McC. Gatch, *Loyalties and Traditions: Man and His World in Old English Literature* (New York: Bobbs-Merrill 1971), 39.
3 C.L. Wrenn, *A Study of Old English Literature* (London: Harrap 1967), 35–56, esp. 36.
4 Ibid., 52.
5 T.A. Shippey, *Old English Verse* (London: Hutchinson 1972), 13.
6 Ibid., 80–113.
7 Stanley B. Greenfield and Daniel G. Calder, *A New Critical History of Old English Literature* (New York: New York University Press 1986), 1–2. Ch. 5 is pages 122–33, including notes.

8 Malcolm Godden and Michael Lapidge, eds, *The Cambridge Companion to Old English Literature* (Cambridge: Cambridge University Press 1991).

9 Ibid., 64 and *passim*.

10 Ibid., 55–70. In the title of this chapter, 'nature' seems to have replaced style for reasons which remain unclear. The 'nature' of this verse has never been described as 'natural,' and the choice of this abstract noun to introduce the only section of the book which clearly commits itself to discussion of the form, as opposed to the meaning, of the poetry must be a considered one. However, it does permit the author to avoid any evaluative analysis, and even to avert any acknowledgment of the criteria implicit in the texts which the rest of the contributors of the volume choose to discuss.

11 Fred C. Robinson, '*Beowulf*,' in Godden and Lapidge, eds, *Cambridge Companion*, 142–59, at 142.

12 Ibid., 153.

13 Patrizia Lendinara, 'The World of Anglo-Saxon Learning,' in Godden and Lapidge, eds, *Cambridge Companion*, 264–81.

14 For a slightly different paradigm, see Allen J. Frantzen, *Desire for Origins: New Language, Old English, and Teaching the Tradition* (New Brunswick, N.J.: Rutgers University Press 1990), esp. 83–90.

15 See Bruce Mitchell and Fred C. Robinson, *A Guide to Old English*, 5th ed. (Oxford: Blackwell 1992), viii, where these texts are described as 'the essential ones for the proper orientation of beginners towards both the literature and culture of Anglo-Saxon England ... important reference points.'

16 A good short introduction to this approach is G.W. Turner, *Stylistics* (Harmondsworth, Middlesex: Penguin Books 1973). Many of the terms used here are elegantly elucidated in Katie Wales, *A Dictionary of Stylistics* (London: Longman 1989). For less sophisticated, but still very helpful, approaches to the subject, see: Geoffrey N. Leech, *A Linguistic Guide to English Poetry* (London: Longman 1969); Raymond Chapman, *Linguistics and Literature: An Introduction to Literary Stylistics* (London: Edward Arnold 1973); and Michael Cummings and Robert Simmons, *The Language of Literature: A Stylistic Introduction to the Study of Literature* (Oxford: Pergamon Press 1983).

17 Bruce Mitchell, *Old English Syntax*, vol. 2 (Oxford: Clarendon Press 1985), 989, § 3959. Syntax is the much-neglected symbiote of metrical analysis, and Mitchell's words in this connection remain true: there is indeed 'room for more work here' (990).

18 C.B. Hieatt, 'Envelope Patterns and the Structure of *Beowulf*,' *English Studies in Canada* 1 (1975): 249–65.

# Grammar, Spelling, and the Rhythm of the Alliterative Long Line

THOMAS CABLE

Laȝamon's *Brut* and the fifteenth-century manuscripts of some of the poems of the Alliterative Revival bracket a period during which the English language changed perhaps more fundamentally than during any other two and a half centuries before or since. It was during this period between the end of the twelfth century and the middle of the fifteenth century that the 'levelling of inflections' gained momentum and carried through to completion, changing English from a moderately synthetic language to a highly analytic one. Because the influx of French vocabulary did not assume large proportions until the second half of the thirteenth century, Laȝamon's lexicon is mainly Germanic except for Latin words borrowed into Old English. During the latter part of this period the historically long vowels also began changing – among the earliest being Middle English [iː] and [uː] to the centralized diphthongs [əɪ] and [əʊ] – in a process that has been perceived with perhaps too much systematicity in hindsight as the Great Vowel Shift. All of these familiar changes were progressing at different rates according to the region, generation, social status, and degree of bilingualism of the speaker as well as the register in which the language was used. Of these changes the one that most affected the rhythm of poetry was the silencing of final -*e*. Indeed, without an understanding of final -*e*, any statement about the rhythm of Middle English poetry is hopeless. Donka Minkova has shown convincingly that the rhythmical function of final -*e* in late Middle English was not only a phenomenon of literary metre but also a part of the phonology of non-literary uses of the language.[1]

It is the systematic phonology of final -*e* that this study focuses on, in contrast with the haphazard representation of final -*e* in the manuscripts. There is a persistent notion that any grammatical construct describing the language of this period must have a direct representation in a manuscript.

The idea is that the manuscripts are our primary evidence and that any grammatical statement must self-evidently be derived from them. This idea drives the view of texts and grammars in Hoyt N. Duggan's important series of articles and culminates in his extraordinary assertion that the metre of Old English poetry cannot be known with certainty because the poems do not exist in more than one copy.[2] The idea persists, even when the scribe, who may have been transcribing a century later than the poet composed, spoke a language quite changed from that of the author and may well have been inclined toward modernizing his text. I would argue that just the reverse is the case – that the rhythmical grammar can be constructed with some certainty for both Old and Middle English poems (although nothing will be said here about Old English) and that for us as well as for the poet the rhythmical grammar has priority; the manuscript representation of the rhythmical grammar is the derivative object. Furthermore, the manuscript is a derivative object whether it exists in a unique copy or in multiple copies, and the projection of an archetypal manuscript is speculative in a way that the construction of a grammar is not.

Consider *The Wars of Alexander* line 1062b, as it appears in the two extant manuscripts, Oxford, Bodleian Library, MS Ashmole 44, and Dublin, Trinity College, MS 213:[3]

```
x  / x x x  /  x
þe hareest on erthe                                            (Ashmole)

x /    x x  x   /
þe aughfulest on erth                                          (Dublin)
```

The poem was composed sometime between the mid-fourteenth century and the mid-fifteenth century. The Ashmole manuscript has been dated to the mid-fifteenth century and the Dublin manuscript to the last quarter of the fifteenth century, possibly as late as 1503.[4] A noun like *erth(e)*, which was of the weak feminine declension in Old English (*eorðe*), would have had *-an* in the dative singular in Old English. The manuscripts are in disagreement about the *-e* ending in this line, as they are in some other lines, such as 1748b:

```
x  /  x x  /  x
& gudnes on erthe                                              (Ashmole)

x  /  x   x   /
& goddesse on erth                                             (Dublin)
```

The Ashmole manuscript happens to contradict its own usage in the very next line, 1749b (a line that does not appear in Dublin):

x ·/ x  x  x /
& sustaynes þe erth                                         (Ashmole)

And in 2159b both manuscripts omit the -e:

þe biggest in erth                                          (Ashmole)

biggest on erth                                             (Dublin)

while in 1722b both manuscripts show the -e:

þat leues in erthe                                (Ashmole and Dublin)

In the manuscripts of *The Wars of Alexander,* final -e on *erth(e)* comes and goes. There is no way, by studying the writing of -e in either of these manuscripts or by comparing the two, to determine whether the metrical phonology of the poem required a final -e on *erth(e).* Of course, this way of stating the matter is too specific. We are interested in *erth(e)* not only for the phonology of that word in itself but also for its phonology as a representative of certain grammatical and metrical categories: a noun that belonged to the weak feminine declension, which occurs as the object of a preposition and as a direct object, at the end of the alliterative long line, and so on. Here, however, we come to what seems to be a persistent confusion – a disagreement among metrists not only about what constitutes appropriate evidence but also, implicitly, about what constitutes the very subject of investigation. The problem is that as soon as one begins discussing grammatical and metrical categories, some metrists see the analysis as moving away from the concrete reality of ink on vellum to something more abstract and more speculative – constructs in the modern grammarian's mind that might or might not have reality. The attitude seems to be that theories come and go, and, in any event, they are derivative from the manuscript, which endures. Several separate considerations are confusingly folded into this view.

In the first place, the ink on vellum may have a tangible, physical reality, but in itself it will not answer the question that is crucial for the rhythm of the lines above: Does the metrical phonology of *The Wars of Alexander* specify the pronunciation of -e in *erth(e)*? It is important to note that this question is different from a central, highly productive question of *A Linguistic Atlas of Late Mediaeval English,* which is: What direct evidence does spelling provide about the written language?[5] Angus McIntosh discusses variants such as *erþe, erthe; him, hym; no3t, noht,* and writes:

> The very fact that such things cannot be correlated with anything in the
> spoken system gives them a special significance and importance. The
> regional distribution of *erþe* and *erthe,* for example – once it is perceived
> that it is not merely haphazard – becomes as interesting a matter from
> the point of view of anyone studying varieties of the written language
> as are the distribution of *vche* and *eche* 'each,' or *mon* and *man* 'man,'
> for anyone studying regional variations in the Middle English sound-
> system.[6]

Critics of grammatical approaches to Middle English metre sometimes combine the specification of grammatical and metrical categories in the approach
that they criticize together with the literalness of the *Linguistic Atlas*'s method
into something that is neither one nor the other. Since presumably no one
would wish to be characterized as anti-grammatical, it may help to illustrate
some of the considerations that are involved in describing a grammar. Then
it should be clear that the thing described, in an important way, has priority
over the manuscript, at least for those categories that are relevant for the
metrical grammar.

In the lines cited above, it may or may not be relevant that all seven
occurrences of *erth(e)* are in grammatical contexts that would have required
a final *-an* in Old English, later developing into final *-e* (six datives as objects
of prepositions and one accusative). It may or may not be relevant that the
metrical context is the end of the line. The point is that these are grammatical
and metrical categories whose relevance must be established independently of
a particular way of writing the manuscript. As it turns out, the evidence
suggests that the relevant category is not 'dative singular' but 'feminine
declension.' At the same time that masculine and neuter nouns were losing
the dative *-e* in late Middle English, many feminine nouns were gaining an
*-e* in the nominative case and thus becoming invariable in what had been the
nominative, accusative, and dative cases. An indication of these opposite
directions of analogical change is this fact: of the nouns from Old English
that occur at the end of the long line and are monosyllabic except for a
possible *-e*, the overwhelming majority in *The Wars of Alexander* – and also
in *Sir Gawain and the Green Knight, Cleanness, The Parlement of the Thre
Ages,* and other poems – were feminine or else had a final vowel in the
nominative in Old English (for example, *time* < *tima*). Lines ending with
prepositional phrases in which the noun has a monosyllabic root and is from
a masculine declension are rare. Yet such prepositional phrases occur freely
at the end of the first half-line. The supporting statistics are laid out in my
*English Alliterative Tradition,* although one suspects that statistical summaries
never have the effect that the compiler wishes.[7]

Notice now that we are using terms such as 'end of the long line' and 'end of the first half-line.' What status do these metrical terms have? The argument here is that they refer to the same kinds of objects that grammatical terms such as 'dative case' refer to and that these objects are different from objects referred to by terms such as 'scribal -e,' 'the spelling of the archetype,' and even 'authorial spelling.' It is not simply that the objects of the second set of terms are derivative from those of the first, and more variable and less predictable. It is that they are not the objects of metre. They are at a further level of abstraction despite their seeming concreteness. A description of the principles of written -e is more abstract than a description of the grammar, because the occurrence or non-occurrence of the written -e depends on the interaction of the grammar with other forces not yet specified.

In comparison with the uncertainty of these other forces, the grammar and the metre are complex but straightforward. For example, 'the end of the long line' occurred in the description above as if it had some significance, although the significance was not made explicit. Traditional metrical discussions have given special consideration to the end of the line, as in Marie Borroff's important study, which disallows final -e within the alliterative long line but leaves open the possibility for its sounding at the end.[8]

It is by discovering these linguistic and metrical concepts in various patterns and combining them in yet further patterns to test the results – by trying out various hypotheses – that we construct the grammar (where 'grammar' includes the segmental phonology and the metrical phonology). For example, *quene* occurs in *Cleanness* 1586 at the end of the long line:

$$x \quad x \quad x \quad / \quad / \; (?)$$
Ho herde hym chyde to þe chambre    þat watȝ þe chef quene

There would be no reason to expect the -e on *quene* to be pronounced if the grammar of the *Gawain* poet followed in every respect the grammar of Old English (where the nominative case of this feminine noun was *cwen*, without an -e). The two most obvious explanations for the pattern before us, one concluding that the -e was silent and the other that it was sounded, both involve a double hypothesis: by one explanation there would be (i) loss of final -e throughout the grammar with no analogical additions of -e and (ii) a metre that allows but does not require an unstressed syllable at the end of the long line; by the other explanation, there would be (i) the spread of final -e to the nominative case in feminine nouns and (ii) a metre that requires an unstressed syllable at the end of the long line. Elsewhere I have given arguments and evidence for choosing the second explanation over the first (see note 7). That discussion did not include consideration of the present line, which, one might add, would also have a final *-e* on *chef*. The grammatical changes in feminine nouns have long been familiar to Chaucerian metrists. As for the metre, the patterning of the final syllable in the alliterative long line involves the collation of grammatical categories in thousands of lines in Middle English. The fact that *quene* is here written with a final *-e* is completely irrelevant to the argument, which involves the analysis of grammatical categories, not the spelling habits of a scribe.

The separation of grammar and spelling can be illustrated by taking a familiar passage from *Sir Gawain and the Green Knight*, stripping it of all final *-e*'s, then projecting the final *-e*'s that would be required by the principles sketched here, and seeing what metrical patterns result. In rough form, the principles require a final *-e* wherever there was an inflectional or derivational syllable in Old English, with certain exceptions. One of the main exceptions has already been named in the discussion above: the dative case is no longer a productive category, the only examples of *-e* in that category being the 'petrified dative' of phrases such as *on live*. Another exception is the verb 'to be' as an auxiliary: plural *wer(e)(n)* from OE *wæron* and *ar(e)(n)* from OE *aron* were contracted to monosyllables when functioning as auxiliary verbs but remained disyllabic as main verbs.[9] In the following passage, Gawain is riding across the countryside in a state of considerable anxiety and discomfort:

| | |
|---|---|
| Bi a mount on þe morn   meryly he rydes | 740 |
| Into a forest ful dep,   þat ferly watz wyld, | |
| Hiȝ hillez on vch a half,   and holtwodez vnder | |
| Of hor okez ful hog   a hundreth togeder; | |
| Þe hasel and þe haȝþorn   wer harled al samen, | |
| With roȝ raged moss   rayled aywher, | 745 |
| With mony bryddez vnblyþ   vpon bar twyges, | |
| Þat pitosly þer piped   for pyn of þe cold. | |
| Þe gom vpon Gryngolet   glydez hem vnder, | |
| Þurȝ mony misy and myr,   mon al hym on. | |

Every line has at least two places where decisions about final *-e* must be made, and one line has four. Clearly, the metre and rhythmical effect of the passage will vary considerably depending on those decisions. The brief reasons for the present readings are as follows: 740 *Mount* from OF *mo(u)nt* and OE *munt* would not have *-e* because the dative case was not generally productive; *morn* from OE *morgen* would not have had *-e* for the same reason except that *on þe morne* appears to be a petrified dative, and the disyllabic structure of the root in OE makes disyllabic structure in ME more likely. 741 *Dep* from OE *deop* would have no grammatical reason for final

*-e*, but *wyld* from OE *wilde* would. 742 *Hi3* from OE *heh* would have *-e* as an adjective before a plural noun; *vch* from OE *ælc* would not have *-e* in this context, although the full story of *vch(e)* is more complex;[10] *half* from the OE feminine *half* would have *-e*; *holt* from the OE masculine and neuter *holt* would not. 743 *Hor* from OE *har* would have *-e* as a plural and *hog* from OF *ahoge* would have *-e* for the same reason, as well as for its OF source. 744 *Ha3þorn* from the OE masculine *haguþorn* would have *-e* after the first element of the compound but not after the second (compare Chaucer Man of Law (Group B) 95: 'Though I come after hym with *hawe*bake'); *wer* as the auxiliary would not have *-e*. 745 *Ro3* from OE *ruh* would not have *-e* because it is not a weak or plural adjective; *moss* from the OE neuter *mos* would not have *-e*. *Aywhere* from OE *æghwær* was one of the two dozen native words that contributed to the 2 per cent of the lines in *Cleanness* that were exceptions by my 1991 scansion.[11] Assuming stress on the second syllable and no analogical *-e,* this line and lines 965b, 1398b, and 1608b in *Cleanness* end on a stressed syllable. My rules as they are presently formulated cannot account for this pattern. 746 *Vnblyþ* would have *-e* as a plural adjective, as would *bar*. 747 Although the distributional evidence available to me is indeterminate about *aywhere*, it strongly suggests that a similar adverb *þer* from OE *þær* acquired an *-e* in ME; *piped* from OE *pipodon*, the preterite plural of a weak verb of class 2, would be *pipede*; *pyn* from the OE feminine noun *pin* would have *-e*, as would *cold*, from OE *cald*, the substantive use of the adjective after a definite article. 748 *Goma* from OE *guma* would have *-e* in place of the *-a*. 749 *Myr* from ON *myrr* would not have *-e*, but *on* from OE *ana* would.

If we project the grammatically determined *-e*'s (marked with x) onto the text as spelled by the scribe, we see that there is both correspondence and lack of correspondence:

```
 x x    /    x   x   /  x    / x x  x  / x
Bi a mounte on þe morne   meryly he rydes              740

x x x / x   x   /     x  / x   x    / x
Into a forest ful dep,  þat ferly watz wylde,

  / x  / x  x   x    x  / x   x    /   x x  / x
Hi3e hillez on vche a halue,   and holtwodez vnder

 x   / x / x   x   / x   x /    x   x / x
Of hore okez ful hoge  a hundreth togeder;

  x  / x x    x  / x  x    x   / x x  / x
Þe hasel and þe ha3þorne   were harled al samen,

  x   /    / x    /     / x  x   /
With ro3e raged mosse   rayled aywhere,                745
```

```
   x    x x  /  x x  / x   x x   / x  / x
With mony bryddez vnblyþe   vpon bare twyges,
```

```
  x  / x  x  xx / xx    x   / x x   x / x
Þat pitosly þer piped    for pyne of þe colde.
```

```
  x  /   x x x     /   x x     / x   x  / x
Þe gome vpon Gryngolet   glydez hem vnder,
```

```
  x    x x  / x x    /      /  x   x  / x
Þur3 mony misy and myre,   mon al hym one.
```

The scribe has sometimes written an -*e* where the grammar does not provide for one (for example, *mounte* in 740) and has sometimes omitted an -*e* where the grammar requires one (for example, *piped* in 747). In the one place where the theory of metre implicit in the present study could use support for a final -*e*, the spelling of *aywhere*, the -*e* does indeed appear. But the argument of the present study is also that the systems of metrical phonology and scribal spelling are different systems; the -*e* of metrical phonology is a different object from that of scribal practice, and it must be established by grammatical principles. The obvious analogy is with the child who learns a language from degraded fragments of language and whose internalized grammar is tested empirically against further degraded fragments – not against an ideal manuscript written by an angel.

Another conclusion to note in this passage is that when the grammatical -*e*'s are supplied, none of the patterns of the a-verse occur in the b-verse, and vice versa. The patterns of the two halves of the line belong to mutually exclusive sets, and they conform to different metrical paradigms.[12]

A final note to make about this exercise is that it follows a strategy of metrical analysis used by Constance Hieatt in a study twenty years ago.[13] There she took a passage from *Sir Gawain and the Green Knight* that Marie Borroff had analysed metrically, brought to it some insights from her own work in Old English metrics, projected the older set of principles onto the Middle English text, and displayed the text again with the insights gained from the superimposition of the two sets of principles. The passage that Hieatt took appeared on pages 207–8 in Borroff's study; my own on page 199.[14] In fairness to Borroff's work, I should emphasize that attention to the etymology of Middle English words and their sources in Old English and Old French was an integral part of her own groundbreaking study. The main difference with the present approach is that Borroff found the etymological information concerning final -*e* more relevant to the rhythm of the wheels than to that of the long line, where she concluded that final -*e* had been lost, at least within the line. And in fairness to Hieatt's work, I should emphasize that the principles of Old English metre that she projected in 1974 and the ones that I project here are sometimes implicitly in contradiction. Part of that implicit contradiction lies in the fact that we now know much more about the Old English types D and E than we knew twenty years ago, as Hieatt's wonderfully clear and accurate 'Brief Guide to the Scansion of Old English Poetry' suggests.[15] Her comments on the impossibility of *hilderinc har open unexpected avenues of theoretical implication, which lead to new problems that any adequate metrical theory must solve. In addition to her own contributions toward solving those problems, some of the solutions have come from metrists represented in the present volume and from others whom she has taught and encouraged.

University of Texas at Austin

## NOTES

1  Donka Minkova, *The History of Final Vowels in English: The Sound of Muting* (Berlin: de Gruyter 1991).

2  See, for example, Hoyt N. Duggan, 'The Shape of the B-Verse in Middle English Alliterative Poetry,' *Speculum* 61 (1986): 564–92, and 'The Evidential Basis of Old English Metrics,' *Studies in Philology* 85 (1988): 145–63.

3  Lines cited are from the edition by Walter W. Skeat, *The Wars of Alexander*, Early English Text Society, ES 47 (London: Trübner 1867).

4  Hoyt N. Duggan and Thorlac Turville-Petre, eds, *The Wars of Alexander*, Early English Text Society, SS 10 (Oxford: Oxford University Press 1989).

5  Angus McIntosh, M.L. Samuels, and Michael Benskin, *A Linguistic Atlas of Late Mediaeval English*, 4 vols (Aberdeen: Aberdeen University Press 1986).

6  Angus McIntosh, 'The Analysis of Written Middle English,' *Transactions of the Philological Society* (1956): 30.

7  Thomas Cable, *The English Alliterative Tradition* (Philadelphia: University of Pennsylvania Press 1991), 66–84.

8  Marie Borroff, *Sir Gawain and the Green Knight: A Stylistic and Metrical Study* (New Haven: Yale University Press 1962) 187–9.

9  See Cable, *English Alliterative Tradition*, 79.

10  See Thomas Cable, 'Standards from the Past: The Conservative Syllable Structure of the Alliterative Revival,' in Joseph B. Trahern, Jr, ed., *Standardizing English: Essays in the History of Language Change in Honor of John Hurt Fisher* (Knoxville: University of Tennessee Press 1989), 52.

11  Cable, *English Alliterative Tradition*, 73. Stress on the first syllable, following the Old English æghwær, is possible here, but this scansion would create problems in the internal rhythm of the verse.

12  For further consideration of this point, with specific reference to *Cleanness*, see ibid., 89–91.

13  Constance B. Hieatt, 'The Rhythm of the Alliterative Long Line,' in Beryl Rowland, ed., *Chaucer and Middle English Studies in Honour of Rossell Hope Robbins* (London: Allen and Unwin 1974), 119–30.

14  Borroff, *Sir Gawain and the Green Knight*, 207–8, 199.

15  Constance B. Hieatt, 'A Brief Guide to the Scansion of Old English Poetry,' *Old English Newsletter* 23, no. 1 (1989): 33–5.

# *The Battle of Maldon* and Beowulfian Prosody

ROBERT PAYSON CREED

In 1990 I published a study of the prosody of *Beowulf*.[1] In 1992 I published a study of the prosody of Caedmon's 'Hymn' showing that this nine-line poem can be scanned in terms of what I shall call 'Beowulfian prosody.'[2] These two poems – *Beowulf*, apparently undatable but showing signs of composition early rather than late in the historical Anglo-Saxon period, and the 'Hymn,' pre-served from the middle of the eighth century – deserve to be regarded as instances of 'classical' Old English verse making. When I was asked recently whether I would like to offer a paper at a conference honouring my long-time friend and colleague Constance B. Hieatt, I decided it was time for me to try to apply Beowulfian prosody to *The Battle of Maldon*, a poem that could have been composed no earlier than the last decade of the tenth century.

My prosody of *Beowulf* grew out of my attempts to work out a way to perform the poem. My goal in the present study is to make possible a reason-ably authentic performance of *The Battle of Maldon*. It is for this reason that I intersperse comments about performance with my prosodic analyses.

## a) The Verse Line and Its Halflines

For my study of *Beowulf*, I began with the text of the poem that survives in the manuscript. Unfortunately, it is not possible to study *The Battle of Maldon* in the late Anglo-Saxon manuscript in which it was written down, since that manuscript was very badly damaged by fire in 1731. Fortunately, the text of the poem – or what was left of it in the already damaged manuscript – was copied down in the decade before the fire.

Soon after the text was copied down, editors began to divide it into verse lines and the verse lines into halflines. The editors have done their work well.

All but three verse lines of the poem conform to the rigorous definition quoted below. The three verse lines that do not conform to the Beowulfian definition have generally been taken to be anomalous. All but six of the halflines that appear in most of the editions of the poem conform to my definition of the halfline.

This fact is important. Scholars have long been able to recognize verse lines and halflines but have so far been unable to define either. I offer what I believe to be the only comprehensive yet appropriately restrictive and acceptable definition of the verse line of *Beowulf*:

> a verse line is a sequence of measures (usually four, but sometimes five or six) that begins either with the first alliterating syllable of an alliteration or with the rest before (or musical augmentation of) the proclitic passage ... to the first alliterating syllable; the verse line ends just before either the first syllable of the next alliteration or the rest before (or musical augmentation of) the proclitic passage to that syllable.    (*Reconstructing*, 206)

More simply put, a verse line is a sequence of measures based on sound-patterning. The sound-patterning that defines a verse line of *Beowulf* or Caedmon's 'Hymn' is what we have come to call 'alliteration.' Although I used the term 'alliteration' in *Reconstructing the Rhythm of Beowulf*, I would now replace such a literate term with one that, while somewhat more awkward, is more accurate. One hears 'alliteration' not simply as repetition but as the establishment of a *link* between *syllabic-initial sounds*; hence, I refer to this phenomenon as *sound-linkage*.

The sound-linkage in *Beowulf*, the 'Hymn,' and *The Battle of Maldon* is created by two stressed syllables, such as *eorl* and *yrhð-* in *Maldon* line 6: *þæt se eorl nolde yrhðo geþolian*; or by three stressed syllables, such as *hicg-*, *hand-*, and *hig-* in verse line 4: *hicgan to handum 7 to hige godum*.[3] Verse line 6 can be said to be built around, or based on, vocalic sound-linkage; verse line 4 can be said to be *H*-based.

The second halfline of a verse line is built around the *last* syllable participating in the sound-linkage. The second halfline of *Maldon* 6 begins with *yrhð-*, which heads the first measure of this halfline. The second halfline of verse line 4 is constructed around – actually *back* from – *hig-*, which heads the *second* measure of this halfline.

I noted earlier that almost every verse line and halfline of *Maldon* conforms to these definitions. There are, however, eleven exceptions. These are the verse lines 1, 29, 32, 45, 80, 172, 183, 224, 240, 271, and 288.

The first exception is the opening passage of the poem. The two words *brocen wurde* are usually designated line 1. The sound-patterning of what is designated line 2 clearly sets off as a verse line the passage beginning with *het*. The two opening words of the poem are thus isolated from the first complete verse line. We can, I think, consider this passage to be *B*-based. It is clear that the two words do not make a complete verse line. But do they make a halfline? I read them instead as a single *measure*, which I will discuss later. The surviving text of *The Battle of Maldon* begins not with a complete halfline but what was probably the second measure of the second halfline.

Only on rare occasions does the *Beowulf* poet compose the second halfline of a verse line around *two* sound-linked syllables.[4] The *Maldon* poet, however, composes two such halflines within a short passage. The first occurs at line 29, the second at line 32. Here are verse lines 29 to 33 as they appear in standard texts:

> me sendon to þe    sæmen snelle                                      29
> heton ðe secgan    þæt þu most sendan raðe
> beagas wið gebeorge    7  eow betere is
> þæt ge þisne garræs    mid gafole forgyldon              32
> þonne we swa hearde    [hi]lde dælon

The second halfline of line 29 contains not one but two sound-linked syllables, *sæ* and *snel*. The second halfline of line 32 also contains two sound-linked syllables, *gaf* and *gyld*. Strict adherence to my definition of the second halfline of a verse line requires that one divide these verse lines into two halflines on the basis of the *last* sound-linked syllable, like this:

> *me sendon to þe sæmen    snelle                                  *29
> *þæt ge þisne garræs mid gafole    forgyldon            *32

No editor has divided either line in this way. Editors have instead preferred to head the second halfline of 29 with *sæmen*, thus suggesting that the *Maldon* poet composed this halfline in a way that the *Beowulf* poet might have regarded as a slip. Perhaps the explanation is that the *Maldon* poet was thinking ahead to *secgan* and the continuation of the sound-linkage on *S*; in effect, the poet lost his place. Verse line 32 poses two problems for the prosodist. Besides having two sound-linked syllables in the second halfline, line 32 seems to consist of five measures. I deal with this problem below. In both lines 29 and 32 the flanking verse lines are properly sound-linked and thus serve to isolate the anomalous passages. In both cases these passages should be divided into halflines as in the standard editions.

Verse lines 45 and 288 handle the sound-linkage in a different way:

gehyrst þu sælida   hwæt þis folc segeð                          45
raðe wearð æt hilde   offa forheawen                           288

The problem here is not that one cannot elicit the verse line from the text and divide it into acceptable halflines, but rather that the passages *hwæt þis folc* in 45 and *offa for-* in 288 function as though they were proclitic to *segeð* and *heawen*, respectively. Since neither *folc* nor *offa* can function as a proclitic, it appears that the poet has, in the first case, simply produced a halfline in which he has reversed the two parts of the final measure, and, in the second, possibly reversed the two measures:

gehyrst þu sælida   *hwæt segeð þis folc                       *45
raðe wearð æt hilde   *forheawen offa                         *288

In verse line 80 the poet would have made a more acceptable verse line had he reversed the two names:

*maccus 7 ælfhere   modige twegen                             *80

Yet verse line 80 can be extracted and properly divided into its two halflines just as it is.

The next exception is verse line 172:

ne mihte þa on fotum leng   fæste gestandan
he to heofenum wlat                                           172
geþancie þe   ðeoda wealdend

The sound-linkage of verse line 171 is on *F*; the sound-linkage of verse line 173 is on *TH*. These two acceptable verse lines isolate a passage that appears to be setting up sound-linkage on *H*. This isolated passage is a complete clause. It can also be analysed into two acceptable measures, as we shall see. Since, then, it can be prosodically scanned, it can be taken to be a surviving halfline of a now partly lost *H*-based verse line. On the other hand, this clause can also be read as an editorial insertion into the poem, a point to which I shall return later.

Verse line 183 occurs in the following context:

7 begen þa beornas   þe him big stodon
ælfnoð 7 wulmær   begen lagon                                 183
ða onemn hyra frean   feorh gesealdon

This generally accepted verse line occurs between a line based on *B* and one based on *F*. But 183 itself contains no sound-linkage. What I suspect happened is something like this: The poet, thinking ahead about *both those fighters who stood by* Byrhtnoþ, then named the fighters *inside* the *B* sound-patterning, which he completes with the second halfline of 183. The line should be kept just as it is. It may perhaps indicate that the *Maldon* poet composed without the aid of writing and that, in this case, the editor or editors, whose work may be apparent elsewhere in the poem, simply did not alter what the poet had said.

Verse line 224 can be elicited from the text on the basis of sound-linkage on *M*, specifically, on *mæg* and (the second) *min*:

> he wæs ægðer min mæg  7  min hlaford                                        224

As we shall see below, there is, however, a more interesting way to perform this verse line than by taking *mæg* and *min* as the sole bearers of sound-linkage.

The next exception is verse line 240:

> wende þæs formoni man    þa he on meare rad
> on wlancan þam wicge    þæt wære hit ure hlaford              240
> forþan wearð her on felda    folc totwæmed

The sound-linkage of line 239 is on *M*, that of 241 on *F*. These two acceptable verse lines isolate a passage in which the sound-linkage is clearly on *W*. A strict application of the rules for dividing a verse line into its two halflines would produce the following division of 240:

> *on wlancan    þam wicge þæt wære hit ure hlaford                     *240

The editors have been right not to divide the line in this way. The second halfline of *240 is impossibly long. But the standard halfline division raises a simple question: Is there any sound-patterning linking the two halflines accepted by most editors? If there is, it can only be on the rarely stressed optative *wære*. I will offer a possible scansion of this puzzling verse line later.

Verse line 271 is, in context:

> hwilon he on bord sceat    hwilon beorn tæsde
> æfre embe stunde    he sealde sume wunde                         271
> þa hwile ðe he wæpna    wealdan moste.

The editorial division of line 271 seems to indicate sound-linkage that would have been unacceptable to the *Beowulf* poet. He adhered to the Indo-Germanic tradition in which a syllable beginning with *ST* creates sound-linkage only with one that begins with *ST*, never with a simple *S* (or *SP* or *SK*).

Verse line 271 is clearly set off: the sound-linkage of verse line 270 is on *B* (although it is possible to read the line as *H*-based because of the two *hwilon*s). The sound-linkage of verse line 272 is on *W*. The *þa* that heads 272 marks a clause boundary. These two acceptable verse lines, 270 and 272, isolate a passage that can be elicited as an acceptable verse line based on *S*. The problem is that a correct division of this line produces the following halflines:

> *æfre embe stunde he sealde    sume wunde                                    *271

Line 271 is, as we shall see, a complete clause that can be scanned into four acceptable measures. Possibly the *Maldon* poet, departing here from tradition, composed a 'verse line' based on rhyme rather than initial sound-linkage.

Three hundred and twenty-two verse lines (of 325) in *The Battle of Maldon* conform, therefore, to the definition of the verse line that I worked out from my analysis of Beowulfian prosody. The only exceptions are lines 1, 172, and 183. Each of these generally accepted 'verse lines' is, however, isolated by the surrounding verse lines, and, as I shall show below, can be scanned as either a single measure (1), two measures (172), or four measures (183).

Four more verse lines, 29, 32, 240, and 271, while they conform to the definition of the verse line, cannot be acceptably divided into two halflines on the basis of sound-patterning. Four of the lines that I have discussed in this section (45, 80, 224, and 288), despite their unusual sound-patterning, can acceptably divide into two halflines.

In *Maldon*, there are not 325 verse lines but rather 323 complete verse lines (counting 183), plus one complete halfline (172), plus what can be counted as one-quarter of a verse line (line 1). The exact count of verse lines and measurable parts of lines is, then, 323.75. The percentage of acceptable verse lines – 322 out of 323.75 – is 99.45. The percentage of acceptable halflines – 638 out of 647.5 – is 98.5. However, despite the fact that 98.5 per cent of the halflines of *The Battle of Maldon* can be acceptably elicited from the verse lines, there are differences between Beowulfian prosody and the prosody of *Maldon*. These differences begin to show up when we examine the halflines in more detail.

## b) Measures and Their Parts

In 1966, I worked out a taxonomy of measure types in *Beowulf* beginning with the most frequent type, which I called the 'alpha.' I did not at that point realize that every measure could be divided into two Parts or understand the importance of this fact. Yet, as I show in *Reconstructing the Rhythm of Beowulf*, the measure types I had worked out not only can but must be so divided in order to make it possible to compare verse lines.

I illustrate each type of measure from *The Battle of Maldon*, using a vertical bar (I) to indicate both the beginning of the measure and the division of the measure into two Parts. Elsewhere in this study I use the vertical bar only to indicate the beginning of a measure:

**Alpha**

I / I x

| | | |
|---|---|---|
| lhicglan to lhandlum | 4a | alpha 2, alpha 1 |
| lcafnle mid his lcynnle | 76a | alpha 3, alpha 1 |
| lguman lto lgulþe | 94a | alpha 4, alpha 1 |
| lhafoc lwið þæs lholtles | 8a | alpha 5, alpha 1 |
| ongunnon llyte lgian þa | 86a | (eta), alpha 6 (?)[5] |
| lhogode lto lwigle | 128b | alpha 7, alpha 1 |
| gað lricene lto us | 93b | (eta), alpha 8 (?)[6] |

**Beta**

I / x I \

| | | |
|---|---|---|
| þ[a] þæt lOffan lmæg | 5a | (epsilon 2), beta 1 |
| het þa lhyssa lhwæne | 2a | (alpha 1), beta |

**Gamma**

I / I \ x

| | | |
|---|---|---|
| 7  lforð lgangan | 3b | (epsilon 1), gamma 1 |
| 7 to lhige lgodum | 4b | (epsilon 2), gamma |
| ... lbrocen lwurde | 1 | gamma |

**Delta**

| / | (x) |

| / (x) | | |
|---|---|---|
| \|brim\| \|liþendra | 27b | delta 1, (gamma 1) |
| \|wigan\| \|unforhte | 79b | delta 2, (gamma 1) |
| yrhðo ge \|þolian \| | 6b | (alpha 2), delta 3 |

**Epsilon**

| (/) | x

| | | |
|---|---|---|
| \| \|þa \|stod on stæðe | 25a | epsilon 1, (beta) |
| \|7 to \|þære \|hilde stop | 8b | epsilon 4, (beta 1) |

**Alpha prime (alpha')**

| / | \

| | | |
|---|---|---|
| bord 7 \|brad \|swurd | 15a | (alpha 1), alpha' 1 |
| ælfnoð 7 \|wullmær | 183a | (gamma 1), alpha' 1 |
| ongan þa \|forð \|beran | 12b | (eta), alpha' 2 |
| he to \|heofenum\| wlat | 172 | (epsilon 2), alpha' 7 |

In the early 1970s, John Miles Foley suggested to me that there was a seventh type of measure, one that functions like an augmented epsilon.[7] The significant feature of this type of measure is that the augmenting syllable(s) is (or are) *not* sounded on the downbeat but on the upbeat. Examples of some of the variations on the epsilon, which I term the 'eta measure,' in *Maldon*, are:

**Eta**

| (/) | \ {x}

| | | |
|---|---|---|
| \| on\|gan þa \|forð beran | 12b | eta, (alpha' 2) |
| \| \|bæd þæt \|hyssa gehwylc | 128a | eta, (beta) |
| \|us \|sceal \|ord 7 ecg | 60a | eta, (beta 1) |
| \|be þam man \|mihte on\|cnawan | 9a | eta, (alpha 1) |

It is crucial to note that every one of these seven types of measure is heard as a variation on the alpha (/ x): The *delta* can be heard as an alpha in which a rest substitutes for an *unstressed* syllable or syllables (/ [x]); The *epsilon* reverses the delta with a rest that substitutes for the *stressed* syllable or syllables ([/] x); The *alpha prime* is the link between the three simpler measure types and the two longer and more complex types, the beta and the gamma. In the alpha prime, the unstressed syllable or syllables of the alpha is (or are) replaced by a stressed syllable or syllables (/ \). In the *beta*, the first stressed syllable of the alpha prime is replaced by a Part that mimics the entire alpha measure (/ x \). The syllables of this Part are *crowded* under the heavy stress (/). The less heavily stressed syllable(s) of the second Part is (or are) heard under the upbeat. In the *gamma*, it is the second stressed syllable of the alpha prime that is replaced by a Part that mimics the alpha measure (/ \ x). The first Part of a gamma exactly equals the first Part of the alpha or alpha prime; the syllables of the second Part are crowded under the upbeat (\).

The most complex variation on the alpha is the type that Foley identified more than twenty years ago and to which he and I gave the name 'eta.' The *eta* is an alpha prime in which the more heavily stressed first syllable(s) is (or are) replaced by either a rest or an unstressed syllable (or unstressed syllables) spoken under the downbeat. The downbeat, however it is expressed, is followed by the obligatory syllable(s) spoken on the upbeat, which may be followed in turn by one or two lightly stressed syllable(s). Note, however, that the syllable(s) spoken on the upbeat may be the only spoken part of an eta.

Two hundred and sixty-six verse lines of *Maldon* consist of four measures, each of which can be readily classified according to my taxonomy. To these 266 four-measure verse lines should be added the two measures of the complete halfline at 172 and the single gamma measure of the opening passage. The total then becomes 266.75 four-measure verse lines, or 82.4 per cent of the verse lines of the poem. These 266.75 verse lines are made up of 1,067 measures and these 1,067 measures of 2,134 Parts.

The fifty-seven remaining verse lines, which I shall discuss in the next two sections, mark the difference between Beowulfian prosody and the prosody of *The Battle of Maldon*. Differences become apparent as early as verse line 7, where the reader encounters the pronoun *he* before the first stressed and sound-linked syllable, *let*. This raises the problem of anacrusis. I think that, as with *Beowulf*, it is not only unnecessary but also misleading to invoke anacrusis in scanning *Maldon*, even though many verse lines (beginning with 7) would seem to demand that the prosodist fall back on anacrusis. In the following two examples I indicate possible anacrusis by placing an x over syllables in anacrusis and a vertical bar before the 'first true measure':

```
 •x  |
he  let him þa of handon    leofne fleogan                                    7

 •x   x      x |
be þam man mihte oncnawan    þæt se cniht nolde                               9
```

One can certainly try to squeeze in a single syllable, even a long syllable like *he*, before the first measure of a verse line. But a longer passage of anacrusis, like the three syllables before *mihte* in line 9, can hardly be squeezed in without seriously affecting the rhythm of the passage. This is, of course, my point. 'Anacrusis' creates its own rhythm, usually a pause followed by an unstressed syllable. If the pause substitutes for a stress, then the performer has simply created an epsilon *measure*. If one assumes that one can perform *Beowulf* or *Maldon* more or less continuously, an assumption borne out by my work on *Beowulf*, then every pause will be accounted for in the rhythm of the continuing performance. For these reasons I do not think that anacrusis has any place in the prosody of *Beowulf*, Caedmon's 'Hymn,' or *Maldon*. I perform each poem without it.

### c) 'Multi-measure' Verse Lines

The prosodist begins to assess the differences between Beowulfian prosody and the prosody of *Maldon* with the so-called hypermetric lines. These verse lines are more correctly designated 'multi-measure,' since they can be shown to consist of five or, much more rarely, six measures. The five-measure verse lines can be divided into those in which the additional measure is in the first halfline, which I shall call '3 plus 2'-measure verse lines, and those in which the additional measure is in the second halfline – '2 plus 3'-measure verse lines. There may be fifteen '3 plus 2' verse lines in *Maldon*: 7, 14, 23, 90, 136, 138, 182, 185, 193, 200, 212, 220, 223, 228, and 277. I am reluctant to assert that all fifteen are unquestionably multi-measure verse lines simply because the poet might have performed at least some of these as *four*-measure lines. I discuss that possibility in the next section.

The first multi-measure verse line, line 7, can be scanned in two ways. In the first scansion, there are five measures, an epsilon followed by four alphas. In the second scansion there are only four measures, an eta followed by three alphas:

```
(/)  x  /   x    x x   /  x      /  x   / x
|⁀ he |let him þa of |handon    |leofne |fleogan                              7

(/)  \    x   x x   /  x      /  x   / x
|he let him þa of |handon    |leofne |fleogan
```

I prefer the first scansion for three reasons. First, since it sets up the sound-patterning, *let* should receive the heavier stress of the first Part of the measure. Second, reading the first measure as an eta forces four syllables into the second Part of this measure. I take up this problem below. Third, when I perform the verse line, the epsilon-alpha suggests to my ear just a bit of hesitation on the part of the young man who is the subject of *let*.

The need for heaviest stress on the syllable that sets up the sound-linkage leads me to read the first measure of all the verse lines listed above, except 220, as an epsilon. In line 220, *sceolon* does not participate in the sound-linkage. Twelve of the remaining thirteen verse lines – line 200 presents a special problem – have *two* sound-linked syllables in the first halfline. It is therefore up to the performer to decide whether to begin each of these lines with epsilon-plus-alpha, or with a single eta. If the performer chooses the latter option, he or she will have to deal with four-syllable second Parts in verse lines 23, 136, 138, 185, 193, and 228. In verse line 14 an eta produces a *five*-syllable Part. The one slight discrepancy here is verse line 200, in which the third syllable of *modiglice* is long and thus initiates a new measure, the third of this halfline:

```
(/) x    x    / x / x    /   x    / x
| þæt þær |modig|lice   |manega |sprǣcon
```

I perform all fifteen of these '3 plus 2'-measure verse lines beginning with an epsilon.

There may be thirteen '2 plus 3'-measure verse lines in *Maldon*: 11, 32, 55, 66, 68, 84, 96, 146, 194, 202, 242, 259, and 282. Verse line 11 is characteristic of most of the '2 plus 3' verse lines:

```
(/)      \   x /  \ (/) x /   x x / x
|eac him wolde |eadric |  his |ealdre gellǣstan
```

A proclitic to the last sound-linked syllable of the series sets up an epsilon measure before the sound-linked measure of the second halfline. This pattern occurs also in lines 32 and 68 where the preposition *mid* is the proclitic; in line 96, where the preposition *for* is the proclitic; in lines 146 and 202, where demonstratives are the proclitics; in lines 84, 194, and 282, where 7 [*and*] is the proclitic; and in line 259, where there are two proclitics, *ne for*.

Despite these apparent similarities, I think there are significant differences among these ten verse lines. While one might argue that the possessive pronoun in line 11, the demonstratives in line 146 and 202, and the Tironian *et* (7) for the conjunction *and* in lines 84, 194, and 282 may be the work of an editor and should thus be ignored in performance, one cannot make the same argument for the prepositions. In these verse lines the proclitic prepositions, and thus the additional measure, must be kept for the sake of sense.

In both lines 55 and 66, the adverb *to* might seem to set up an eta measure before the two final measures of the verse line. But, because of the stress on the formative *-lic*, an eta reading is unlikely for line 55. Verse line 66, on the other hand, can be scanned in two different ways:

```
  /  x x x    / x  (/) \   /  \   x  / x
Ihæþene æt Ihilde  I  to Iheanlic me Iþinceð                         55

  /  (x)  /   \   x  (/) \  /    x  x  / x
Ilucon  Ilagustreamas I  to Ilang hit him Iþuhte                     66

  /  (x)  /   \   x   (/) \   x  x  / x
Ilucon  Ilagustreamas Ito lang hit him Iþuhte                        66
```

I prefer the first reading for line 66 for two reasons. First, *lang* completes the sound-linkage; second, the three-measure halfline seems to me to convey better the feeling of impatient men longing to fight. I therefore begin all thirteen '2 plus 3' verse lines with an epsilon.

Two verse lines in *Maldon* can perhaps best be scanned in six measures, '3 plus 3.' One is the very unusual line 240, already discussed because of its puzzling sound-patterns. If *wære* completes the sound-linkage in verse line 240, it also begins an alpha measure the second Part of which contains four syllables. Nevertheless, I prefer line 240 as follows:

```
 (/) x    /  x   x    /  x   (/) x   /  x x x x  / \
I   on Iwlancan þam Iwicge  I    þæt Iwære hit ure Ihlaford           240
```

Verse line 72 also appears to be an example of '3 plus 3':

```
 (/) x  /  \   x  / (x)(/) x   /   \  x    /  (x)
I   se Iflod ut gelwat  I    þa Iflotan stodon Igearowe              72
```

If, however, one ignores the demonstratives, this line is transformed into a four-measure line of simplicity and power:

```
  /   \   x  / (x)       /    \ x   /   (x)
*Iflod ut gelwat      Iflotan stodonIgearowe                        *72
```

Line 72, like line 11 and others, may have been 'improved' by an Anglo-Saxon editor. It is possible to conjecture that the editor provided the pronouns, the demonstratives, and the Tironian *et*-signs as semantic cues for a reader, knowing that anyone who spoke the lines aloud would not speak these words.

## d) The *Maldon* Poet's Violations of the 'Rule of Three'

The *Beowulf* poet rarely speaks more than three syllables in a single Part. In the 2,340 Parts of the two sample passages I analysed from that poem, only five (0.2 per cent) contain more than three syllables. On this basis I formulated what I call the 'Rule of Three.' Poets followed this rule – unconsciously, I believe – for the very good reason that trying to speak more than three syllables under either a downbeat or an upbeat is likely to cause the speaker to garble the words.

The *Maldon* poet does not observe this rule as rigorously as does the *Beowulf* poet. There are twenty-eight violations of the rule in *Maldon*: verse lines 10, 14, 20, 28, 34, 35, 40, 46, 59, 64, 70, 81, 83, 87, 108, 117, 159, 164, 167, 171, 174, 216, 220, 235, 240, 249, 272, and 289. For the details of these violations, see Table 1.

In verse lines 10, 14, 220, and 240 the violation occurs in the second Part of an alpha measure. In line 28 the violation occurs in the second Part of a gamma measure, and in line 174 in the first Part of a beta measure:

| | |
|---|---|
| / xx  x   x<br>lwacian æt þa w[i]ge   þa he to wæpnum feng | 10 |
|    / x  x  x  x<br>þa lhwile þe he mid handum   healdan mihte | 14 |
| /    x x   x x<br>ne sceolon me on þære þeode   þegenas ætwitan | 220 |
|            / x  x x x<br>on wlancan þam wicge   þæt lwære hit ure hlaford | 240 |
| / \   x  x  x<br>lærænde to þam eorle   þær he on ofre stod | 28 |
|           /   x  x \<br>ealra þæra wynna   þe ic on lworulde gebad | 174 |

It is worth noting that lines 10, 28, and 220 would conform to the rule if the demonstrative were left out. Line 174 would conform if the verbal prefix were left out. The *Maldon* poet is much fonder of these 'little words' and unstressed syllables than is the *Beowulf* poet.

There are twenty-two more halflines that begin with a measure the second Part of which violates the 'Rule of Three.' I list these verse lines in Table 1. Again, leaving out the possessive pronoun (lines 20, 70), the demonstrative (lines 35, 40, 81), the usually unstressed adverbs *þær* and *þa* (lines 64, 108, 171), and the verbal prefix *ge* (lines 159, 167, 289) would bring eleven of these verse lines into conformity with the rule.

Note that the second Part of the first measure of verse lines 164 and 249 actually contains *five* syllables. Line 164 may indicate a virtuosic performance.

The adverb *raþe* consists of two short syllables, unlike all the verbs in this position except *sceole* in verse line 59. Line 249 is harder to explain. The five syllables in the second Part can be performed only at the risk of garbling the passage. I prefer to perform line 249 as an epsilon followed by an alpha.

The *Maldon* poet composes at least twenty-eight Parts that violate the 'Rule of Three.' These Parts account for 1.05 per cent of the total of 2,647 Parts in the poem. If this percentage seems insignificant, the reader should translate it into the fact that the *Maldon* poet violates the rule five times more often than does the *Beowulf* poet. It is the former's willingness to crowd so many Parts with four or even five syllables that accounts for the chief difference between the *Maldon* poet and the *Beowulf* poet.

Table 1    Violations of the 'Rule of Three'

| Halfline | | | Halfline | |
|---|---|---|---|---|
| measure | measure | measure | measure | |
| Part 1    Part 2 | | | | |
| I (/) I \    x    x x | I | | | |
| 7    bæd þæt hyra | randas | rihte | heoldon | 20 |
| ne    þurfe we us | spillan | gif ge | spedaþ to þam | 34 |
| we    willað wið þam | golde | grið | fæstnian | 35 |
| we    willað mid þam | sceattum | us to | scype gangan | 40 |
| hi    willað eow to | gafole | garas | syllan | 46 |
| ne    sceole ge swa | softe | sinc ge | gangan | 59 |
| ne    mihte þær for | wætere | werod to þam | oðrum | 64 |
| ne    mihte hyre | ænig | oþrum | derian | 70 |
| þa    noldon æt þam | forda | fleam ge | wyrcan | 81 |
| þa    hwile þe hi | wæpna | wealdan | moston | 83 |
| bædon þæt hi | upgang | agan | moston | 87 |
| hi    leton þa of | folman | feolhearde | speru | 108 |
| ge    hyrde ic þæt | eadweard | anne | sloge | 117 |
| eode þa ge | syrwed | secg to þam | eorle | 159 |
| to    raþe hine ge | lette | lidmanna | sum | 164 |
| ne    mihte he ge | healdan | heardne | mece | 167 |
| ne    mihte þa on | fotum leng | fæste ge | standan | 171 |
| ic    wylle mine | æþelo | eallum ge | cyþan | 216 |
| þa    hwile þe he | wæpen mæge | | | 235b |
| ne    þurfon me embe | sturmere | stedefæste | hælæð | 249 |
| þa    hwile ðe he | wæpna | wealdan | moste | 272 |
| he    hæfde ðeah ge | forþod | þæt he his | frean gehet | 289 |

## e) The Scansion of Other Problematic Lines

In several verse lines in *Maldon* the sound-linkage seems to occur in an unusual measure or Part. In verse line 49 the performer is, I think, forced to
indicate the sound-linkage in an eta measure:

$$\overset{/}{\text{|brimmanna}}\overset{\backslash}{}\overset{x}{\text{|boda}}\overset{/\;(x)}{}\overset{(/)\;\backslash}{\text{|abeod}}\overset{/}{\text{|eft}}\overset{x}{\text{ongean}}\overset{\backslash}{} \qquad 49$$

The alternative would be to perform *a-* in *abeod* as an epsilon. But then *-beod*
would be a delta (/ [x]) and the three-measure halfline would have a rest in
its middle measure. It seems better to perform the verse line as above.

I scan the isolated halfline at line 172, discussed above, as an epsilon and
an alpha prime 7:

$$\overset{(/)\;x\;x}{\text{|}}\overset{}{\text{he to}}\overset{/}{\text{|heofenum}}\overset{\backslash}{\text{wlat}} \qquad 172$$

The second halfline of line 271, also discussed above, can be scanned
either as an eta plus a gamma 1, or – to bring out the rhyme – as an eta with
a four-syllable second Part plus an alpha:

$$\overset{/}{\text{|æfre}}\overset{x\;x\;x}{\text{embe}}\overset{/}{\text{|stunde}}\overset{x}{}\overset{(/)\;\backslash}{\text{|he}}\overset{x}{\text{sealde}}\overset{/}{\text{|sume}}\overset{\backslash}{\text{wunde}}\overset{x}{} \qquad 271$$

$$\overset{/}{\text{|æfre}}\overset{x\;x\;x}{\text{embe}}\overset{/}{\text{|stunde}}\overset{x}{}\overset{(/)\;\backslash}{\text{|he}}\overset{x\;x\;x}{\text{sealde sume}}\overset{/}{\text{|wunde}}\overset{x}{}$$

Verse line 45, discussed above, raises a very interesting question. Taking the
line as it appears in the text, I would scan it as follows:

$$\overset{(/)\;\backslash}{\text{|gehyrst}}\overset{x}{\text{þu}}\overset{/\;\backslash}{\text{|sælida}}\overset{(/)}{\text{|}}\overset{x}{\text{hwæt}}\overset{x}{\text{þis}}\overset{/}{\text{|folc}}\overset{\backslash}{\text{segeð}} \qquad 45$$

I scan my more Beowulfian version like this:

$$\overset{(/)\;\backslash}{\text{|ge}}\overset{x}{\text{hyrst}}\overset{/\;\backslash}{\text{þu}}\overset{}{\text{|sælida}}\;\;{}^{*}\overset{(/)}{\text{|}}\overset{x}{\text{hwæt}}\overset{/}{\text{|segeð}}\overset{x}{\text{þis}}\overset{\backslash}{\text{folc}} \qquad *45$$

In verse line 288, which I discussed along with line 45 earlier, the poet builds
the first halfline around *H* sound-linkage but then fails to complete this
linkage until the second measure of the second halfline. In terms of the
rhythm, there is nothing wrong with the poet's completing the sound-linkage

with the second measure of the second halfline. That description fits the practice of both the *Beowulf* poet and Caedmon in two-fifths of their verse lines. What does not fit their practice is the placing of an alpha measure (or any of the four other measures that begin with a stressed syllable) before the measure that completes the sound-linkage. When either of the two other poets completes the sound-linkage with the second measure of the second halfline, that halfline begins with either an epsilon or an eta. Keeping it as it is, line 288 is best performed as four alphas:

|raðe wearð æt |hilde    |offa for|heawen                                    288

The rhythm of these verse lines rather than the unusual sound-patterning should probably guide the performer.

Two final verse lines call for comment. I scan the first measure of both verse lines 50 and 174 not as an eta with crowded second Parts but as somewhat unusual alphas – because of their lack of sound-linkage:

|sege þinum |leodum  |' miccle |laþre spell                                50

|ealra þæra |wynna   |' þe ic on |worulde gebad                           174

### f) The Prosody and Sound of *The Battle of Maldon*

The prosodist familiar with Beowulfian prosody can scan 266 verse lines (82 per cent) of *The Battle of Maldon* with no difficulty. The *Maldon* poet has composed these verse lines exactly as the *Beowulf* poet or Caedmon might have composed them. The prosody of *The Battle of Maldon* can be said, then, to be essentially the same as the prosody of *Beowulf* and Caedmon's 'Hymn.' This is the most important point to be made about the prosody of *Maldon*: It is a variation on the 'classical' prosody of *Beowulf* and Caedmon's 'Hymn.' The two quantitative differences between *Beowulf* and *Maldon* lie in the *Maldon* poet's use of more multi-measure verse lines and his willingness to crowd many more Parts with four or even five syllables.

The qualitative differences between the two poems are more interesting. At times it seems that one can directly contrast the *Maldon* poet's mode of expression with the *Beowulf* poet's:

|wiglaf wæs |haten                                               (*Beowulf* 2602a)

```
  _(/)___  \ x   /   \
|se waes haten |wulfstan
```
(*Maldon* 75b)

It turns out, however, that the *Maldon* poet can, if desired, name a warrior almost exactly as the *Beowulf* poet does:

```
(/)  x   x  /  x  \   /  \   / x
|  waes min |ealda faeder  |ealhelm |haten
```
(*Maldon* 218)

The effect of the *Maldon* poet's demonstrative in line 75b is, then, to insist that it was *that one named Wulfstan* who was chosen to hold the causeway. With line 75b, then, the poet seems to be taking the audience to the very scene of the battle.

Since there is something a bit clumsy about the really complex etas like the one in 9a (*be þam man mihte on-*), one tends to look for reasons for such passages. Perhaps a reasonable explanation is that the *Maldon* poet was trying to express ideas that either had not been expressed before by traditional poets or had only been expressed in more traditional ways – by means of proverbs, for example. One can imagine the *Beowulf* poet commenting on the account of Offa's son releasing his beloved hawk with a *swa sceal* proverb.

In telling of Byrhtnoþ's generalship, too, the *Maldon* poet uses complex etas:

```
 __ (/)__  \   x    /   x
|hu   hi sceoldon |standan
```
19a
```
 __ (/)_  \   x  x  /  (x)    / x x x /    x
|þa   he haefde þaet |folc    |faegere geltrymmed
```
22

At times one wonders whether the poet wasn't simply trying to recreate Byrhtnoþ's actual words:

```
   (/) \   x   /  \   (/)   x   x  /    \
|'gehyrst þu, |saelida,  |   hwaet þis |folc segeð?'
```
45

That explanation at least makes some sense out of the unusual sound-linkage of this verse line. And, it perhaps justifies the eta reading in the second halfline of verse line 49 that I discussed earlier.

Sometimes the peculiar syncopated lilt of the eta simply sounds just right:

```
   /   x x   /  x   (/) \  x / x  \
|sege þinum |leodum  |  miccle |laþre spell
```
50
```
 (/)  \   x   /   \  (/) \ x   /    \
|  hloh þa |modi man |  saede |metode þanc
```
147

This analysis of the prosody of *The Battle of Maldon* shows, I think, that the poet knew the old oral tradition well. But the *Maldon* poet had much to say that seemed to be pressing against the limits of that tradition. In composing verse that conveys a sense of immediacy, of the complexity of generalship in the world of the 990s, and even of the very voices of the fighters, the *Maldon* poet seems to have been, like the *Beowulf* poet, a virtuoso of the tradition.

University of Massachusetts at Amherst

NOTES

1  Robert Payson Creed, *Reconstructing the Rhythm of 'Beowulf'* (Columbia, Mo.: University of Missouri Press 1990). To assist the reader who has not yet read the book, I summarize the main points here. This summary will also make it easier to understand my use of certain terms like *measure* in my analysis of *Maldon*. The book begins by demonstrating the hypothesis that the verse lines of *Beowulf* can only be read from the manuscript lines by attending to stressed, (initial-)sound-linked (i.e., 'alliterating') syllables. The book then falsifies every other hypothesis for determining the verse lines of the poem – syllable counting, counting only certain syllables, attempting to rely only on clause or phrase boundaries, etc. Then the book demonstrates that the first ($A$) and last ($A'$) sound-linked syllable of each successive series of sound-linked syllables head the key constituents of the verse line. $A$ and $A'$ divide the verse line into two halflines: $A$ heads the key constituent of the first halfline, $A'$ the key constituent of the second halfline. $A$ heads the *measure* from which the remaining measure – rarely measures – of the *first* halfline can be determined; $A'$ serves the same function for the *second* halfline. The remaining measures are then determined in one of the following ways: (1) by a sound-linked syllable that occurs between $A$ and $A'$, *unless A* is preceded by a proclitic passage; (2) by a stressed but not sound-linked syllable that follows $A$ or $A'$; or (3) by a passage that is proclitic to either $A$ or $A'$. By a proclitic passage I mean one that contains no sound-linked syllable. A proclitic passage of three syllables or fewer generates a preceding *rest* that may indicate one of the points at which musical accompaniment or augmentation would have been most clearly heard. Finally, every measure is shown to be divisible into two *Parts*; the first Part indicates the heavier downbeat, the second Part the lighter upbeat that completes the simple rhythmic pulse of every measure of the poem. Every measure of *Beowulf*, Caedmon's 'Hymn,' and *The Battle of Maldon*, as the present work demonstrates,

can be shown to be a variation on the simplest and most frequently occurring measure, which I call 'alpha 1' (a single long stressed syllable followed by a single unstressed syllable whether long or short).

2 Robert Payson Creed, 'The Archetypal Verse Line in Caedmon's "Hymn" and *Beowulf*,' in Joan H. Hall, N. Doane, and R. Ringler, eds, *Old English and New: Studies in Language and Linguistics in Honor of Frederic G. Cassidy* (New York: Garland Publishing 1992), 31–45.

3 I quote the text of *The Battle of Maldon* from a composite that I prepared for this study. The composite is based on two sources: (1) E.V.K. Dobbie's text of the poem on pages 7–16 in *The Anglo-Saxon Minor Poems*, The Anglo-Saxon Poetic Records, vol. 6 (New York: Columbia University Press 1942) and (2) E.V. Gordon's text on pages 41–62 in *The Battle of Maldon* (New York: Appleton-Century-Crofts 1968). Gordon does not divide verse lines into halflines, as Dobbie does, but Dobbie does not include the 'accent' marks as Gordon does. Where an editor adds a letter or letters I enclose the added material in square brackets. Where an editor changes a letter or the order of letters I italicize the change. I stripped out all editorial punctuation and capitalization and then analysed this composite text in an eight-column grid.

4 The possibility that the *Maldon* poet does not admit sound-linkage ('alliteration') between 's' and 's plus consonant' seems to me to be falsified by verse line 282, where *si-* (in *sibyrhtes*) sets up the sound-linkage that is completed by *swið-* (in *swiðe*). On the other hand, it seems likely that the *Maldon* poet, unlike the *Beowulf* poet, hears the *g* before a back vowel (as in *gafole*) as a different sound than the *g* before a fronted vowel like *y* (as in *forgyldon*).

5 The alpha 6 reading depends upon keeping minimal stress on *þa* even though a word at the end of a halfline tends to acquire a heightened degree of stress.

6 See the previous note. Alpha 9, if it occurred, would run something like this: *\*hogode to þære ...*

7 John Miles Foley, 'Formula and Theme in Old English Poetry,' in B.A. Stolz and R.S. Shannon III, eds, *Oral Literature and the Formula* (Ann Arbor, Mich.: Center for the Coordination of Ancient and Modern Studies 1976), 207–32. In the early seventies, Foley and I were willing to read certain passages containing the sound-linked syllable as etas. Except under special circumstances, I now read all sound-linked passages as alphas, alpha primes, etc., preceded by epsilons. In my *Reconstructing the Rhythm of 'Beowulf'* I have little to say about the eta measure, even though I am certain that it offers the best reading of certain verse lines.

# The Poet's Self-Interruption in *Andreas*

JOHN MILES FOLEY

The *Andreas* poet proceeds quite a distance – 1477 lines, to be exact – in his retelling of the apocryphal account of Matthew and Andrew among the Mermedonians before he ungraciously interrupts his own performance. He does so in order to vouchsafe his uncertainty about continuing, to question his own capability to carry the tale through to its conclusion. Since this self-imposed intermezzo is unique in surviving Anglo-Saxon poetry, there exists no ready model or analogy to help us with its interpretation, and we are left to ascribe to this otherwise competent poet an admission of lack of religious learning or poetic ability, a failure of nerve, or perhaps even a dark night of the soul.[1]

What I propose to offer in this paper is another explanation for the interruption, and in the process to take the opportunity to consider what impact some recent developments in literary theory, folklore, and anthropological linguistics may have on our reception of the poem as a whole. The key to this approach will lie in recognizing that the *Andreas* is indeed a *performance* – not the imagined improvisation of an oral bard, to be sure, but nonetheless a kind of performance. From this insight and the empirically justifiable argument that the Old English poem is an interestingly augmented translation of a (probably Latin) version of the Greek Πράξεις Ἀνδρέου καὶ Ματθεία εἰς τὴν πόλιν τῶν ἀνθρωποφάγων,[2] we will be able to ascertain what the poet means when he quite heavy-handedly puts down his verse making in order to comment on it, exiting the planned program to construct his own metanarrative. As dislocating as his temporary abandonment of the versified story may seem, it will in fact aid us in better understanding the nature of the medium with which he and his counterparts work, and particularly of the way in which that medium fosters a unique combination of traditional resonance and individual craft. In short, this paper will suggest how to avoid disenfranchising either the traditional oral roots of Old English verse or the peculiar, quite singular, genius of the *Andreas* poet.

## Spectrum, Register, and Reception

Anthropologists and folklorists have left us no responsible alternative but to abandon the Great Divide thesis of oral versus written literature. These categories have shown themselves to be insufficient to the task of parsing the worldwide assortment of verbal art – as in South Africa, where electronic news infiltrates highly politicized praise-poetry; as in Anglo-American balladry, where broadsides compete with the palimpsest of memory for influence on a given singer or version; even in the former Yugoslavia, where people who use *litterae* for correspondence or the consultation of manuals never resort to reading and writing in the transmission of stories and customs. Life has proven more complex than the 'strong thesis' of Parry, Lord, and others allowed: real societies and real individuals seldom line up neatly across the imagined Great Divide.[3]

Given this complexity, together with the undeniable if selective prominence of writing in the medieval period, some scholars have opted to 'write off,' so to speak, the influence or even the existence of oral tradition. If probably written and probably oral poems show similar characteristics, we were told some years ago,[4] then all's one and we are relieved of the responsibility of fashioning an oral, or even a composite, poetics. I would point out that admitting complexity and assimilating to the culturally dominant model – *our* writing and reading, the very medium we use to define ourselves and earn our bread – are not the same thing. A 'hard Maloneism' or 'hard Bensonism' is just as unattractive as a 'hard Parryism,' and just as likely to lead us astray in our efforts to understand Old English poetry.

I prefer to accept the realistic messiness resulting from the interaction of oral traditions with written and print or electronic media as the base condition, and to attempt to deal with the situation as best we can. Toward this end I have found two concepts extremely helpful: the idea of a spectrum in lieu of a typology, and secondly, the linguistic notion of a 'register' of language.[5] The first of these concepts is nothing more than common sense: we simply envisage the assortment of reported interactions between oral traditions and texts as a spectrum of theoretically infinite shadings, granting to the worldwide assortment of expressive forms the same diversity and heterogeneity we customarily grant other cultural manifestations. The second distinction, that of a 'register' of language, is borrowed from anthropological linguistics, where it denotes a variety of language differentiated not by geographical area or by chronology, but by social function. Even today each of us manages a large repertoire of registers, whether we know it or not; many of us speak differently to children than to academic administrators, for example, and the language I am using in this published paper differs somewhat from that employed in its oral antecedent. Registers are, in short, codes that we use in appropriate situations; the result of inappropriate deployment is miscommunication of one sort or another – as in the time I 'mislexically' directed a colleague in Belgrade to a fourteenth-century Turkish veranda (a *čardak* – complete with implicit hookahs, pashas, and beys) when all the poor fellow wanted was the porch.

We can extend this idea of register to the Anglo-Saxon poetic language, a specialized variety of Old English that follows certain rules in its metrical, lexical, and syntactic dynamics. The prosody, vocabulary, and stylistic traits we associate with Old English verse are some of the defining features of its integrity as a register or, as the Native Americanist Dell Hymes has so aptly put it, a 'way of speaking.' Comparative research has demonstrated, at least to my satisfaction, that this register at some point arose from an oral tradition, but has not demonstrated exactly what connection our extant texts – and they *are* texts – might have had to this prior and perhaps ongoing tradition. And here our investigations have stalled: we are loath to hypothesize too much, and so the usual tendency has been to acknowledge a distant debt to oral tradition, and then to treat the Old English poems as if they were fully and unambiguously 'our' kind of poetry. I think this is an inadequate response to the challenge presented by a poetic register that has, after all, managed to persist long past the *adventus litterarum*, and I would suggest, in concert with recent work by Katherine O'Brien O'Keeffe and A.N. Doane,[6] that this inadequacy is traceable to a discontinuity in reception – that it is, in short, our problem.

Another way to look at our problem is to confront the riddle posed by the persistence of traditional forms in the poetry. Notice that I have now deleted the 'oral' term in the equation; since we are dealing with manuscript witnesses, it seems untenable to speak of their contents as 'oral,' unless one finds refuge in the double designation 'traditional oral.' At any rate, I cannot defend using the unadorned term 'oral' to speak about Anglo-Saxon verse; not only is that category much too generic and subdividable to be of much heuristic value, and not only must medievalists deal with textual reflections, but we should also stipulate that even a known transcription of an oral performance amounts to an intersemiotic translation from an event to a thing. With these caveats in mind, let us try the question of the persistence of traditional forms. Why does the *Andreas* poet, or any other poet, continue to depend upon them? Are these artists antiquarians by nature? Do they, as G.S. Kirk has been so quick to claim for the South Slavic bard,[7] have only a limited grasp of what they are doing? Surely the canonical Parry-Lord explanation from utility – the ease of composition under the pressure of oral performance – must be disqualified if it is likely that these poets were composing in writing.

*To lang ys to reccenne*, but, as I have tried to show elsewhere,[8] a poet uses a given register because it indexes the context in which he or she wants the communication to be received. Thus Homer, or whatever group of poets antiquity was identifying with the name Homer, uses the hexameter diction first and foremost because it establishes the interactive context of ancient Greek heroic poetry in which the present performance or text is to be placed. Even when Homer or his colleagues turn away from *The Iliad* and *The Odyssey* toward the composition of chiefly lyric Hymns, their employment of the hexameter register signals the mythic background against which these prayers and praises are sung. Likewise, the South Slavic bards invoke a mythic context for events and characters merely by resorting to the decasyllabic register that is the medium of most of the genuinely heroic poetry, while women, bearers and performers of other kinds of poetry, summon a different arena by turning to an octosyllabic 'way of speaking.'[9]

If the poetic register, that specialized variety of language tied to situation and social function, is so evocative of context, thus enriching any particular performance with unspoken but still immanent resonance, then why should a poet abandon its unique qualities as an expressive instrument simply because he or she begins to read or write? To phrase the same matter in another way, how can such a poet afford to lose the traditional resonance inherent in such a specially coded language? To forgo the inimitable advantages of the 'dedicated' medium (to have recourse to an analogy from computing) is to cut oneself off from a body of implication that is directly accessible in no other way. Small wonder that, *pace* the Great Divide theorists, wordsmiths clung stubbornly to a highly stylized, artificial diction and scenic repertoire; until other stylistic means could be devised that permitted a comparable aesthetic advantage, what reason could they have had to do otherwise?

Of course, there is another crucial dimension to this situation, one that our only-too-ready assimilation of Old English poetry to contemporary textuality often shields from view. I speak of the audience, or reader, the other bookend to the communicative act, whom we ignore or make monolithic at our peril. Many recent developments in literary theory have aimed at upgrading the audience to full partnership in the making of the work of art, by recognizing that reception is not at all a foregone conclusion but itself a complex, multifaceted process. The school of Receptionalism, for instance (pioneered by Hans Robert Jauss and Wolfgang Iser),[10] positions the 'work' midway between the text and its perceiver, with 'reality' constituted as much by the plethora of readers as by the physical object of the text. As I have attempted to illustrate elsewhere,[11] this model translates easily to traditional texts and even traditional oral performances, with allowances made for the endemic heterogeneity of the audience and the focusing factor of traditional signification. Young and old, female and male, familiar and unfamiliar may be present in the same audience, each with his or her own predispositions; in this case, however, the very consistency of register – in both its semantic and metonymic dimensions – will to an extent counteract the centrifugal responses of an otherwise diverse audience. Within the 'performance arena' defined by the use of a given register – the communicative equivalent of selecting a channel for transmission and reception – the answer to Stanley Fish's famous question is: 'Yes, there *is* a "text" in this class.'

We must therefore see Old English poetry not as an oral or written phenomenon, but as a poetry in which individual artists employ a traditional register. Let us recognize that traditional oral forms persist in manuscripts not because they are merely useful, or charming, or stylistically correct, but because they continue to encode an immanent context, a referential background that deepens and complicates whatever more particular events occupy the foreground in a given work. And let us not forget the audience, both their demands and their responsibilities as partners in the signifying loop. Without audiences and readers willing and able to listen, the most splendid old oak will make no sound when it falls, and the most densely coded traditional utterance may appear only pedestrian or awkward – Homer or his counterparts 'nodding.' All three of these principles ask no more than a reasonable complication of the work of art, paying attention not only to *what* but also to *how* it means.

### Adding Traditional Insult to Textual Injury

As a brief example of how the *Andreas* poet uses the traditional register, I summon what may seem at first sight an unlikely witness: the description of Andrew's first of four miserable nights in prison. All day long his faith has been tested by physical torture, and the night brings only a continuation of that scourging in the form of a mental assault. To the expectable notation of his suffering the poet adds the following:[12]

> Snaw eorðan band
> wintergeworpum;   weder coledon
> heardum hægelscurum,   swylce hrim ond forst,
> hare hildstapan,   hæleða eðel
> lucon, leoda gesetu.   Land wæron freorig;

cealdum cylegicelum    clang wæteres þrym,
ofer eastreamas    is brycgade,
blæce brimrade.    Bliðheort wunode
eorl unforcuð,    elnes gemyndig,
þrist ond þrohtheard,    in þreanedum
wintercealdan niht.    No on gewitte blon,
acol for þy egesan,    þæs þe he ær ongann,
þæt he a domlicost    dryhten herede,
weorðade wordum,    oððæt wuldres gim
heofontorht onhlad.                    (ll 1255b–1269a)

Of course there is absolutely no precedent for this passage in the Greek *Praxeis*, and for good reason: it represents an appearance of the ubiquitous and much discussed 'exile theme' first analysed in detail by Stanley Greenfield.[13] As such, it is a decidedly Anglo-Saxon gloss on the Greek narrative, a 'traditional translation,' if you will. For the *Andreas* poet has done no more – and no less – than to index the idea of psychological torture of the solitary saint by appeal to a ready and resonant analogy – the equally solitary, equally miserable figure of exile. Read outside of this paradigm, the passage seems strange and awkward: we wonder why the poet branches off to such a lyric expostulation, and we may even be curious about the sudden change in the weather! Read against the *anhagan* indexed by the Exile pattern, however (against the Wanderer, Seafarer, and their kin), this moment in the story of Andrew appears in a new light, viewed from inside the syncretic poetics of Old English traditional verse.

## Before and After: Source and 'Translation'

With the idea of a 'traditional translation' in mind, that is, with the notion of a target language that offers its own repertoire of expressive possibilities, let us consider what happens just before and after the poet's self-interruption at 1478–91. First, here is a literal rendering of that portion of the *Praxeis* that corresponds to *Andreas* 1450–77:

> And standing apart [Andrew] spoke: 'For I know, O lord, that you have not forsaken me.' And when it was evening they took him back and threw him into the prison, having bound his hands behind him. And he was exceedingly exhausted and enfeebled. And the men of the city spoke among themselves: 'Perhaps he will die this same night, and we will not find him living tomorrow.' For he was exhausted, and his flesh was spent.

And the lord appeared in the prison, and having extended his hand he
spoke to Andrew: 'Give me your hand, and arise whole.' And having looked
upon the lord Jesus, he gave his hand to him and arose whole, and falling
down he worshipped him and spoke: 'I thank you, my lord Jesus Christ.'

I now append the twenty-eight-line section from *Andreas*, marking with an asterisk (*) those half-lines that have a direct precedent in the *Praxeis* and with a
plus sign (+) those that are variations on the asterisked half-lines. We will have
occasion to comment on certain of the marked and the unmarked verses below.

```
*Ða worde cwæð   wigendra hleo:                         1450
'Sie ðe ðanc ond lof,   *þeoda waldend,
to widan feore   +wuldor on heofonum,
*ðæs ðu me on sare,   +sigedryhten min,
ellþeodigne   *an ne forlæte.'
   Swa se dædfruma   dryhten herede                     1455
halgan stefne,   *oððæt hador sig[e]l
*wuldortorht gewat   *under wadu scriðan.
Þa þa folctogan   feorðan siðe,
egle ondsacan,   *æðeling læddon
*to þam carcerne;   woldon cræfta gehygd,               1460
magorædendes   mod oncyrran
on þære deorcan niht.   *Þa com dryhten God
*in þæt hlinræced,   +hæleða wuldor,
ond þa wine synne   wordum grette
*ond frofre gecwæð,   +fæder manncynnes,                1465
+lifes lareow.   *Heht his lichoman
*hales brucan:   'Ne scealt ðu in henðum a leng
searohæbbendra   sar þrowian.'
   *Aras þa mægene rof;   *sægde meotude þanc,
*hal of hæfte   heardra wita.                           1470
Næs him gewemmed wlite,   ne wloh of hrægle
lungre alysed,   ne loc of heafde,
ne ban gebrocen,   ne blodig wund
lic(e) gelenge,   ne laðes dæl
þurh dolgslege   dreore bestemed,                       1475
ac wæs eft swa ær   þurh þa æðelan miht
lof lædende,   ond on his lice trum.
```

The pattern of asterisked half-lines indicates, in a kind of gross anatomical
sketch, the relationship of the *Praxeis* source to the Old English versification.

The *Andreas* poet is essentially retelling the story fairly closely, but hardly slavishly; in the normal manner of the traditional register, the skeleton of the narrative is fleshed out with formal variations as well as augmentations of different sorts, and there is no attempt to provide a literal translation. In addition, there are small insertions into the story that have no basis in the *Praxeis*. All of these divergences, some of them familiar items in the traditional poetic wordhoard, illustrate the poet's individual artistry, the deftness with which he moulds the target idiom to resonate with stylistic overtones.

At the microcosmic level, the relatively common phrase *wigendra hleo* (1450b) illustrates the poet's predilections in translation. Customarily used in the poetic register to denominate a figure of patently martial heroic achievement in defence of a people (Beowulf, Hrothgar, and Sigemund in *Beowulf*; Edmund in *Capture of the Five Boroughs*), it can also be applied to God, in his capacity as protector of the human race. The narrator of the *Advent Lyrics* refers to God in this way toward the end of the eleventh lyric, and the *Andreas* poet has Andrew call his as-yet-unrecognized divine companion 'protector of warriors' during their sea journey earlier in the poem. As a traditional phrase, *wigendra hleo* thus refers fundamentally to a heroic figure who has performed bravely for the sake of his people, and this indexical meaning can readily be transferred in the poetry, from the secular protector to the Christian God who defends the larger human flock.

But neither the core assignment of meaning nor its ready transposition to the world of Christian thought and action can explain the last two occurrences of *wigendra hleo*, both of them in *Andreas*. The final one, at 1672b, names the holy man Andrew as 'protector of warriors,' thus assigning the meek and much-beleaguered saint to the cadre of heroic figures mentioned above. He is given this resonant title by none other than God himself, who is ordering Andrew to return to the land of the Mermedonians to secure their incipient conversion (1672–4):

> Wuna in þære winbyrig,   *wigendra hleo*,
> salu sinchroden,   seofon nihta fyrst;
> syððan ðu mid mildse   minre ferest.

He dutifully spends the prescribed seven-day period among the former cannibals, and his ministrations prove effective: in a continuation of the traditional translation, the poet tells us that this *wuldres þegn* (1678b) was the reason for their growth in faith. Without doubt the traditional characterization of Andrew as *wigendra hleo* harmonizes well with the saint's achievements – for he clearly accomplishes as much in the field of proselytizing as his onomastic confrères do on the field of battle.

Traditional characterization, by implicit reference to the type encoded in the phrase 'protector of warriors,' also lies behind the occurrence of *wigendra hleo* at 1450b. At this juncture the holy man, having echoed Christ in asking God '*hwæt forlætest ðu me?*' (1413b) and having received God's pledge of support and corroborating visual symbol of the beautiful groves of trees blooming where he had moments ago shed his blood (1448–9), now addresses his creator with thanks (1450–4, quoted above). One could explain this instance of 'protector of warriors' as looking ahead – after the interruption – to the time when Andrew will miraculously loose the destructive waters (1498 and following), or perhaps with more immediate logic to the closing moments of the poem when, as we have seen, Andrew returns to Mermedonia to consolidate the Christian conquest. But I believe we more fully understand the expressive method and more readily foster a continuity of reception if we interpret this metonymic title as applying to the whole of Andrew's hagiographical existence, that is, to the poem's activities from start to finish. Andrew's actions are heroic, this traditional phrase is telling us, on a par with those of the mythic paragons Beowulf, Hrothgar, and Sigemund; equal in their way to the political and historical deeds of Edmund; parallel to the saving grace of God himself. Such indexed parity is the fundamental poetic function of *wigendra hleo*, a highly resonant item in the traditional register.

A second feature apparently added by the poet to the lines preceding his self-interruption provides an interesting echo of earlier passages. This is the brief 'catalogue of healing' (1471–7) that expands upon the saint's miraculous restoration. First come the two lines that correspond straightforwardly enough to the *Praxeis*:

> And having looked upon the lord Jesus, he gave his hand to him and arose whole, and falling down he worshipped him and spoke: 'I thank you, my lord Jesus Christ.'

> Aras þa mægene rof;  sægde meotude þanc,
> hal of hæfte  heardra wita.                                              (1469–70)

We then hear an extrapolation on the holy man's transfiguration, presented as a rhetorical series of negatives that have no precedent in the Greek: we learn now that the Old English saint's countenance was not defiled, nor was the hem of his garment torn off, nor a lock of hair from his head, nor was a bone broken, nor a bloody wound visible on his body, nor any part of his body drenched with blood because of a cruel wound. The poet emphasizes that he became once again as he was before, through God's agency.

This enumeration corresponds to three earlier passages in the *Andreas* that likewise have no precedent in the *Praxeis*, namely the three descriptions of the wounds inflicted on the prisoner, one description for each of the three days of torture. Of course, these prior catalogues are presented not as a negative series emphasizing the saint's restoration, but as horrifying accounts of the severity of his ordeal. I quote a short selection from each of them:

> Wæs þæs halgan lic
> sarbennum soden,   swate bestemed,
> banhus abrocen;   blod yðum weoll,
> haton heolfre.                                                      (1238b–41a)

> Swat yðum weoll
> þurh bancofan,   blod lifrum swealg,
> hatan heolfre;   hra weorces ne sann
> wundum werig.                                                      (1275b–78a)

> wæs se halga wer
> sare geswungen,   searwum gebunden,
> dolgbennum þurhdrifen,   ðendon dæg lihte.          (1395b–97)

More than mere textual echo, however, these lexical and narrative corre-spondences call attention to the poet's use of the traditional poetic register. For the first three passages represent realizations of a constituent element – 'The prisoner's wounds are described' – within a thrice-repeated pattern that has been identified as the 'Scourging theme' in *Andreas*, a pattern that, significantly, has no basis in the Greek source.[14] Alerted to this narrative matrix, we may 'reread' the transfiguration of the saint in a different light. The third day of torture, like the first two, has involved the following: (1) the enemy arrives with a large troop, (2) the enemy leads the prisoner out and drags him around the city, (3) a description of the prisoner's wounds, (4) the enemy leads the prisoner back to his cell, and (5) the prisoner confronts night and mental torture. Although the *Praxeis* typically makes no mention of the final element on this third day, the heathen in *Andreas* are pictured as practising their evil psychological designs anyway (1460b–62a):

> woldon cræfta gehygd,
> magorædendes   mod oncyrran
> on þære deorcan niht.

Then, in opposition to their machinations, as well as to the Exile theme we noted above during the first night, and to the attack of the *atol aglæca* and his troop during the second night (1311 and following), God enters Andrew's cell. What is more, he comes not to test but to reward Andrew for his per-severance, and the poet underlines the reversal idiomatically and through the poetic register by, in effect, subtracting the afflictions that were thematically added to the saint's misery in earlier passages, enumerating them, as we have seen, in a catalogue. It is as if the *Andreas* poet were balancing the terrible afflictions visited upon the holy man with a point-by-point dismissal of his physical suffering. In a rhetorical *tour de force* that is *both* traditional *and* individual, the poet deepens the 'translation' by a personalized selection from the wordhoard.

The same general strategy, which we might label 'indexed translation,' informs *Andreas* after the poet's self-interruption. Immediately below are, first, the *Praxeis* passage that corresponds to *Andreas* 1492–1508a, and, second, the Old English poetic excerpt itself. As before, I have marked with an asterisk (*) those verses with a direct precedent in the *Praxeis* and with a plus sign (+) those that constitute variations on such lines:

> And Andreas, having looked into the middle of the prison, saw a pillar standing and an alabaster statue lying on the pillar. Andrew unfolded his hands seven times and spoke to the pillar and the statue upon it: 'Fear the sign of the cross, which the heavens and the earth dread, and let the statue on the pillar bring up much water through its mouth as a purge, so that those in this very city may be punished.'

```
*He be wealle geseah    wundrum fæste
under sælwage  *sweras unlytle,
+*stapulas standan    storme bedrifene,
+eald enta geweorc;  *he wið anne þæra,                    1495
+mihtig ond modrof,  *mæðel gehede,
+wis, wundrum gleaw,  +word stunde ahof:
'Geher ðu, marmanstan,    meotudes rædum,
*fore þæs onsyne    ealle gesceafte
*forhte geweorðað,    þonne hie fæder geseoð              1500
heofonas ond eorðan    herigea mæste
on middangeard    manncynn secan!
*Læt nu of þinum staþole  *streamas weallan,
+ea inflede,   nu ðe ælmihtig
hateð, heofona cyning,    þæt ðu hrædlice                 1505
on þis fræte folc    forð onsende
wæter widrynig  *to wera cwealme,
+geafon geotende.'
```

Two half-lines in this passage stand out as especially familiar and obviously traditional: *storme bedrifene* at 1494b and *eald enta geweorc* in the very next verse. The first of these finds numerous structural and lexical echoes throughout the Anglo-Saxon poetic corpus, perhaps none closer in both metonymic and lexical content, than the exile-linked occurrence in *The Wife's Lament*, where *min freond siteð / under stanhliþe storme behrimed* (47b–48). The second phrase, either, as here, as *enta ærgeweorc*, or as the metrically shorter *enta geweorc*, likewise resonates throughout the canon, occurring in *The Wanderer* (87a), *The Ruin* (2b), *Maxims 2* (2a), and of course *Beowulf* (1679a, 2717b, and 2774a) as well as earlier in *Andreas* (1235a). The immediate contexts for the 'old work(s) of giants' range from a meditation on the transience of the world to the great age of cities to the hilt of the magic sword that Beowulf presents to Hrothgar, and on to the pillars of the dragon's hoard; the earlier instance in *Andreas* applies to the streets and byways through which the saint was dragged as the Mermedonians tortured him. What these usages share, however, is not the particular topical circumstances in which they appear, or any literal relationship to giants and their works, but rather the idiomatic value of retrojection into the deep past. By employing *eald enta geweorc*, the poets index the subject of their immediate concern among other objects or structures consigned to the same category. Thus the *Andreas* poet employs the phrase a second time to render the columns, soon to produce the miraculous purging flood, metonymically ancient and therefore suitably mysterious.

Given that neither 'beaten upon by storm' nor 'old work(s) of giants' has any precedent whatever in the *Praxeis*, and that both are traditional and thus bear extrasemantic associations (exile and age/mystery, respectively), we may use their example to propose an underlying poetic strategy more pervasive and systemic than the particular phrases alone can suggest. Scholars have often remarked on the plasticity of the Old English poetic language, and on the necessity of that flexibility for success in satisfying metrical requirements, especially the alliterative constraint. Even when the matter of oral tradition is not brought into the equation, the spectre of mechanism – of compounding elements that seem not to enter into the core meaning of the ongoing narrative, for instance, and may even be considered extraneous – looms threateningly close to the discussion. I would propose an alternative to this way of thinking, and also to the idea of 'mere' stylistic devices or a purely textual logic, by arguing that it is precisely in such 'throwaway' verses, which may at first sight seem accommodating but somehow supernumerary, that the excellent poet shows his or her true command of the poetic art. Because the *Beowulf* poet can index the sword-hilt – with all of its endemic mystery – in a ready traditional category of objects and structures of great age and indeterminate provenance, he reveals an ability to compose the poem not *in spite of* the traditional idiom but rather *through its unique agency*. Similarly, phrases such as the two examined here allow the *Andreas* poet to harness the metonymic power of the register in service of his 'indexed translation,' in which the story told in the *Praxeis* or a close relative becomes a work of identifiably and authentically Anglo-Saxon verbal art.

**Performance and Performance Anxiety**

Now that we have some sense of the extent to which the *Andreas* poet has indexed his translation by adding phrases and ideas unprecedented in his source and unique to his compositional register, we may attempt to place his self-interruption in a fresh context. Let us begin by quoting the passage in full (1478–91):

> H(w)æt, ic hwile nu    haliges lare
> leoðgiddinga,    lof þæs þe worhte,
> wordum wemde,    wyrd undyrne.                               1480
> Ofer min gemet    mycel is to secganne,
> langsum leornung,    þæt he in life adreag,
> eall æfter orde;    þæt scell æglæwra
> mann on moldan    þonne ic me tælige
> findan on ferðe,    þæt fram fruman cunne                    1485
> eall þa earfeðo    þe he mid elne adreah
> grimra guða.    Hwæðre git sceolon
> lytlum sticcum    leoðworda dæl
> furður reccan;    þæt is fyrnsægen,
> hu he weorna feala    wita geðolode,                        1490
> heardra hilda,    in þære hæðenan byrig.

If performance amounts, in the words of folklorist Richard Bauman, to 'the nexus of tradition, practice, and emergence in verbal art,'[15] then what we have learned about the Old English poeticizing of the Andrew story qualifies it as a kind of performed work. It is also a performance in the sense advocated by Receptionalist critics like Jauss and Iser, who envisage the work of verbal art as an emergent co-creation by author and reader or audience. In both cases there exist gaps of indeterminacy – like the questions of the thrust of *eald enta geweorc* examined above – that can be bridged only by the reader's or audience's bringing to bear certain knowledge that, strictly speaking, cannot be 'found' in the given text. Whether we are considering a modern novel or an early medieval poem, then, all experiences of texts can be understood as (inevitably idiosyncratic) performances.

The *Andreas* poet, for his part, is performing the Andrew story within the limits and with the aid of the traditional poetic register. His is, as we have remarked, a kind of indexed translation, with the narrative rendered idiomatically in a target language. At one point during the performance – to be precise just after completion of the third of the three Scourging episodes – he acknowledges a degree of what we would nowadays call 'performance anxiety,' exiting the story-line for a moment to detail his own shortcomings as an interpreter of the tale in Old English. Observing that his account has already been extensive, the poet stresses that it is far beyond his ability to describe the saint's suffering from beginning to end, that such an immense task should be left to someone *æglæwra* (literally, 'more learned in the law') than he, probably a person better schooled in the scriptures.

While this is a logical enough conclusion about the poet's quandary, in that it posits an impediment that would seem debilitating enough to cause anxiety and perhaps the resultant interruption, it oversimplifies a complex situation. We can understand the quandary and motivation for the break in more depth if we start by recognizing that the *Andreas* poet is actually performing at two levels: he is re-creating the *Praxeis* story, and, secondly, he is employing the traditional register for that re-creation. When he interrupts himself and recounts the problems that stand in the way of continuing, the poet exits the first of these levels of performance – the story of Andrew – but not the second. That is, he continues to employ the traditional idiom even as he describes how difficult his task is, and how unprepared he is to go on. An analysis of the phraseology employed during the intermezzo confirms this impression: of the twenty-eight half-lines that the passage comprises, only a single one (1479b) is unparalleled in the rest of the poetic corpus.

Such fluency in the register, in the 'way of speaking' that constitutes the vehicle of Old English poetry, is all the more remarkable when we consider that the interruption must represent undiscovered generic territory for the poet: on available evidence, this is a unique 'genre,' wholly without a model or rules, and yet he carries on idiomatically and without apparent hesitation. In this fluency the *Andreas* poet is not unlike many traditional artists in other cultures – some of whom use literacy for certain purposes – who know their compositional registers so thoroughly that they can create 'new' kinds of discourse within the idiom. Our fieldwork team recorded just such an event in central Serbia in 1975, from an epic bard named Milutin Milojević in the village of Velika Ivanča. Milojević had just finished a performance of a long narrative and a poetic recitation of the members of his army battalion (another new genre!) when we asked whether we could take his photograph for our records. In response he spontaneously composed the following four lines:

> Ja od Boga imam dobrog dara,
> Evo mene, mojega slikara;
> Kogod 'oće, ko me lepo čuje,
> On mene lepo nek slikuje.

> Yes, from God I have a fine gift,
> Here comes my photographer;
> Whoever wishes, whoever hears me well,
> Let him take my picture well.

Milojević had never had his picture taken before, so we may be sure that these were 'new' lines. But they were at the same time also highly traditional lines, in the sense of having innumerable parallels in the South Slavic epic register. This poet was memorializing a unique event not in the unmarked conversational prose we presume as a norm for such activities, but wholly within the epic 'way of speaking.'

Of course I will not claim that the *Andreas* 'translator' was an oral poet whose methods were in every respect congruent with those of Milutin Milojević, whose novel composition is cited here only to illustrate how dynamic and pliable an instrument a traditional register really is. And it is such a register, which can support a tremendous range of composition from the most 'canonical' to the most occasional forms, that the presumably learned and literate Old English poet seems able to employ, even when conveying his doubts about continuing activities presently under way. What does it mean, then, when he calls for a person *æglæwra* than he to complete the translation?

Clearly he is not describing his ability to use the dedicated 'way of speaking,' since he seems to be able to compose even in an unknown genre. Just as clearly, access to the raw data of the story of Andrew cannot be the problem: his general fidelity to the sequence and detail of the *Praxeis* version, broken chiefly by traditional glosses that index his translation into the Anglo-Saxon world, argues strongly for the presence of a text that he himself can consult, probably a Latin intermediary of the Greek story. What I suspect the *Andreas* poet may be longing for is neither the one nor the other of these desiderata, but rather their combination or 'fit.' In other words, a person 'wiser in the law' would be a poet who could more easily adapt his fluency to this particular compositional task, who could match register and source text with more success or authority. Further, I would suspend judgment on whether the poet 'truly' feels inadequate or whether this is another Anglo-Saxon avatar of the modesty topos, but in either case I believe that he longs for a syncretic poetics.

Could the particular episode on which he is soon to embark – Andrew's summoning the retributive flood from the statue's mouth – have stimulated his hesitation at precisely this point? Having just finished the three Scourging episodes, for which he has successfully fashioned a traditionally indexed rendering, did he sense an impending lack of fit between his traditional idiom and the next episode? Did the translation of this structured narrative event – based on a text, we must keep in mind – match poorly with the scenic contents of his repertoire? (We need to remember here that the interruption placed no narrative demands on that repertoire, and that its source was not a predetermined text but his own thoughts and reactions.) But these are questions for another time, as are the stylistic designations contained in the curious and tantalizing phrases *lytlum sticcum* and *fyrnsægen*. For now, perhaps it is enough to say that the *Andreas* poet's self-interruption, taken in the context of the surrounding 'indexed translation,' offers us a unique perspective on the craft of poetry in Anglo-Saxon England. Without recourse to untenable and exclusivist typologies, we can take account of the traditional oral register used by this presumably literate and highly individual artist, and perhaps understand how a syncretic poetics helps us toward a continuity of reception and toward a better appreciation of his remarkable performance – including both its undeniable creativity and its patently traditional resonance.

University of Missouri


NOTES

1 Kenneth Brooks, most recent editor of the poem, observes that '[the poet] seems to be making a rhetorical disclaimer that he does not know the whole story of St. Andrew, in order to condense his poem.' *Andreas and the Fates of the Apostles* (Oxford: Clarendon Press 1961), 112. Cf Frederick Biggs, 'The Passion of Andreas: *Andreas* 1398–1491,' *Studies in Philology* 85 (1988): 413–27; James W. Earl, 'The Typological Structure of *Andreas*,' in John D. Niles, ed., *Old English Literature in Context: Ten Essays* (Woodbridge and Totowa, N.J.: Boydell and Brewer 1980), 66–89; and John P. Hermann, *Allegories of War: Language and Violence in Old English Poetry* (Ann Arbor: University of Michigan Press 1989), 140–1.

2 Claes Schaar in *Critical Studies in the Cynewulf Group* (1949; rpt New York: Haskell House 1967), 23, found the Greek text the most likely even-

tual source for the Old English poem, although he posited a Latin intermediary because Greek was little known in Anglo-Saxon England. The most thorough consideration was conducted by Robert Boenig, who reported in *Saint and Hero: 'Andreas' and Medieval Doctrine* (Lewisburg, Pa: Bucknell University Press 1991) that 'the Greek text is by far the closest in structure and language of any surviving version of the Andreas legend to both *Andreas* and the two Old English prose versions'; cf also Boenig tr., *The Acts of Andrew in the Country of the Cannibals: Translations from the Greek, Latin, and Old English* (New York: Garland 1991), which contains translations of all relevant texts and sources.

3 See especially Ruth Finnegan, *Oral Poetry: Its Nature, Significance, and Social Context* (Cambridge: Cambridge University Press 1977); and John Miles Foley, *Oral-Formulaic Theory and Research: An Introduction and Annotated Bibliography* (New York: Garland 1985); and *The Theory of Oral Composition: History and Methodology* (Bloomington: Indiana University Press, 1988; rpt. 1992); and the variety illustrated in the journal *Oral Tradition*.

4 Especially Larry D. Benson, 'The Literary Character of Anglo-Saxon Formulaic Poetry,' *PMLA* 81 (1966): 334–41. For a history of oral-formulaic theory and Old English poetry, cf Alexandra Hennessey Olsen, 'Oral-Formulaic Research in Old English Studies: Part I,' *Oral Tradition* 1 (1986): 548–606, and 'Oral-Formulaic Research in Old English Studies: Part II,' *Oral Tradition* 3 (1988): 138–90.

5 I advert to Dell Hymes's sense of registers as 'major speech styles associated with recurrent types of situations,' as explained in 'Ways of Speaking,' in Richard Bauman and Joel Sherzer, eds, *Explorations in the Ethnography of Speaking*, 2nd ed. (Cambridge: Cambridge University Press 1989): 433–51, 473–4, at 440. This distinction stems ultimately from the linguistic theories of M.A.K. Halliday, who in *The Linguistic Sciences and Language Teaching*, with Angus McIntosh and Peter Strevens (London: Longmans 1964), conceived of register in terms of three controlling variables: *field of discourse* ('the area of operation of the language activity,' 90), *mode of discourse* (spoken or written, with many more layers of taxonomy possible), and *style or tenor of discourse* ('the relations among the participants,' 92). For a full discussion of register in oral and oral-derived works, see John Miles Foley, *The Singer of Tales in Performance* (Bloomington: Indiana University Press 1995), ch. 2.

6 See Katherine O'Brien O'Keeffe's *Visible Song: Transitional Literacy in Old English Verse* (Cambridge: Cambridge University Press 1990), and A.N. Doane's 'Oral Texts, Intertexts, and Intratexts: Editing Old English,' in Jay

Clayton and Eric Rothstein, eds, *Influence and Intertextuality in Literary History* (Madison: University of Wisconsin Press 1991), 75–113.

7 See Geoffrey S. Kirk, *The Songs of Homer* (Cambridge: Cambridge University Press 1962), 100, and John Miles Foley, *Traditional Oral Epic: The 'Odyssey,' 'Beowulf,' and the Serbo-Croatian Return Song* (Berkeley: University of California Press 1990; rpt 1993), 44–5.

8 See Foley, *The Singer of Tales in Performance*, ch. 3 ('The Rhetorical Persistence of Traditional Forms'); cf also John Miles Foley, *Immanent Art: From Structure to Meaning in Traditional Oral Epic* (Bloomington: Indiana University Press 1991), chs 1, 2, and, with specific application to *Beowulf* and other Old English poetry, ch. 6.

9 In the Serbian village of Orašac, where my research team worked in the mid-1970s, women performed a variety of octosyllabic genres, among them charms (*bajanje*), lyric songs (*lirske pesme*, also called *ženske pesme*), and funeral laments (*tužbalice*), while men were responsible for heroic epic (*junačke pesme*), genealogies (*pričanje*), and other decasyllabic forms. For further discussion and references, see ch. 4 of Foley, *The Singer of Tales in Performance*.

10 See especially Wolfgang Iser, *The Implied Reader: Patterns of Communication in Prose Fiction from Bunyan to Beckett* (Baltimore: Johns Hopkins University Press 1974); *The Act of Reading: A Theory of Aesthetic Response* (Baltimore: Johns Hopkins University Press 1978); and *Prospecting: From Reader Response to Literary Anthropology* (Baltimore: Johns Hopkins University Press 1989); and by Hans Robert Jauss, *Toward an Aesthetic of Reception*, tr. Timothy Rahti, Theory and History of Literature, 2 (Minneapolis: University of Minnesota Press 1982); 'The Identity of the Poetic Text in the Changing Horizon of Understanding,' in Mario J. Valdés and Owen Miller, eds, *Identity of the Literary Text* (Toronto: University of Toronto Press 1985), 146–74.

11 See Foley, *Immanent Art*, ch. 2.

12 All quotations from *Andreas* are taken from Brooks, ed, *Andreas*. A fuller discussion of the passage below is available in Foley, *Traditional Oral Epic*, 351–4.

13 See Stanley B. Greenfield, 'The Formulaic Expression of the Theme of "Exile" in Anglo-Saxon Poetry,' *Speculum* 30 (1955): 200–6.

14 Cf Foley, *Traditional Oral Epic*, 344–54.

15 Richard Bauman, *Verbal Art as Performance* (Prospect Heights, Ill.: Waveland Press 1977), 48.

# Alliterative Licence and the Rhetorical Use of Proper Names in *The Battle of Maldon*

M.S. GRIFFITH

*The Battle of Maldon* contains a rich hoard of personal names. The poet refers directly to some three-dozen people in the space of 325 lines, and two-thirds of these are involved in the battle. Apart from the poet of *Widsith*, no other Old English poet shows such a developed interest in proper names, and the *Maldon* poet is not only interested in the names of the participants. He frequently tells us who is related to whom; at one extreme, for example, we are told the name of Ælfwine's father, Ælfric, of his grandfather, Ealhelm, and that he is a kinsman of Byrhtnoþ. Ten of the fighters are given named fathers. The poet often notes the occupation or rank of warriors, whether high or low (*burþen, ceorl, ealdorman, gysel, geneat, þegn*): their places of origin are sometimes mentioned (Ælfwine of Mercia, Leofsunu of Sturmere, Æscferþ of Northumbria); and the poet occasionally points out whether warriors are young, like Wulfmær, Ælfwine, and the unnamed kinsman of Offa, or old, like Byrhtnoþ and Byrhtwold. He is especially concerned to differentiate warriors who bear the same names: Godric, the son of Odda, from Godric, the son of Æþelgar, Eadweard the tall from Eadweard the chamberlain, and Wulfmær the young, the son of Wulfstan, from Wulfmær, the nephew of Byrhtnoþ. Doubtless, one purpose behind this unusual specificity was to demonstrate that the whole of Anglo-Saxon England, North and South, high and low, young and old, father and son, was united in opposition to the Viking invaders. Quite possibly, also, the poet's audience knew a good deal about the battle, and about who died there, and the poet was giving them no more than they expected, a properly informed celebration of the warriors' heroism. Whilst we may speculate about the poet's motive, there can be little doubt that the fact that the text is studded with proper names focuses our attention upon the individual participants in the Anglo-Saxon army who are, of course, contrasted with the entirely anonymous opposing force. It is the aim of this paper to examine the various stratagems that the poet uses to heighten our awareness of the names, and the evidence falls fairly conveniently into three sections: alliterative and metrical, onomastic word-play, and the special link that the poet draws between Byrhtnoþ and Byrhtwold.

The poem's unorthodox use of the alliterative and metrical rules is, of course, well known and commented upon by its editors and is usually interpreted as evidence of lateness of date when the poetic tradition is assumed to have been declining. E.V. Gordon, in his stout defence of the poet's art, still acknowledges that: 'His verse does not always follow the strict rules formulated by Sievers from the practice of the older poets.'[1] More recent critics have expressed more diverse opinions. E.S. Sklar sees the irregularities as characteristic of late Old English popular, rather than classical, poetry,[2] whilst D.G. Scragg attributes less importance to these features and places new emphasis on the author's 'general competence in the inherited alliterative metre' and his 'considerable skill in his handling of the alliterative technique.'[3] Nonetheless, almost all the critics have been at some pains to defend the poet from the charge of incompetence, and the attempt to assimilate a sense of the poem's general quality with an awareness of its specific technical abnormalities has often produced conclusions about the text's style which verge on the contradictory. The view expressed by S.B. Greenfield and D.G. Calder is representative: 'Though the poet may not have used Old English metrical types with great versatility, nor his poetic diction and formulas with great originality or imagination, and though he used considerable formulaic repetition, he nevertheless produced a spirited and esthetically effective poem.'[4] No one, to the best of my knowledge, has ever suggested that these irregularities might be an aspect of the poet's artistry and integral to his composition, rather than 'glaring faults.'[5] An examination of the relevant lines and verses is necessary. Judged by the accepted rules of alliteration, and following the scansion of Sievers-Bliss, three categories of anomalies occur.

A) Lines without alliteration on the main stresses:

| | |
|---|---|
| he let him þa of handon   leofne fleogan[6] | 7 |
| Ælfnoð and Wulmær   begen lagon | 183 |
| æfre embe stunde   he sealde sume wunde | 271 |

In the first, non-functional alliteration falls on the finite verb *let*, but the noun *hand* should carry the alliteration.[7] Line 183 may be corrupt; many emendations have been suggested, but none is convincing.[8] According to the normal rules, *s-* and *st-* cannot alliterate in line 271, and it seems that rhyme here is used to compensate for the lack of alliteration.[9] If Bazell and Scragg are right to argue that all *s*- clusters in the poem alliterate only with themselves,[10] then line 282, *Sibyrhtes broðor, and swiðe mænig oþer*, likewise shows rhyme compensating for absence of alliteration.

B) Lines containing postponed alliteration:

i) a-verses

| | |
|---|---|
| Ælfere **7** Maccus,   modige twegen | 80 |
| wende þæs formoni man,   þa he on meare rad[11] | 239 |
| scyldburh tobrocen.   Abreoðe his angin[12] | 242 |
| he wæs on Norðhymbron   heardes cynnes[13] | 266 |
| Ðurstanes suna,   wið þas secgas feaht[14] | 298 |

ii) b-verses

| | |
|---|---|
| feoh wið freode   **7** niman frið æt us[15] | 39 |
| Gehyrst þu, sælida,   hwæt þis folc segeð? | 45 |
| wigan wigheardne   se wæs haten Wulfstan | 75 |
| Raðe wearð æt hilde   Offa forheawen | 288 |

All of these verses contain a syllable which would normally bear main stress which precedes the alliterating syllable. Such postponement of the alliteration is rare in the corpus, and because of this, it is often assumed to be evidence of corruption when it does occur and is emended out of existence. Lines 669 and 1230 of *Andreas*, for example, display postponed alliteration if the manuscript forms are accepted, but the poem's main editor, K.R. Brooks, 'corrects' them, on the grounds that only 'poems of loose metrical structure such as *Maldon*'[16] sink to the use of such 'defective' assonance.[17] If some texts show occasional postponement which is almost certainly the product of corruption,[18] others show sufficient use of this irregularity for their editors at least to have entertained the possibility that some other explanation is required. C. Williamson accepts the authenticity of the postponement in his *Riddle* 1, line 66 (Anglo-Saxon Poetic Records, 3.36) and remarks in his footnote to the line that this feature 'appears to be a not uncommon exception to the rule, cp. *Rids*. 2.8, 53.14, 57.12, 71.2, and 87.6.'[19] A. Campbell thought that this, and comparable kinds of alliterative licence, were features of lay (referring, for example, to *Finnsburg* 28b and *Hildebrandslied* 51b), and occurred in epic verse only as fossilized survivals, but labelled *Maldon*, despite the relative frequency of such features there, a short epic rather than lay.[20] At this juncture, I will only note that some kinds of licence may be causally related, and that we should not be surprised to find examples of postponed alliteration and verse-end rhyme in the same text, for both show that the poet sometimes felt that the second and the fourth stresses in the line were more important than the first and third.

In addition to these two groups, there is a third group of verses which displays abnormality. These are a-verses which, because of their particular metrical shape, ought to contain double alliteration according to the general rules established by A. Bliss's *The Metre of 'Beowulf,'*[21] but which fail to do so. The most important general rule is that double alliteration is compulsory or quasi-compulsory in a-verse metrical types in which the first sense-group or breath-group is shorter than the second. There are six examples in *Maldon* of single alliteration or lack of alliteration in such a-verses:[22]

| | | |
|---|---|---|
| 1A*1a | Ælfere and *M*accus | 80 |
| 1A*1a | Ælfnoð and *W*ulmær | 183 |
| 1A1a | *ea*rd gesecan | 222 |
| 1A*1a | *O*ffa gemælde | 230 |
| 1A*1a(ii) | *L*eofsunu gemælde | 244 |
| 1A*2b | *O*ffa þone sælidan | 286 |

The alliterating sound – where there is one – is italicized. Four of these are type 1A*1, whose basic rhythmical paradigm is / x l x / x, and 92 per cent of a-verses of this kind in *Beowulf* show double alliteration. One is 1A*2, or / x l x (x) / \, 100 per cent of the instances of which contain double alliteration in *Beowulf*. The final example is of the simpler form 1A1, / l x / x, which occurs with 95 per cent double alliteration in *Beowulf*. Although the poet of *Beowulf* may have interpreted the normal metrical rules quite strictly, his poem does not differ from other Old English poetic narratives in the extremely high occurrence of double alliteration in these metrical types.[23] Scanning *Maldon* using the methods of Bliss shows that this poem is not dissimilar in this respect: 1A1 occurs in 97 per cent of cases with double alliteration, 1A*1 with 86 per cent double alliteration.[24] In these metrical types the poets clearly felt a strong pressure to produce heavy alliteration, and seem to have allowed exceptions only where there was good reason for doing so. The *Beowulf* poet, for example, also allows single alliteration to pass in phrases which are syntactically analogous to *eard gesecan*. In 3078a *wræc adreogan*, a stressed and alliterating object precedes an infinitive. Verses like 1174a *nean ond feorran*, 2269a *dæges ond nihtes*, 72a *geongum ond ealdum*, and 1611a *sæla ond mæla*, in which copulative conjunctions link parallel forms, comprise one of the commonest kinds of exception.[25] In such stereotypical word pairs, semantic contrast ('far and near,' 'day and night'), and rhyme (*-æla*) might have been felt to offset the lack of heavy alliteration. Although the exceptions in *Maldon* are not of this kind, most of them do share a common feature.

The common thread running through the majority of the examples in the three categories of alliterative abnormality is the appearance of proper names, and, in particular, personal names. We must, however, first consider whether this empirical correlation is statistically significant. As *Maldon* contains a large number of proper names and a relatively large number of alliterative irregularities, is it surprising that there are verses that illustrate both features? Fifty-eight of the poem's 648 verses, or 9 per cent, include proper names, whilst nine of the sixteen verses with alliterative abnormalities (80a and 183a being irregular in two ways), or 56 per cent, contain proper names. That is, proper names are six times more frequent in the abnormal verses than in normal ones. Five of the nine verses with postponed alliteration have proper names in them, a proportion six times greater than in normal verses. Whilst all twenty cases of type 1A*1 in the poem that do not contain proper names do have double alliteration, only five of the nine of the same type with proper names do so. There is, then, a very significant, and therefore presumably causal, correlation between technical irregularity and the use of names in the poem.

How is this unusual situation to be explained? Textual corruption might account for an occasional metrical or alliterative deficiency, but it clearly cannot account for patterned abnormality, for, in that case, we would have to assume that the scribe, for some inexplicable reason, had an especial difficulty in copying proper names. Perhaps, as some have suggested, the poet was just incompetent, but, if so, we must grant too that his failing is of a very specific kind, and also, given that some of these instances could be corrected in the simplest of ways by reversal of word order (*Ælfere and Maccus* = *Maccus and Ælfere*; *se wæs haten Wulfstan* = *Wulfstan [se] wæs haten*), that his incompetence was perverse. More plausible is the possibility that some or all of these oddities might be explained as the products of metrical licence. At the best of times, proper names are difficult for poets to handle. In a highly regulated poetics, like Old English, they might be expected to pose some acute problems. The potential difficulties were alleviated by the fact that the Anglo-Saxon nobility (and those of other Germanic tribes too) gave their children names which were in a number of ways ready fashioned for use in poetry. Aristocratic names are generally dithematic, and the poets were experts at handling compounds; many names incorporate poetic diction; above all, members of the same family most frequently had names which alliterated with each other. Where, however, a poet chose to compose a piece about a historical Anglo-Saxon battle at which the native army seems to have been united rather more by comradeship and ties of personal loyalty than by blood relationship, this last advantage did not pertain. Perhaps, then, we should regard a verse like *Ælfere and Maccus* in the same light as the *Beowulf* poet's *Iofore ond Wulfe* (2993a). Ongenþeow is slain by brothers whose names happen not to alliterate, and so the verse lacks the expected heavy alliteration. Both poets appear to accept that needs must when the story drives. Perhaps, too, verses like *Offa gemælde* and *Leofsunu gemælde* show an excusable laxness, for as Bliss points out: 'it would be unreasonable to restrict the useful verb *gemælde* to proper nouns beginning with *M-*,'[26] and the only other example in the corpus of *gemælde* shows the same licence – *Genesis B* 790 *Adam gemælde*. That this is a conventional, or formulaic, type of permissiveness is shown not only by the facts that all three examples of *gemælde* are in verses of the same structure and that the poet of *Genesis B* was not at this point slavishly copying his model, which has only the more prosaic *quað Adam*, but also by the fact that *(ge)mælan* is a poetic word. There are only five occasions in *Maldon* on which poetic words occur in the second stave of the a-verse but do not share in the alliteration (as we should normally expect them to do according to the rules of rank). Apart from the two under discussion, the other three are 26a *wicinga ar*, 42a *Byrhtnoð maþelode*, and 309a *Byrhtwold maþelode*. It is instructive to note that in four of the five the second stave is occupied by a verb in the third person singular preterite indicative meaning 'spoke,' which is preceded by a personal name. The poets had set ways of introducing speakers; that some of these show the use of licence reflects the difficulty of the poetic moment, and probably shows too that such verses as *Offa gemælde* were felt to be analogous to those like *Byrhtwold maþelode*, in which the metrical pattern did not demand double alliteration.

But at what point does licence itself become a rhetorical trope? The almost complete absence of technical anomalies from most of the poetry suggests that poets and audiences generally disliked such deviations, but, if some few kinds of permissiveness – in the handling of personal names and the introductions to speeches – had become acceptable, then these must, by definition, have been absorbed into the customary rhetoric of the poetry, and could be recognized by the audience and exploited by the poets. In short, the fact that the *Maldon* poet is using more frequently and more extremely a feature found elsewhere in the poetry is exactly what suggests that this is rhetoric and not incompetence. If the postponed alliteration in *se wæs haten Wulfstan* can be corrected by reversal of the word order, then the problem of the lack of double alliteration in the a-verse of *Beowulf* 2602 *Wiglaf wæs haten   Weoxstanes sunu* can similarly be corrected by reversal of the verse order, for metrical type 3E1 / x x l / may be used in the a-verse with single alliteration, but the similarity of phrasing and syntax, *X wæs haten, wæs haten X*, suggests that this is a traditional licence (compare also *Genesis A* 1240a *Sem wæs haten*, *Psalm 50.*1a *Dauid wæs haten*) which is used more extremely in *Maldon*.

If such anomalies do form an aspect of the *Maldon* poet's artistry, we should expect them to be used in conjunction with other stylistic devices to create particular effects. By way of illustration, compare lines 79–81 and 182–4:

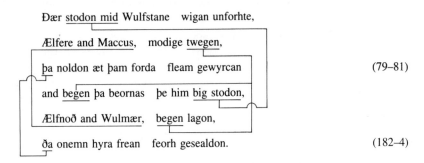

In both passages, there is a marked similarity between the pictures: two warriors stand beside a third who is more important. Repetitive phrasing and parallel syntax underline this resemblance: 79a *stodon mid* – 182b *big stodon*; 80a *Ælfere and Maccus* – 183a *Ælfnoð and Wulmær*; 80b *twegen* and 182a, 183b *begen*; *þa*, the first word in lines 81 and 184, is nominative plural of *se* used as a relative pronoun, and these are its only two occurrences in the poem. Both of these are followed by a prepositional phrase (*æt þam forda*, *onemn hyra frean*), and the direct object of the clause as head stave of the line (*fleam, feorh*). In addition, lines 80–1 and 183–4 are metrically identical (80a, 183a 1A*1a; 80b, 183b 2A1a; 81a, 184a a1e; 81b, 184b 1A1a). Finally, of course, the paired names in verses 80a and 183a are the source of the alliterative defects in those lines, and represent the only instances of coupled names in the a-verse which fail to alliterate properly (contrast 192a *God-[w]ine and Godwig*, and 304a *Oswold and Eadwold*, where the names of brothers fulfil the normal requirements). Clearly, by the use of a variety of techniques, the poet establishes a close relationship between these passages. But why should he have chosen to do this? He may have had various motives. First, these sections are part of a larger pattern in the poem which shows warriors acting in groups of three: as we have seen, three defend the cause-way together, and Byrhtnoþ dies with two warriors who may be presumed to have had a close relationship with him; also, the cowardly sons of Odda, Godric, Godwine and Godwig flee to the wood together, and Byrhtwold appears in close proximity to the brothers Oswold and Eadwold, whose names chime with his, and to whom he may possibly have been related; Wistan slays three in the throng. Secondly, the stylistic links draw our attention to the important service done to Byrhtnoþ by the family of Ceola: his son, Wulfstan, is picked by the *ealdorman* to hold the causeway, and his grandson, Wulmær, dies right beside him. Structurally also, these echoes seem to be purposeful: it is often said that *Maldon* is a battle of two halves, and the turning point is the death of the hero and the flight of the cowards. These passages form respectively the first and the last combats of the first half of the battle. The alliterative anomalies in 80 and 183, then, are not accidental, but are important and integral and link their contexts. In these verses, the common purpose and shared loyalty of the warriors is actually highlighted by the technical abnormality, and by the use of a kind of dissonance, of a surprising clash of sound, the poet focuses our interest onto the names themselves.

When dealing with proper names in medieval literature, it is essential to recognize that the medieval interest in etymology and onomastics differed profoundly from our own. This is not the place for a proper discussion of this subject, but, in brief, medievals believed that names were the key to the nature of things. As Jacques Le Goff put it: 'To name something was already to have explained it ... To name things and realities was to know them and to take possession of them ... The *res* and the *verba* did not oppose each other; each symbolized the other.'[27] The main source for this view was Isidore of Seville's *Etymologiarum Libri*, which E.R. Curtius referred to as 'the basic book of the entire Middle Ages' that established etymology and name-play as 'among the fundamentals of grammar and rhetoric ... an obligatory "ornament" of poetry.'[28] Old English poetry has been shown by various critics to be quite typical in this respect, and onomastic analysis has cast light on various textual cruces.[29] Much of this work, of course, has concentrated on the interpretation of scriptural names and Old English poets' use of exegetical etymologies. Nonetheless, the medievals were also interested in the interpretation of vernacular names. Perhaps the single richest source of such onomastic glossing is medieval hagiography, and lives of Anglo-Saxon saints provide some examples. Felix of Crowland and the Old English *Martyrology* both interpret Guþlac's name to mean 'war-gift' (*belli donum* and *belli munus* respectively).[30] Wulfstan of Winchester's *Life of St. Æthelwold* incorrectly, but conveniently, explains the saint's name as a compound of *æþel* and *wolde*, from *willan* – *nomine, mente et opere beniuolus* ('in name, mind and deed, well intentioned').[31] *The Life of Dunstan* by William of Malmesbury interprets the central figure's name straightforwardly as *montem et petram* ('hill and rock'),[32] and Osbern's life of the same saint includes a similar etymology.[33] Walter Daniel's *Life of Ailred of Rievaulx* equally straightforwardly explains: 'The great counsellor had a fitting name, for the English *Alred* is in Latin *totum consilium* or *omne consilium*. Well is he placed in the counsels of an earthly king, whose very name gives forth the sound, "all counsel."'[34] Similar etymologizing is to be found in other monastic Latin literary genres, both verse and prose. Alcuin, in his *Letters*, addresses Hehstan as *altapetra* and Arno as *aquila*.[35] Æþelwulf's historical poem *De Abbatibus* Latinizes the author's name as *clarus lupus*.[36] The end of Æþelweard's *Chronicle* explains the name of King Edgar as *contim beatam*, 'where the first word is for *contus*,' hence 'blessed spear,' and puns on the author's own name, for *patricius quaestor* means 'noble public servant.'[37] William of Malmesbury discusses two interpretations of Aldhelm's name in the *Gesta Pontificum*, preferring *galea uetus*, 'old helmet,' to Faricius's *senex almus*, 'kind old man.'[38] The manuscript of *Hemming's Cartulary* contains three lines of complimentary verses which appear to interpret the name Wulfstan as *lupus … lapis*.[39]

Given this context, and in view of the fact that many Old English names had obvious meanings, it would be surprising if Old English poetry did not show evidence of some interest in the meanings of vernacular names.[40] A number of the critics of *Beowulf* have tried to demonstrate the aptness of names like Æschere, Heremod, Heardred, Hondscio, Hygd, Hygelac, Modþryþ and others as descriptions of the figures they label.[41] Constance Hieatt's 'Modþryðo and Heremod: Intertwined Threads in the *Beowulf*-Poet's Web of Words'[42] is worthy of mention here. The nickname Unferth – if nickname it is – has attracted the most attention,[43] but the failure of an agreed interpretation to emerge underscores the perilousness of this critical approach. Where the Latin texts deal in explicit etymologizing, the Old English poets subtly weave name-play into their composition. But what is subtlety to one critic may be another's chimera. Before I investigate the *Maldon* poet's possible use of onomasia, it is worth briefly noting the difficulties that the analysis faces. We must ask ourselves whether the elements of the names would have been recognized by the poet. Phonetic change quite frequently obscures these elements. Contraction may have rendered the first element of *Sibyrht* (*sige-*) unintelligible; loss of secondary stress in names, and that most important late Old English sound change, the centralization of vowels in unstressed syllables, may well have made more acute the problem of deciphering final elements, though traditional spellings may have counterbalanced this. Except where contemporary texts provide clear and explicit evidence, we cannot at this historical remove know what folk etymologies would have appealed to the poet. We cannot even be sure that the original meaning of some name elements was still available to a late tenth-century, or early eleventh-century poet. Were OE *noþ*, 'temerity, daring,' frequently attested in the language, then it would be very tempting to interpret Byrhtnoþ's name as 'clear daring,' and to regard the hero's *ofermod* as an extension of his name-meaning.

However, though *noþ* is common as a name element, it occurs only once as a separate lexeme with this meaning, in *Juliana*, and so it would be clear rashness on our part to assume that the meaning of the word was known to the poet.

With the exception of the hero and possibly of Byrhtwold (whom I shall turn to later), the *Maldon* poet does not devote much space to characterization, and seems at first sight to be more concerned with the warriors' common qualities than with their individuality. Accordingly, names like Wulfstan and Æscferþ are appropriate to the figures they label only in the general sense that they are suitable for aristocratic warriors, rather than in the specific ways that have been suggested for many of the names in *Beowulf*. On closer inspection, however, many of the warriors' words and actions do appear to be affected by their names, or their patronymics. Lines 225–35a of the poem show this and other typical aspects of the poet's style:

Ða he forð eode,    fæhðe gemunde,

ðæt he mid orde    anne geræhte,

flotan on þam folce,    þæt se on foldan læg

forwegen mid his wæpne.    Ongan þa winas manian,

frynd and geferan,    þæt hi forð eodon.

Offa gemælde,    æscholt asceoc:

'Hwæt, þu, Ælfwine,    hafast ealle gemanode,

þegenas to þearfe.    Nu ure þeoden lið,

eorl on eorðan,    us is eallum þearf

þæt ure æghwylc    oþerne bylde,

wigan to wige …

The passage shows some use of variation (*foldan/eorðan, winas/frynd/geferan, gemanode/bylde, eorl/þeoden*), but, like the rest of the poem, rather less than is normal. The text shows, however, a very high and unusual degree of lexical repetition, and this section is representative in this respect.[44] Repetitions are underlined. Doubtless, many modern readers find such a style to be otiose and weak, and this is one of the main reasons why some critics have questioned the poem's quality. It must be acknowledged, however, that many of these repetitions form patterns which highlight some of the main ideas. With their words the warriors exhort each other in need, by their deeds they set each other an example. Ælfwine's own advance (*he forð eode*), as much as his powerful but unrecorded exhortation (*manian*), emboldens his fellows to advance (*hi forð eodon*), and Offa immediately pays tribute to Ælfwine's prompting (*gemanode*). The *winas*, the friends in need, are helped by Ælfwine, a friend in name, word, and deed. If the usual emendation is accepted, the name element *wine* occurs elsewhere in the poem only in Godwine (transcript: *godrine*), and the simplex *wine* appears only once more, in line 250. The repetition here, and the absence of the use of (-)*wine* in the rest of the poem suggests that elements of the personal names are being incorporated into this web of words. The poet exploits the poetic resource of Ælfwine's name, for *wine* is a poetic word, and thereby indicates that he lives up to his name.

Echoes and cross-references permeate the poem. Critics have noted, because the poet tells us, that Godric the cowardly son of Odda is sharply contrasted with Godric the valiant son of Æþelgar: 187a *Godric fram guþe*, 321a *Godric to guþe*; 187b *and þone godan forlet*, 321b *Oft he gar forlet*; 325 *Næs þæt na se Godric þe ða guðe forbeah*. What has not been noticed is that by similar repetitions Æþelgar's son is made to resemble Æscferþ, son of Ecglaf, the Northumbrian hostage, and the motivation for the comparison lies in their names and in the similarity of their actions, though their social positions are different. Of all the names and patronymics in the poem, only these two contain elements meaning 'spear': *æsc* and *gar*, and only Æscferþ and Æþelgar's son frequently fire forth darts (269 *ac he fysde forð flan genehe*;[45] 321b–22a *Oft he gar forlet, / wælspere windan*). Others shake spears (Byrhtnoþ, Offa, Dunnere, Byrhtwold), and spears are mentioned quite frequently. Eadric carries one, Wulfstan kills a Viking with his *franca*, and Wulfmær plucks out and returns the spear that fatally wounds his lord, but only these two act so energetically with these weapons. Their names have shaped their behaviour, or at least the poet's view of it.

More often than is usual in the poetry, the *Maldon* poet alliterates a line on the same word, or on words that are etymologically related. There are some nineteen instances of this,[46] including *beot, boda, abeodan* (27, 49); *flod, flota, flowan* (65, 72); *freod, frið* (39); *standan, stede* (19, 127); *wig, wiga, wigend* (75, 235, 302), and so on. He also links words that are phonetically very similar and which he may have thought were cognate (for example, *hream, hremm* 106; *feallan, fealo-* 166; *leof, lif* 208). That this is probably a stylistic device and not verbal paucity is illustrated by cases in which the repetition brings out the meaning of a name. The adjective *æþele* is used only twice, in lines 151 and 280, and on both occasions it alliterates with a name whose first element is *Æþel–*:

| þurh ðone æþelan   Æþelredes þegen | 151 |
| Swa dyde Æþeric,   æþele gefera | 280 |

Byrhtnoþ and Æþelric are the only warriors distinguished by the description 'noble.' In the case of the latter, it is difficult to believe that the loss of *-l-* obscured the etymology. Surely, the poet calls him noble because he is called Noble. The former example is more complicated. Byrhtnoþ, as an *ealdorman*, might properly be labelled *æþele*, and he certainly lives up to this description, but, though the adjective refers to *þegen*, it immediately precedes the name Æþelred, and it is possible, given the bad reputation that this king acquired, that the description stands in ironic juxtaposition with his name. R. Quirk has suggested the existence of ironic alliterating collocations in the poetry, commenting, for example, on *Beowulf* 2850: 'When Beowulf's ten cowardly comrades rejoin Wiglaf after the fatal combat, it is said of them, "hy scamiende scyldas bæran" (2850). The lexical and metrical connexion between *scamiende* and *scyldas* points the irony of their external equipment and their internal inadequacy.'[47] *Maldon* provides two other possible examples:

| Godric fram guþe,   and þone godan forlet | 187 |
| gar and god swurd.   Us Godric hæfð | 237 |

There is, of course, no grammatical relationship here between the adjective *god* and the name Godric, but the alliterative connection, strengthened by the strong assonance and the probable etymological link between the two, establishes an ironic semantic relationship between them. If Godric meant 'good power' to an Anglo-Saxon, then it turned out to be a spectacularly inappropriate name for the man who, though showered with gifts by his lord, gallops away on Byrhtnoþ's horse the moment, as it seems, that the *ealdorman* is dead.

When the Anglo-Saxons gave their children names like 'noble counsel' or 'all protector,' it is reasonable to argue that they did so either in the pious hope that such names would act as reminders to their bearers to live up to their epithets, or more performatively because parents thought such names would destine their children to be as they were called. Both of these are plausible interpretations of the relevant passage in the *Encomium Emmae Reginae*:

> And so they washed this very dear child, as is the custom of all Christians, in the sacred baptismal font, and gave him a name which conveyed in a measure an indication of his future excellence. For indeed he was called

Hörthaknútr, which reproduced his father's name with an addition, and if the
etymology of this is investigated in Germanic, one truly discerns his identity
and greatness. 'Harde', indeed, means 'swift' or 'strong', both of which
qualities and much more could be recognised in him above all others ...[48]

Perhaps, then, when the poet calls Wulfstan, 'wolf rock,' by the adjective
*wig-heardne*, 'battle-hard,' a description not used of any other warrior, he
did so not just because he believed, as William Camden put it, that 'the
names and natures of men were suitable,' but also because he felt, as
Camden continued, that 'fatal necessity concurred herein with voluntary
motion in giving the name.'[49] The poet, after all, like many heroic poets and
battle poets, had a strongly developed interest in destiny. Those who die in
battle are repeatedly called 'doomed' (*fæge men* 105, *fæge cempa* 119,
*fægean men* 125, *fæges feorhhus* 297), and the repetitive style itself conveys
a sense of the inevitable. The poet's use of a number of traditional battle
themes – like the *flyting* and the beasts of battle – gives the impression that
this is a battle like all others, and that all battles happen in set ways. To
know whether the poet forecast the final defeat from the beginning we would
need to have the lost opening, but we may reasonably assume that the audience knew the outcome, and the poet hints in a number of ways that the
result will not be victory: the seemingly invincible Vikings are the enemy;
many of Byrhtnoþ's troops appear to be young and inexperienced; and from
the death of the hero onwards, no one speaks of victory, but of vengeance,
promises, and death.

    In the midst of the catastrophe, an old voice succinctly iterates a final
determination that is lyrical but brief. The famous words that begin Byrhtwold's speech are followed by these lines:

> A mæg gnornian
> se ðe nu fram þis wigplegan   wendan þenceð.
> Ic eom frod feores:   fram ic ne wille,
> ac ic me be healfe   minum hlaforde,
> be swa leofan men,   licgan þence.                  (315b–319b)

If Wulfstan of Winchester understands Æþelwold's name to mean 'well-
intentioned,' might not our poet, a contemporary or near-contemporary of
Wulfstan, have understood Byrhtwold to mean 'clearly determined'? The
second element, *-wold*, occurs too in Oswold and in Eadwold, whose appearance immediately precedes that of Byrhtwold, but not elsewhere. No one
speaks of intention more clearly than this old retainer. The verb *þencan*, 'to

intend,' is used twice here by Byrhtwold, and only once in the rest of the
poem, by Dunnere. *Fram ic ne wille*, 'I will not leave here,' he affirms. The
omission of the infinitive of motion (or the independent use of the auxiliary)[50]
throws stress on *wille*; and the use of the uncontracted form, *ne wille*, perhaps
makes the syntax even more emphatic.[51] The dominance of the speaker's
purpose in his words is further underscored by the metrical patterning by
which the verb in each case occupies the last stave of the line. In fact, these
lines provide personal confirmation of Byrhtwold's intention to follow his
own injunction to the warriors to harden their hearts:

> Hige sceal þe heardra,    heorte þe cenre,
> mod sceal þe mare,    þe ure mægen lytlað.                    (312–14)

The poem has not mentioned *hige* since the narrator's comment at the
opening of the fragment that Byrhtnoþ told the young men to think of good
courage (*hicgan ... to hige godum* 4). Some critics, and in particular S.B.
Greenfield in *The Interpretation of Old English Poems*, have remarked upon
the way in which the poet seems to invite a comparison between these two
figures. Greenfield observes the similarity of lines 42 and 309 (*Byrhtnoð
maþelode, bord hafenode: Byrhtwold maþelode, bord hafenode*) and notes that
in the poem only these two figures are introduced in this identical fashion;
that the phrasing *bord hafenode* occurs nowhere else in the corpus, and
*hafenian* only once elsewhere; that where others either raise a shield or
brandish a weapon, these two both raise their shields and shake their spears.
He might have mentioned too that only these two brandish an *æsc*, and that
this poetic word occurs in the singular in the corpus only at these two points.
These similarities are given aural force, as he notes, by the rhyming of the
weak preterite *-ode* endings. He concludes: 'I am inclined to believe in the
implications of meaning generated by the formulaic echo in these two
passages which envelop the speeches and actions of the English, and which
make their own stylistic contribution to the heroic ethos of the *Battle of
Maldon*.'[52] Whilst Greenfield perhaps overestimates the structuring function
of the repetition, we can, nonetheless, agree that the repetition is remarkable.
It is also much more extensive than Greenfield acknowledges. Byrhtnoþ and
Byrhtwold are the only two warriors who are manifestly old: the first is said
to be *har hilderinc*, the second *eald geneat*, and of only these two is the
adjective *frod* (140, 317) used, a word which seems to mean 'wise' and to be
complimentary, as well as meaning 'old.' When the narrator says of the
*ealdorman, Frod wæs se fyrdrinc*, he shows respect for his battle experience
in directing his *franca* through his young opponent's neck; and when

Byrhtwold says of himself, *Ic eom frod feores:   fram ic ne wille*, he is not displaying false modesty, but seems to be saying something like 'I'm not going to flee like a fool.' Both are examples of an Old English poetic type-figure, the *senex fortis*, the old man who is not weakened or enfeebled, but who robustly transcends his agedness by his virility.[53] As befits their role, they are the only warriors who *teach* their fellows: where Dunnere, Oswold and Eadwold ask their comrades to persevere (*biddan* 257, 306), Ælfwine and Godric encourage them (*byldan* 209, 320), Ælfwine exhorts them (*manian* 228, 231), and Oswold and Eadwold also embolden them (*trymian* 305); Byrhtnoþ does most of these, and orders them too (*hatan, passim*), but only the two old men *instruct* the warriors. Byrhtnoþ *rad and rædde, rincum tæhte* (18), and Byrhtwold *beornas lærde* (311b). As the key figures of authority, they are the only ones who speak emphatically of obligation and necessity:

Feallan sceolon

hæþene æt hilde ...                                                    (54b–55a)

Ne *sceole* ge swa softe   sinc gegangan:
us *sceal* ord and ecg   ær geseman                                    (59–60)

Hige *sceal* þe heardra,   heorte þe cenre,
mod *sceal* þe mare                                                    (312–13)

In times of need in tight situations, words must be used urgently and resolutely to oppose unwanted outcomes: the giving of Danegeld and the loss of fighting strength. It is also appropriate for the *senex fortis* to enjoy battle. The narrator tells us with gruesome relish that, after Byrhtnoþ has stabbed one Viking through the neck, and another through the heart:

Se eorl wæs þe bliþra:

hloh þa modi man ...                                                   (146b–47a)

Earlier, in his speech to the Viking messenger, Byrhtnoþ promises battle and refers to it in a time-honoured and poetic way as *guðplega*, 'battle-play.' Nobody else talks of it in this way until Byrhtwold speaks:

A mæg gnornian

se ðe nu fram þis wigplegan   wendan þenceð.                           (315–16)

Undoubtedly, the old retainer means that those who flee will mourn because they will be known to be cowards and traitors to their lord, but perhaps, by using the term *wigplega*, 'war-game', he means also that they will grieve for having missed out on a good battle, and a famous last stand.

Though different in rank, Byrhtnoþ and Byrhtwold are fundamentally similar in nature and role, in what they say and in what they do. It is also true that they are similar in name, sharing the first element, *byrht*. They are the only two named warriors at the battle whose names include this element; Byrhtelm, the hero's father being presumably long since dead, and the presence of Sibyrht being unknown. Though the spelling *byrht* is normal in the late tenth century, the consistency of this spelling in the transcript may possibly suggest that the poet was attentive to this detail. In any case, we can say that the lexical similarity between lines 42 and 309 is not disguised by orthographic variation: with the exception of the change of -*noþ* to -*wold*, the lines are identical. If the poet made up the name Byrhtwold, then he must have made it similar to the hero's quite deliberately once he had decided to see them as examples of a single stereotype. If his was a historical name, then the poet only did what came naturally to him, seeing similar natures in similar names, just as the brothers Oswold and Eadwold speak in unison, and just as Ælfere and Ælfnoþ are spoken of in similar lines, and just as the brothers Godric, Godwine, and Godwig act identically – though here in contradiction of their names.

In this contradiction we find an explanation for the curious obviousness of the poet's statement that Godric, son of Æþelgar, was not the Godric who fled from the battle. After all, how could he be? The sons of Odda have long gone and the poet's comment that *hit riht ne wæs* surely precludes the possibility that this is a temporary absence for which restitution will later be made; in addition to which we have been told that the one is the son of Odda, the other of Æþelgar. Though others at the battle bear identical names, none is distinguished so very explicitly, but then none differs so completely in behaviour. Uniquely in the poem, the two Godrics are identical in name but opposite in nature. The behaviour of the first Godric has bleached the name of meaning and is an affront to all who bear his name. The second Godric is Godric as he should have been, a proper Godric who restores the integrity of the name by his powerful contribution to the battle. The Vikings have won, but the deserters have not. The battle is lost, but heroism lives on. *Næs þæt na se Godric    þe ða guðe forbeah* (325): that was definitely not the Godric who fled the field; in this ringing double negative lies the poet's justification for celebrating a contemporary defeat in antique heroic expression. Moral and linguistic order are restored by a call to arms and a defence of poetry.

New College, Oxford

## NOTES

1 E.V. Gordon, ed., *The Battle of Maldon* (Manchester: Manchester University Press 1976), 29.
2 E.S. Sklar, '*The Battle of Maldon* and the Popular Tradition: Some Rhymed Formulas' *Philological Quarterly* 54 (1975): 409–18.
3 D.G. Scragg, ed., *The Battle of Maldon* (Manchester: Manchester University Press 1981), 29.
4 S.B. Greenfield and D.G. Calder, *A New Critical History of Old English Literature* (New York: New York University Press 1986), 152.
5 A. Bliss, *The Metre of 'Beowulf,'* 2nd ed. rev. (Oxford: Basil Blackwell 1967), 101.
6 All quotations from the poem are from Scragg's edition, see n3 above. Verses 32b and 192b are not examples of double alliteration in the b-verse, but show that palatal and velar *g* no longer alliterated.
7 Cf *Beowulf* 758a, 1537a. For suggested emendations, see Bliss, *Metre of 'Beowulf,'* 105.
8 See Scragg, *Battle of Maldon*, 79.
9 On rhyme in *Maldon*, see E.G. Stanley, 'Rhymes in English Medieval Verse: From Old English to Middle English,' in E. Kennedy et al., eds, *Medieval Studies Presented to George Kane* (Wolfeboro, N.H.: D.S. Brewer 1988), 24–5.
10 See C.E. Bazell, 'Notes on Old English Metre and Morphology,' in H.E. Brekle and L. Lipke, eds, *Wortbildung, Syntax und Morphologie: Festschrift zum 60. Geburtstag von Hans Marchand*, (The Hague: Mouton 1968), 17–18, and Scragg, *Battle of Maldon*, 52. If they are wrong, then 29b *sæmen snelle* is irregular.
11 Assuming that the intensifying prefix, *for-*, is stressed.
12 Analogous examples are very rare. Cf *Beowulf* 707.
13 In Old English, as in Modern English, the second syllable of the place-name probably carried the main stress.
14 The irregularity may be connected to the genealogical difficulty of lines 297–300.
15 The infinitive is normally a stressed element; see E.G. Stanley, 'Verbal Stress in Old English Verse,' *Anglia* 93 (1975): 307–24, esp. 321–4.
16 K.R. Brooks, ed., *Andreas and the Fates of the Apostles* (Oxford: Oxford University Press 1961), 67.
17 Ibid., 85, and also 106.
18 For example, *Soul I* 83–5, beside the better reading in *Soul II* 78–9. See D. Moffat, ed. and tr., *The Old English 'Soul and Body'* (Woodbridge: D.S. Brewer 1990), 76.

19  C. Williamson, ed., *The Old English Riddles of the 'Exeter Book'* (Chapel Hill, N.C.: University of North Carolina Press 1977), 139.

20  A. Campbell, 'The Old English Epic Style,' in N. Davis and C.L. Wrenn, eds, *English and Medieval Studies Presented to J.R.R. Tolkien on the Occasion of His Seventieth Birthday* (London: Allen and Unwin 1962), 16–17 and 25.

21  Bliss, *Metre of 'Beowulf,'* esp. 36–9, 44–50, 122–3.

22  Excluding 271a, where lack of alliteration precludes scansion, and 161a, which is normal if *hr-* has simplified to *r-*.

23  See, for example, J. Roberts, 'A Metrical Examination of the Poems *Guthlac A* and *Guthlac B*,' *Proceedings of the Royal Irish Academy* 71C (1971): 91–137; E. Clemons, *A Metrical Analysis of the Old English Poem 'Exodus'* (PhD diss., University of Texas 1961).

24  The following are the relevant a-verses with double alliteration.

    1A1: 8, 12, 13, 18, 39, 54, 95, 104, 110, 113, 123, 126, 131, 153, 161, 208, 212, 214, 227, 228, 229, 233, 235, 245, 248, 253, 259, 274, 302, 312, 313, 315, 324.

    1A*1: 4, 10, 21, 31, 44, 55, 76, 101, 103, 118, 133, 150, 182, 187, 192, 223, 232, 236, 240, 250, 292, 296, 304, 305, 321.

25  See also the discussion of word pairs in C. Kendall, *The Metrical Grammar of 'Beowulf'* (Cambridge: Cambridge University Press 1991), 112–15.

26  Bliss, *Metre of 'Beowulf,'* 102.

27  J. Le Goff, *Medieval Civilization*, tr. J. Barrow (Oxford: Basil Blackwell 1988), 331.

28  E.R. Curtius, *European Literature and the Latin Middle Ages*, tr. W.R. Trask (London: Routledge and Kegan Paul 1953), 496–7. Excursus XIV, 495–500, contains many examples of name-play in medieval literature.

29  See especially F.C. Robinson, 'Some Uses of Name-meanings in Old English Poetry,' *Neuphilologische Mitteilungen* 69 (1968): 161–71; 'The Significance of Names in Old English Literature,' *Anglia* 86 (1968): 14–59; 'Anglo-Saxon Onomastics in the Old English *Andreas*,' *Names* 21 (1973): 133–6; R. Frank, 'Some Uses of Paronomasia in Old English Scriptural Verse,' *Speculum* 47 (1972): 207–26.

30  B. Colgrave, ed., *Felix's 'Life of Saint Guthlac'* (Cambridge: Cambridge University Press 1956), 174, and G. Herzfeld, ed., *An Old English Martyrology* Early English Text Society OS 116 (London: Oxford University Press 1900), 56. See also W.F. Bolton, 'The Background and Meaning of Guthlac,' *Journal of English and Germanic Philology* 61 (1962): 595–603.

31  Wulfstan of Winchester, *The Life of Saint Æthelwold*, ed. M. Lapidge and M. Winterbottom (Oxford: Oxford University Press 1991), 14–15.

32  See W. Stubbs, ed., *The Memorials of Saint Dunstan*, Rolls Series (London: Longman 1874), 5: 254–5.

33  Ibid., 3: 73.

34  Walter Daniel, *Life of Ailred of Rievaulx,* ed. F.M. Powicke (London: Nelson 1950), 8.

35  See W.F. Bolton, *Alcuin and Beowulf: An Eighth Century View* (London: Edward Arnold 1979), 80–2. Note also D.A. Bullough's argument that Alcuin's Letter to Speratus is addressed to Unuuona, Bishop of Leicester, because the Latin name is a translation of the Old English *un-wana,* 'not-lacking,' in 'What Has Ingeld to Do with Lindisfarne?' *Anglo-Saxon England* 22 (1993): 114–15.

36  Æþelwulf, *De Abbatibus,* ed. A. Campbell (Oxford: Oxford University Press 1967), xxii and 63.

37  Æþelweard, *Chronicle,* ed. A. Campbell (London: Nelson 1962), xiii and 56.

38  William of Malmesbury, *Gesta Pontificum Anglorum,* ed. N.E.S.A. Hamilton, Rolls Series (London: Longman 1870), 332.

39  See N.R. Ker, '*Hemming's Cartulary*: A Description of the Two Worcester Cartularies in Cotton Tiberius A xiii,' in R.W. Hunt et al., eds, *Studies in Medieval History presented to F.M. Powicke* (Oxford: Oxford University Press 1948), 71–2.

40  For an opposing view, note F.M. Stenton, 'Personal Names in Place-Names', in A. Mawer and F.M. Stenton, eds, *Introduction to the Survey of English Place-Names* English Place-Name Society (Cambridge: Cambridge University Press 1924), 1: 168: 'The men who coined the names *Friþuwulf,* "peace-wolf", and *Wigfriþ,* "war-peace", were not concerned about their meaning.' Anglo-Saxons were, however, content to interpret a single element of a dithematic name, as is illustrated by Wulfstan's famous sobriquet, 'Lupus.'

41  See, for example, K. Malone, 'Royal Names in Old English Poetry,' *Names* 1 (1953): 153–62; R.E. Kaske, '"Hygelac" and "Hygd,"' in S.B. Greenfield, ed., *Studies in Old English Literature in Honor of Arthur G. Brodeur* (Eugene: University of Oregon Press 1963): 200–6; A.L. Harris, 'Hands, Helms, and Heroes: The Role of Proper Names in *Beowulf,*' *Neuphilologische Mitteilungen* 83 (1982): 414–21.

42  C.B. Hieatt, 'Modþryðo and Heremod: Intertwined Threads in the *Beowulf*-poet's Web of Words,' *Journal of English and Germanic Philology* 83 (1982): 173–82.

43  For the most important views, see M.W. Bloomfield, '*Beowulf* and Christian Allegory: An Interpretation of Unferth,' *Traditio* 7 (1949–51): 410–15, and F.C. Robinson, 'Elements of the Marvelous in the Characterization of Beowulf: A Reconsideration of the Textual Evidence,' in R.B. Burlin and E.B. Irving, eds, *Old English Studies in Honour of John C. Pope* (Toronto: University of Toronto Press 1974), 119–37.

44  On the technique of 'word-echo,' the re-use of a word within a few lines, see J.O. Beaty, 'The Echo-Word in *Beowulf* with a Note on the Finnsburg Fragment,' *PMLA* 49 (1934): 365-73; J.L. Rosier, 'The Literal-Figurative Identity of *The Wanderer*,' *PMLA* 79 (1964): 366–9, and W.F. Bolton, 'The Dimensions of *The Wanderer*,' *Leeds Studies in English* 3 (1969): 7–34, esp. 16–21.

45  *Flan* may mean 'arrow' or 'spear'. Nobles in this period did not use bows, however, and a hostage, to be useful, must have been aristocratic. The latter is, therefore, the preferable translation.

46  In addition to the fifteen listed by E.D. Laborde, *Byrhtnoth and Maldon* (London: Heinemann 1936), 87, note also lines 19, 187, 237, 280. For evidence of the poet's possible interest in place-name etymology, note Laborde's suggestion (ibid., 122) that *scir wæter*, l. 98, may be a play on the other name of the Panta, the Blackwater (*blac* = 'bright').

47  R. Quirk, `Poetic Language and Old English Metre,' in A. Brown and P. Foote, eds, *Early English and Norse Studies* (London: Methuen 1963), 156.

48  A. Campbell, ed., *Encomium Emmae Reginae*, Camden 3rd Series 72 (London: Office of the Royal Historical Society 1949), 35.

49  William Camden, *Remains Concerning Britain* (London: J.R. Smith 1870), 55.

50  See B. Mitchell, *Old English Syntax* 2 vols. (Oxford: Oxford University Press, 1985; corr. 1987), 2: 421.

51  Contracted forms are general in the south and west; uncontracted forms in the north and east: see ibid., 1: 478–80. There are exceptions in texts from both dialect areas, however, and a number of these are probably for reasons of emphasis. Some exceptions in verse may have a metrical cause.

52  S.B. Greenfield, *The Interpretation of Old English Poems* (London: Routledge and Kegan Paul 1972), 56–8.

53  See J.A. Burrow, *The Ages of Man: A Study in Medieval Writing and Thought* (Oxford: Oxford University Press 1988), 130–4.

# Simplifying Resolution
# in *Beowulf*

JAMES KEDDIE

Sievers's 'Theory of Five Types' has never been quite satisfactory – not even
to Sievers – but has been so useful for the more sophisticated texts such as
*Beowulf* that it has been used for want of something better. It has been used,
slightly modified, as the basis for so many theories of metre that to discard
it altogether would disqualify a century of scholarship.[1] Sievers was right, I
think, to look for a series of patterns underlying Old English metre, but wrong
to assume that the devices of later or other systems – caesuras, feet, strict
syllable counts – should apply. However, the most fundamental flaw in
Sievers's theory, the flaw which does most to deny the existence of a simple
metrical template of the type found in other languages, rests on an assumption
made by Sievers almost without discussion, and quietly rejected by many
metrists since, an assumption rooted in an untenable view of resolution.

Resolution is a metrical concept in need of definition, a concept whose
practical ramifications go well beyond the notation on the page that it
represents for most theorists. The only unarguable use of resolution occurs in
a lift when two short syllables are joined to take the place of the normal one
long syllable; I would deny that resolution occurs in drops – or in half-
stresses, to which I deny special status. The concept of resolution in drops is
inspired by Sievers, who, although he does not use the term 'resolution' for
it, claims that all unstressed syllables adjacent to each other must be taken
together to form a single drop.[2] When you resolve two short syllables to form
a lift, the practical reality of what you do corresponds to its theory: together
the two short syllables occupy the same amount of time as one long syllable.
If, however, you run together as many as six unstressed syllables to form one
drop, these syllables are going to occupy as much time as six drops composed
of one syllable each – you cannot resolve unstressed syllables in the same

sense in which you can resolve stressable syllables. It is quite true that a drop in certain positions may be expanded to contain several syllables, but it does not follow that any series of two or more unstressed syllables must form one rather than two drops: Sievers himself discovers verses that give the lie to this assumption, for instance *þæt hine on ylde* (*Beowulf* 22a), where the only lift is on the first syllable of *ylde*. Although a number of metrists object, often tacitly, to this assumption on Sievers's part, none seems fully to have realized how crucial it is to Sievers's whole theory, perhaps because Sievers avoids discussing the theoretical basis for his claim. If you cannot have two unstressed drops side by side in a verse, as Sievers claims, because they always resolve into one, then you automatically disqualify a number of theoretically possible arrangements of two lifts and two drops. If you allow adjacent drops, then all possible combinations of two lifts and two drops are allowable. There are only six such possible combinations, which I will label AA to FF in conjunction with the Sievers Type to which they most closely correspond:

*Possible Combinations of Lifts and Drops*

| Lift/drop combination | | | Sievers Type and stress profile[3] | |
|---|---|---|---|---|
| AA | L d L d | **wuldr**es **Weald**end | A | / x l / x |
| BB | d L d L | on **flod**es **æht** | B | x l / x l / |
| CC | d L L d | þone **God** sen**de** | C | x l / l / x |
| DD | L L d d | **ymbsitt**endra | D | / / l \ x |
| | | **flota** fāmī**heals** | | / l / x \ |
| EE | L d d L | **weorð**myndum **þāh** | E | / \ x l / |
| FF | d d L L | Hwæt we **Gār-dena** | | – |

My contention is that these six patterns are the metrical templates kept in mind by the poet when composing, and that he used them in such a way that a first-time reader of the poem – given a basic knowledge of syllable lengths and parts of speech – could tell immediately which of the six Types was being used.[4]

Sievers absolutely forbids only one combination, my FF, which has to have adjacent unstressed drops because a half-stress cannot precede a full stress: x \ / \ cannot occur.[5] Naturally enough, Types AA, BB, and CC correspond with the Sievers Types because they do not involve adjacent drops. Sievers gets around the problem in his D and E Types by insisting that one drop consist of a half-stressed syllable, so that two unstressed syllables are not side by side. As it happens, a majority of E Types do have a half-stressed syllable in second position, / \ x l /. According to Bliss, however, the most common D Type in *Beowulf* is / l / x x, my basic DD template, with no half-stress in the verse, and the second of Sievers's two D Types (/ | / x \) occurs less frequently. If you accept Bliss's analysis, the poet has managed to create several hundred lines that would be defective according to Sievers's typology.[6]

By denying adjacent drops, Sievers initiated a tradition of confusing linguistic or syntactical stress with metrical stress. The following table of 'half-stresses' shows how anomalous is Sievers's attitude to them:

*Half Stresses*

| Sievers Type | linguistic stress | Lift/drop pattern | | metrical stress |
|---|---|---|---|---|
| A-Type | / \ / \ | L d L d   / x / x | AA | snellīc særinc |
|  | / x \ x | L d L d   / x / x |  | wilgesīþas |
| B-Type | x x / \ / | d L d L   x x / x / | BB | secean wynlēas wīc |
| C-Type | x / \ x | d L L d   x / / x | CC | þa sēlestan |
|  | x / / \ | d L L d   x / / x |  | oft Scyld Scēfing |
| D-Type | / / \ x | L L d d   / / x x | DD | merelīðende |
| E-Type | / \ x / | L d d L   / x x / | EE | murnende mōd |
| A3-Type | x x / \ | d d L L   x x / / | FF | eft was anræd |
| A*-Type | / \ x / x | L d L d   / x x / x | AA | Bēowulf wæs brēme |
| D*-Type | / x / \ x | L d L d   / x / x x | AA | gomela iōmēowlan |
| E*-Type | / \ x x / | L d d L   / x x x / | EE | wīgspēda gewiofu |

In the first A-Type example, both drops consist of a syllable which is linguistically and grammatically stressable; however, because *-lic* and *-rinc* form the second part of a compound they take a lower level of stress than *snel-* and *sæ-* – they are half-stressed, but they form the drops. In the second A-Type example, *-siþ-* is the second element of a compound with a lower level of stress than *wil-*; it is half-stressed, but it forms a lift. In the first C-Type example, the second lift consists of a half-stress which is merely a formative element, incapable of standing on its own; in the second example, the equally weighty syllable *-ing* forms the drop, because two more heavily stressed syllables precede it. In Types A, B, and C, stress is relative: the two heaviest stresses form the lifts. A half-stressed syllable may form a lift or a drop, as the purely metrical situation demands. Sievers does not allow the same flexibility to D and E Types, whose linguistic stress profile is fixed by him in defiance of the evidence of the poem. This anomalous special status accorded to the half-stress leads directly to the idea of the expanded A* and D* Types. If you apply the relativity concept to them, then both fit within my AA Type. Because there are two full stresses in each to form the lifts, then the half-stress forms part of the drop. Thomas Cable suggested this possibility for the expanded A*, a possibility which logically should be extended to expanded D*.[7]

Given that the poet has six patterns from which to choose, a number of constraints will operate to limit his unbridled use of them. These constraints include the avoidance of ambiguity for the reader or reciter, the need to maintain a sense of on- and off-verse in poetry without strophic divisions, and the nature of the language itself, both general and local.[8] Obviously, in an inflected language where the root syllable is routinely stressed, AA Types will predominate without any effort by the poet – indeed, despite any effort by the poet to avoid them. Equally obviously, in such a language FF Types, with two adjacent stresses following two unstressed syllables, will be difficult to construct, or would be were it not for resolution.

Once you admit the possibility that an FF pattern might exist, then a number of verses which have traditionally been forced into other patterns can be seen to fit it without resolution – I count seventy-seven of them. For example, in verses such as *swa he nu git deð* (1058b), the final verb has traditionally been stretched into a diphthong to convert a natural FF into an unnatural CC. Given that metrical stress is relative, then a verse such as *no he þone gifstol* (168a), where the final word is a two-noun compound whose second element has half-stress, fits the FF pattern. This verse has traditionally been taken as a Sievers Type A3. Considered as a subtype of Type A, the A3 has two faults in that the first position lacks both stress and alliteration. For example, the stress profile for a verse such as *fand þa ðær inne* (118a) is x x x / x, impossible for Sievers, who attempted to explain the discrepancy by letting the initial finite verb, *fand*, form a lift. That verb, however, does not alliterate, and Kuhn's Laws have since removed any real doubt that such verses contain only one stress.[9] In any case, not all A3 verses include an initial finite verb or other particle. In *oð þæt him æghwylc* (9a), *æghwylc* is the only word that may be stressed. The more than 400 such verses in *Beowulf* are, then, serious errors according to Sievers, an unlikely number for so skilled a poet. Considered as subtypes of FF, however, A3s have both first stress and alliteration correct, but lack a second stress – a relatively minor fault. Treating A3 as a subtype of FF has the further advantage of allowing us to simplify the rule for alliteration: all verses *must* alliterate on the first stressed syllable, and on-verses *may* also alliterate on the second.

A3-Type FF verses are, of course, confined to the on-verse, more useful there perhaps because a verse ending with two full stresses has an air of finality that makes it unsuitable where the off-verse continues the sense. However, FF Types with a second lift formed through resolution occur in both on- and off-verses, and typically do not have an extended string of unstressed syllables forming the drops. Though resolved FF Types generally replace Sievers C Types, by no means all or even most of the resolutions occur in the second and third syllables of trisyllabic verbs and compounds. Four hundred and forty-two FF Types form a second lift through resolution, of which half, 220, resolve a separate word.[10] This separate disyllabic word may be a noun, as in *scop him Heort naman* (78b), an adverb, as in *Þanon woc fela* (1265b), a verb, as in *þe hie ær drugon* (15a), or indeed any word of stressable quality in final position. When the first lift of an FF is the first element of a trisyllabic compound, then the second lift is formed by resolving the second and third short syllables. Most often, these two syllables belong to a word capable of standing on its own, as in *buton folcscare* (73a), where *-scare* is a noun. In a few cases (19), the two resolved syllables form an inflected ending, as in *ic him þenode* (560b). This last use of resolution is likely to be more controversial, since it may be objected that the unstressed inflected ending of a verb is too weak a site for resolution. However, without resolution the same weak site must form a lift on its own: *ic him þenode,* x | x | x | / \ x . If the purpose of resolution is to supply a stressable position where none naturally exists, it seems likely that a poet would prefer to resolve two short syllables in what would be recognizably the final position of the verse rather than to use an unstressed single syllable to take full metrical ictus.

A simple law of resolution, such as 'Resolution is mandatory whenever it is possible,' would be very convenient. Unfortunately, resolution cannot be simplified to that degree. Resolution can occur in the first or second lift, or rarely in both lifts of any Type, and of course it follows that it occurs only in words capable of carrying stress: nouns, adjectives, or displaced particles (including verbs). Resolution in the first lift of any Type causes no problem of recognition, since it is either in initial position or preceded by an unstressed syllable. A potential source of confusion could arise when the second lift is resolved in a Type such as DD where two lifts are adjacent. When a two-part compound such as *sundwudu* or *mundbora* begins a verse, a compound whose second element, *wudu,* is technically resolvable, it never is resolved; such a compound always introduces a Type AA or EE. Were *sundwudu* to be resolved, it would form the first and second lifts of a DD, and would have to be followed by a word of stressable status consisting of two short syllables which also would normally be resolved (since Type DD is normally restricted to four positions, and non-stressable monosyllabic words do not end either the clause or a DD verse), for example, *\*sundwudu samod.* This embarrassment of resolvable syllables, four in a row, and complete suspension of resolution in the second stressable word would be confusing to the reader, who is better served by having a restricted choice of possibilities at the opening of verses with initial stress. There are 108 such cases of suspended resolution; whether the reader looks ahead to the next word to discover an AA or EE or simply knows from long practice that a *sundwudu* compound never is resolved in initial position is impossible to prove, though it seems likely that a competent reader or listener would notice any deviation from normal practice. When a compound such as *sundwudu* is the second word of an AA- or DD-Type verse, resolution is not involved; with *sund-* forming the second lift, *-wudu* would form the drop or drops and not be resolvable.

My claim that the profile Sxx never introduces a DD Type agrees in substance with Bliss's classification of verses of the *sundwudu sohte* kind as Type A; however, Bliss uses a different definition of resolution, and makes a number of different assumptions about the processes at work in such verses. Although he does not resolve the second element of the compound to form a lift, he does resolve it to form a drop, able to do so under the provisions of Sievers's claim of special status for the half-stress. Bliss notes correctly that 'the sequence / \ x / x … is studiously avoided by the *Beowulf* poet when the first three syllables belong to the same word' (*Metre of 'Beowulf,'* § 34); in other words, the profile / \ x always introduces an E Type. Bliss then assumes that in a verse such as *brimclifu blican*, if the second element of *brimclifu* is left unresolved, then the stress-profile of the word will be equivalent to that of *murnende* in *murnende mod*, / \ x, and so must be followed by a monosyllable to form an EE Type, / \ x | /. But *brimclifu* is not equivalent to *murnende*: it has a short second syllable. Bliss's assumption that the first syllable of *-blicu* may bear half-stress because it has what he calls secondary stress, but may and must also be resolved with another syllable to form a half-stress, is self-contradictory.

In his approach to resolution, Bliss uses a modified version of Kaluza's Law, which takes for granted the Sievers Types. Kaluza noted a difference in vowel quantity in the final syllable of words used in different positions in the verse, which he ascribed to whether or not the words were resolved. He pointed out that a word with the stress profile / x x has a short vocalic ending when it introduces a Type A, *sundwudu sohte*, but a long-vocalic ending when it introduces a Type E, *mundbora wæs*, or ends a Type D, *wis wordcwida*. He explained the difference as caused by resolution requirements: the two short syllables in a Type A must be 'resolved' to form a drop, but the two short syllables in the Types D and E must be left unresolved to form two drops. By extension, he assumed that disyllabic words resolved to form the final lift of Types B and E must follow the same rules, with short vocalic endings subject to resolution, and others not.[11] Bliss points out that the Law does not work for Types B and E; noting that a verb with an apparently short vocalic ending may form the second word of a D Type, *sele hlifade*, he further concludes that short vocalic endings are not necessarily resolved in a word with the profile / x x, but that a long-inflected ending precludes resolution in such a word (*Metre of 'Beowulf,'* § 40). Bliss did not, of course, consider the possibility of resolving such words in a C Type, since he considered the FF Type prohibited. In attempting to rehabilitate Kaluza's Law, Robert Fulk confines its operation to nouns and adjectives, the class which contains most short-vocalic endings and forms the first word in the relevant A Types.[12]

Fulk concedes, however, that a word with the profile Sxx in a Sievers C Type does not necessarily follow Kaluza's Law. In fact, the same word in the same case may occur in both A, E, or D Type, and C Type, whatever the status of its vocalic ending: *goldsele gumena* (1253) and *sipðan goldsele* (715); *mundbora wæs* (2779) and *Wes þu mundbora* (1480); *geong gold-hroden* (2025) and *eode goldhroden* (640). In my system, such compounds in a C Type are resolved to form an FF, but whether resolved or not, there is no consistent link between inflectional length and resolvability in lifts. The only consistent application of the phenomenon noted by Kaluza is in the 'resolution' of the first drop of an A Type, a site where my system does not accept resolution. A short-vocalic ending is one that regularly disappeared following a long stem, and presumably enjoyed a relatively inconspicuous existence following a short stem. In a different set of A Types where the words have the stress-profile / x x | / x, for example, *mistige moras* (162), Bliss proposes that the medial vowel of the first word was syncopated in pronunciation, and should be ignored in the scansion (*Metre of 'Beowulf,'* § 51). A similar stratagem may have been in place for short-vocalic endings in verse-initial compounds. I agree with Thomas Cable that resolution of the first drop of an A Type is an anomaly, and that verses of this sort are 'simply type A with a disyllabic first dip that is heavier than usual but not so heavy as to break into two positions' (*English Alliterative Tradition*, 141–2).

Although Kaluza's Law has no relevance to resolution of lifts, it does shed some light on the nature of drops. The essential difference between a compound with the profile / x x in Type AA, and one in DD or EE, is that the two short syllables fill one drop in the AA, but fill two adjacent drops in the others. If it makes sense to have an insignificant second vowel in the single drop in the AA, it makes equal sense to have a significant vowel form the second of two adjacent drops. Clearly the preference is for long-vocalic endings in Types DD and EE. All of the EE Types have them, although the number (seven, excluding the two instances of *irena cyst*) is too small for generalizations. In my Type DD with the profile Ss-xx, in 50 of the 68 examples the second word has a consonantal ending, and in 11 of the rest the final vowel is the *-a* never found in Bliss's short-vocalic ending group.[13]

However, a long-vocalic ending was not always available for the DD. Bliss speculates in giving his list of DD Types with 'apparently' short-vocalic endings and tertiary stress (*Metre of 'Beowulf,'* § 39), that verbs such as *hlifade* may in fact have had different standards for quantity than nouns. That remains a possibility. However, the list in § 39 consists almost entirely of verses with verbs (49 of 51) in the off-verse (49 of 51). Such verbs were simply not available for use as the first word in an AA Type in the on-verse. They could not take stress in first place preceding a word entitled to primary stress, and Kendall points out that his transformational rule for verses in the clausal dip without nouns or adjectives never generates an AA Type in the on-verse (*Metrical Grammar*, 24). A poet wishing to use a trisyllabic verb such as *hlifade* in a stressed situation had very limited options as to its placement. Kuhn's Laws make the end of the off-verse the logical place for it, and Types DD and FF the most accommodating templates.

In the FF-Type patterns where the resolvable sequence consists of a separate word in final place, as in x-x-S-S, then not surprisingly the resolved final word may contain any of the three endings found by Bliss in the B Type: consonantal *beran* 48b, long-vocalic *hraðe* 224b, short-vocalic *wine* 2047a.[14] In the FF-Type patterns where the resolvable sequence consists of the second element of a compound with the stress profile / x x (the Sievers C Type), the same is true. Of the 51 examples in the on-verse of one FF pattern xx-Ss, where the second lift is resolved, 25 are consonantal, like *goldhroden* in 614a, and vocalic endings may be long, like *wigfruma* 664a, or short, like *goldsele* 1253a. In the FF Type, adjacent drops in the same word can occur only in a four-position verse: if the verse is any longer, then separate words may form the two drops. Of the 50 on-verses with the particular pattern xx-Ss, where the second lift is resolved, 32 have both drops in a word with a consonantal ending, such as *æfter*. Most of the vocalic endings occur in verbs such as *hæfde*, adverbs such as *fore*, or pronouns such as *ðinra*: there are two cases of the short-vocalic *þone*, which also shows up in the drops of the DD Type. Here too, then, the preference is for long-inflected endings in the formation of adjacent drops. Since, as Fulk points out, most short-vocalic endings occur in nouns or adjectives, the poet would expend no great effort in finding appropriate words, since nouns and adjectives cannot possibly occupy the drops of an FF Type. If Kaluza's Law does not affect resolution, it is not, however, irrelevant to metre in its broadest sense, or to consideration of the historical development of the language. Clearly, it is significant that a specific class of compounds is preferred where a low degree of stress is required to form a single drop, and that a different class is preferred where adjacent drops are required.

When a reader encounters a compound of the *sundwudu* type at the end of a verse with an initial unstressed syllable, the choice is quite clear: resolution is necessary. The reader knows that the verse cannot be a BB Type; in the whole poem, only a dozen or so of the thousand-plus BB Types contain in the first lift a word of the pattern /xx, usually an inflected word, never a compound like *sundwudu* – and always unambiguous. Also, it cannot be a CC Type, since -*wu*- is short and cannot take stress on its own; if -*wudu* is resolved, then a CC Type would require a final unstressed monosyllable not possible at the end of a verse. Since the verse already has two unstressed initial positions and one lift, -*wudu* must resolve to make a Type FF.

Resolving to make FF-Types simplifies C Types in a number of ways: it makes consideration of secondary and tertiary stress irrelevant, and reduces many five-position verses to four positions. It also dramatically reduces the contexts for suspension of resolution, forcing us to face the question of what suspension of resolution actually is, and, in turn, to consider what resolution is. Only three contexts for suspension of resolution remain, besides the verse-initial *sundwudu* or *mundbora* type: a CC Type, of which there are close to 90 in the poem; 17 verses containing inflected forms of *cyning* and participles such as *wesend*; and an AA Type which corresponds to two of Bliss's categories, 2A3b and 2A1b, for which he gives a combined total of 79. If there are three contexts for suspension of resolution, there is now only one reason for it: resolution is suspended to prevent the creation of verses with only three metrical positions.[15]

That in itself is a considerable simplification of the traditional position, and perhaps I should leave it at that. But the existence of a category – the AA variety – which invokes suspension of resolution on the last two syllables to provide a weak second lift, when the verse already contains two perfectly good stresses, fills me with suspicion.[16] It would be a thoroughly clumsy way for the poet to compose, especially since 'suspended resolution' in an A Type *always* follows a word with the stress-pattern / \ , never a word with the pattern / x: *feasceaft guma*, not *\*fæger guma*. I would like, then, to consider what resolution is in practice.

What it cannot be is stress on or lengthening of only the first of the two resolved syllables. If it were, my FF Type would be worthless, indistinguishable in practice from the C Type it often replaces. Fortunately for my theory, the same objection arises with regard to EE Types with resolution on the final lift: if only the first resolved syllable were stressed, then the verse would be indistinguishable in practice from an AA. For example, if you pronounced 876b *uncūðes fela*, it would sound like an AA. For resolution to make any sense, it must involve heavy intonation of the two short syllables which together occupy the same timespan as one long syllable: *uncūðes fela*. If that is so, then three possibilities arise for suspension of resolution in CC Types. One is that you do not suspend at all, but resolve as usual, giving a three-position verse with only one drop: *in geardagum* (1b), x-Ss. This possibility should not be ruled out automatically. Other Germanic dialects have poetry with three-position verses; we have no right to assume that number of positions was more important than number of stresses. The second possibility is to suspend resolution completely, failing to stress either of the resolvable syllables, so that the pattern becomes x / x x : *in geardagum*. Such a pattern is similar to that known to exist in the FF one-stress subtype (the 'A3'), in having four positions and one stress. The third possibility is to stress the first resolvable syllable, leaving the second to form the final drop: *in geardagum*. In the CC Type, such a course would not be rhythmically confusing, as it would reproduce the basic stress pattern, x / \ x. If the first resolvable syllable was stressed without being lengthened, however, then the verse would have essentially three-and-a-half positions. If the first syllable was stressed and lengthened, there would be the risk of confusion over vocabulary, unless care was taken never to involve words where change of vowel-length would lead to change of meaning. For example, one of the CC Types with suspended resolution is *geond widwegas* (840a), usually translated as 'over the wide ways, from near and far.' If *-we(g)-* is lengthened, then the meaning changes to 'over the wide wave, across the sea.' Even if *-we(g)-* is stressed without lengthening it, there tends to be confusion over meaning. Of the three possibilities, I prefer full suspension, x-Sxx, because of the near-parallel in FF Types; but this can be only a personal preference.

When similar logic is applied to the AA Types, problems are caused by the half-stress in second position. If the second word is resolved, a very dense line results, consisting of three positions all capable of forming a lift. If only the first resolvable syllable is stressed without lengthening it, the problem is as severe: try saying **guðrinc monig** or **magodriht micel** in such a way that the short stressed third position outweighs the heavy consonants of the second position. In these particular verses a series of consonants rather than a long vowel provides length; even if the reciter uses pitch to differentiate metrically stressed syllables, as is possible, the result is less than satisfactory. What you get in practice is something that sounds like a DD with a steadily reducing level of stress, rather than an AA. DD is, of course, what you get if you do suspend resolution on the second word, since the half-stress in second position becomes a lift. Hans Kuhn points out that the poet is extremely careful not to use words such as *monig* and *swefan* in positions where they cause metrical problems.[17] Since such words are entirely replaceable by others, presumably they are used in this situation because they need no stress, rather than because the poet could find no better way to form an AA Type. You could formulate some sort of rule for suspension of resolution in such a case: 'suspension of resolution occurs to prevent three-position verses where the first two positions are capable of forming lifts, in which case an AA Type forms a DD instead,' or something equally involved. But such a procedure stops the reader in the midst of the analysis, producing a triple problem of recognition, decision, and performance – an undesirable situation. It would make much more sense metrically if these AA Types were, in fact, easily recognizable DD Types without suspension of resolution being invoked, that is, if the second word was obviously unstressed. I believe that enough of them are unstressed to justify disqualifying the whole category as AA, despite the few problem verses that remain.

The AA 'suspended resolution' category comprises a number of identifiable subgroups, which may for convenience be placed in five general classes, for each of which I shall give a typical example:[18]

First: *Goldfag scinon* (994b) is one of a group where, if you postulate a Type DD with the outline Ss-xx, the verb occupies the first dip of the clause, and so according to Kuhn's Laws should be unstressed, even though it is in final position in the line. Kuhn, of course, did not envisage a Type in which both lifts were initial and the third position was a drop.[19]

Second: *Guman ut scufon* (215b) is one of an allied group with the stress pattern / | / | x x, where a verb in final position is preceded by a modifying adverb or an adverbial preposition. I agree with Sievers, who points out that, except for simple intensifiers such as *micle*, such words take over the stress and alliteration of the word they modify, if they precede that word (*Altgermanische Metrik*, § 26). Bliss makes a narrower definition of what constitutes a definitive adverb.[20]

Third: *Hleoburh wera* (1731b) and *wælreow wiga* (629a) are typical of verses formed by two words in a compound-like relationship, usually noun plus possessive noun or adjective plus noun.[21] Sievers is somewhat ambiguous on this subject. Three 'equal' nouns are allowed, he says, when one is subject to the preceding noun in a grammatical relationship. Two nouns so bound constitute a single nominal form treated like a compound. He adds that noun formulations of more than two parts are rare.[22] His view of their rarity is perforce driven by his view of the stress patterns available to the poet. I treat these verses as essentially a single compound with the basic DD pattern.

Fourth: *Frumcyn witan* (252a) is one of a group where an infinitive follows a compound: Kendall argues that infinitives and participles do not necessarily take stress, though in general he means in verse-initial position. Sievers refers to infinitives as the noun forms of verbs, and assumes that they have primary stress.[23] If *witan* in a verse such as this is treated as essentially a noun in a grammatical relationship with the compound that precedes it (which is its object), then perhaps the same logic that applies to the 'compounds' in the previous paragraph may apply here.

Fifth: *Guðrinc monig* (838b) is one of seven verses with *monig* in final position, part of a larger group ending in similar words. Sievers describes pronominal adjectives of indeterminate quantity as enclitic and unstressed; Kendall describes them as proclitic and of indeterminate stress.[24] I can see no evidence that the stress of such words is determined by their position: their stress seems indeterminate both before and after the word they qualify. The practical course would be to treat them as unstressed unless the metre demands that they achieve stress through resolution to form the final lift.

An interesting group consists of varieties of *cyning*; indeed, the distribution of the word in *Beowulf* almost demonstrates in microcosm the uses of resolution. *Cyning* is always resolved except where it forms the last word of a DD Type with the profile Ss-xx, or where the rule against forming the second lift of a DD by resolving the second element of a compound applies. The word is used 57 times in the poem, shown by Klaeber as separate 28 times; as the second element of a compound (as in 84b *woroldcyninga*) 27 times; and as the first element of a compound twice: *cyning-bald* and *Kyning-wuldor*. In 9 of the off-verses, *cyning* is the resolved final lift of an FF; in 6, it is the unresolved final word of a DD with the profile Ss-xx. Its use is metrically similar to that of adverbs such as *fela* and *tela*, predominantly used at the end of the off-verse to form a DD or FF.

Klaeber's compound examples are evenly distributed between on- and off-verse, thanks largely to the heavy use of *þeodcyning* in the on-verse between lines 2579a and 3086a. When *cyning* is classified as the second element of a compound, it can be considered an unresolved pair of drops without controversy, as it is in 2563a *god guðcyning* and 54a *leof leodcyning*, where alliteration clearly shows that the first two positions take stress, and resolution would cause a three-position verse.[25] I propose that a number of Klaeber's separate examples should be treated as equivalent to such compounds: those where *cyning* is preceded by a proper name (as in *Hiorogar cyning* 2158b), by a conventional or heroic epithet (as in *rumheort cyning* 2110b), or where the relationship of *cyning* to the word preceding it is shown by the genitive case (as in *fyll cyninges* 2912b, and *feorh cyninges* 1210b). Klaeber generally limits compounds to two elements; the examples I give extend the treatment to three, with 2158b equivalent to *Frescyninge* at 2503b, and with 2110b equivalent to *guðcyning* at 199b and elsewhere. If the two genitive-case examples are considered equivalent to compounds, they can be included alongside the 9 other examples of inflected forms of *cyning* considered compounds by Klaeber.[26]

One inflected form of *cyning* which presents no problem is in *Hwilum cyninges þegn* (867b), where it may be resolved to help form a BB, xx-Sx-S. The other relevant verses are: 1210b *feorh cyninges*; 2912b *fyll cyninges*; 2a *þeodcyninga*; 1039b *heahcyninges*; 1155b *eorðcyninges*; 1684b *woroldcyninga*; 2382b *sæcyninga*; 2503b *Frescyninga*; 2694b *þeodcyninges*; 3180b *wyruldcyninga*. These have in common the difficulty that resolving *cyning* would lead to a three-position verse. *Wuldurcyninge* (2795a) is different in that, if *cyning* is resolved, then the verse formed is a normal AA with the profile Sxsx. Klaeber and others propose to shorten the first element to *wuldr* to bring this verse into line with the others; I propose to leave it problem-free. Kuhn discusses the inflected forms along with the participles *umborwesende* (46b), *cnihtwesende* (372b and 535b), *sawlberendra* (1004b), and *umborwesendum* (1187a) in an influential article in which he concludes that the first syllables of *cyning*, *wesend*, and *berend* took metrical stress without resolution when the situation required.[27] That conclusion, while it could be happily accepted by those who regularly suspended resolution on two-syllable *cyning* to form a C Type where I would posit an FF, needs re-examination.

Since in all of the examples the relevant syllables form the second element of a compound (or equivalent), they cannot be resolved under the provisions of the general rule for Type DD: a DD cannot be formed by resolving the second element of a compound. The question arises whether a reader who knew that a DD could not be formed through resolution would expect to find a DD at all in a verse such as *heahcyninges*. A long syllable need not undergo stress; if, however, metrical stress does require length, as I suspect, then -*cy*- cannot form a lift on its own. While -*nin*- can, it is debatable whether arsis would ever fall on the second syllable of a compound element whose first syllable is unstressed. In a normal verse such as *secgan hyrde*, the stress pattern dictated by the length of the syllables, long-short-long-short, coincides with the stress pattern of intonation required by the morphological nature of the words, high-low-high-low. In the verses under discussion, no such coincidence is possible, long-short-long-short being at odds with high-high-low-low. A compromise is possible in which a high-pitched short syllable -*cy*- is followed by a low-pitched stressed long syllable -*nin*-, to give an AA which conforms to form without offending sense, but such a compromise would give a unique metrical situation. The alternatives are a DD with a second lift which is stressed but not long, or a DD with a single initial stress. The difference between these two is largely one of notation, since a speaker would likely pronounce the verse in exactly the same way whether one chose to transcribe it Ssxx or Sxxx. Because my theory is based on the assumption that a lift must be occupied by a 'long' syllable, it would make sense for me to describe this type of verse as a one-stress DD with the profile

Sxxx; the syllable *-nin-* would have to be treated as a formative ending not capable of bearing stress, since under the relativity provision the verse would normally have to be designated AA. Kuhn points out that the poet is reluctant to use this construction, replacing it with an alternative where possible; in the circumstances, it seems foolish to add to the numbers by forcing a line such as *umborwesende*, which makes a perfectly good AA, into the mould through syncopation.[28] If altering the MS reading is permitted, it would make more sense to expand 1004b to *sawolberende* in order to achieve another trouble-free AA, thus leaving this small category to consist of two examples of *cnihtwesende* and 10 examples of inflected *cyning*. However, whether one counts the category as twelve or fourteen, it remains a problem.

To sum up, I propose that resolution is a metrical tool whose use is quite simple. It cannot be used in a drop, whether the drop is half-stressed or not. It forms a lift using two short syllables in a stressable position where a long syllable is not available. Stressable positions include the second element of a compound or trisyllabic verb where that element forms the second lift in final position. Resolution is mandatory, except where its use would lead to a verse with only three positions, and except for compounds of the *sundwudu* type in verse-initial position.

The position on resolution put forward here is part of a larger metrical theory which cannot be adequately discussed, let alone justified, in a short paper. Its aim is to preserve as much as possible of Sievers's monumental work, while questioning his assumptions on half-stress and resolution – assumptions whose grounds were not adequately established by Sievers. There are several advantages to having six very simple Types, rather than Sievers's more specific Five Types with numerous subtypes: to use all of the possible combinations of lifts and drops, rather than all but one, gives a more satisfactory theoretical basis for a metrical system, and a *raison d'être;* the simpler stress profile of, for instance, the DD Type accommodates both of Sievers's profiles plus others which seem to breach Sievers's rules for the Type; fewer and simpler Types make it easier to see how a reader of Old English poetry might have been able to recognize and decode the metre as he read; and the simpler Types answer Kuhn's criticism, that the Sievers Types worked well for *Beowulf* but not for less sophisticated works, by applying to a broader range of texts.[29] Small as the difference is between the Sievers Types and those that I propose, the change in the rules for resolution, if accepted, would have some far-reaching effects. One is that the 'metrical evidence'· would often no longer lend support to theories of whether particular words had a particular level of stress. For example, in a verse such as *Hwæt, wē Gār-dena*, Sievers's identification of the verse as a C Type insists that the first syllable of *dena* must be weightier than the second syllable. If the verse is regarded

as an FF Type, with *dena* subject to resolution, then the only important consideration metrically is that both syllables of a stressable word are short: the
metre does not otherwise distinguish between their quantity. A second effect
is that the phenomena dealt with in Kaluza's Law would no longer be tied to
resolution, although they would still be of importance linguistically. Much
work remains to be done on the possible ramifications of the simplified system of resolution suggested in this paper. The absence of a sound theoretical
basis for a few of the elements of Sievers's theory that are often taken for
granted makes that work necessary.

University of Western Ontario

## NOTES

1 Sievers, of course, discarded his Theory of Five Types late in life in favour
of another so arcane that Hans Kuhn refused to discuss it because he could
not understand it: 'Über die späteren Arbeiten und Lehren von Sievers, die
sogennante Schallanalyse, bin ich leider nicht imstande zu urteilen, denn ich
verstehe sie nicht,' 'Die Altgermanische Verskunst,' *Germanische Philologie, Festschrift für Otto Behaghel* (Heidelberg, 1934), 25. Although he
preferred the system of Andreas Heusler, Kuhn himself admitted that the
Five Types were useful for more polished works such as *Beowulf* (ibid., 24),
and assumed in setting out his own laws that the Types had some validity.
John C. Pope, whose own theory has similarities with Heusler's, admits as
great a debt to Sievers: *The Rhythm of 'Beowulf,'* rev. ed. (New Haven: Yale
University Press 1966), vii. The system of notation set out by A.J. Bliss in
*The Metre of 'Beowulf,'* 2nd ed. (Oxford: Blackwell 1962; rev. 1967), perhaps the system most in use, is essentially the Sievers Types taken to an
extreme level of descriptive complexity – a somewhat ironic fact, since Bliss
is even better known for his version of Kuhn's Laws, and Kuhn is quite
scathing about the efforts of Sievers's *Anhänger* to make a simple system
unnecessarily complicated (ibid., 22–3). Perhaps the extent to which the
scholarly community has invested in Sievers helps explain why theories
critical of major aspects of Sievers's work, such as David L. Hoover's *A
New Theory of Old English Meter* (New York: Lang 1985), are often dis-
missed without much discussion.
    Sievers's influence inevitably extends beyond metre. For instance, in his
chapter on accent, Campbell begins the section on half-stress with 'the Old
English metrical system shows that many words had both a stressed and a
half-stressed syllable,' *Old English Grammar* (Oxford: Clarendon Press

1959), § 87. A number of assumptions about the existence and nature of secondary and tertiary stress depend on the Sievers Types.

2 Sievers in discussing drops says only that 'generally' every series of unstressed syllables will form a single drop: 'Im allgemeinen hat jede ununterbrochene reihe sprachlich unbetonter silben als einheitliche senkung zu gelten,' *Altgermanische Metrik* (Halle: Niemeyer 1893), § 10.1. However, his decision to exclude Types with adjacent drops consisting of unstressed syllables makes it clear that this has the force of a rule.

3 I use the symbols '/,' '\,' and 'x' as they have been used traditionally by Sievers and others to show, respectively, fully stressed, half stressed, and unstressed syllables. The symbol 'l' shows a word-division in the Klaeber edition. Although my own system accords no metrical status to half-stressed syllables not in a lift, it is sometimes useful to record these. Where I wish to emphasize metrical stress rather than another kind of stress, I use 'S' for a stressed position and 'x' for an unstressed position, in imitation of Geoffrey Russom, *Old English Meter and Linguistic Theory* (Cambridge: Cambridge University Press 1987). I use the term 'linguistic stress' to mean stress on a long syllable in a word capable of metrical stress.

All quotations from *Beowulf* are from F. Klaeber, ed., *Beowulf and the Fight at Finnsburg*, 3rd ed. (Lexington, Mass.: Heath 1950).

4 In making the claim that each Type was recognizable, I accept the suggestion made by Calvin B. Kendall in *The Metrical Grammar of 'Beowulf'* (Cambridge: Cambridge University Press 1991), 13ff, that particles, finite verbs, and equivalent words in initial position in the on-verse did not usually bear metrical stress even if they bore alliteration.

5 In his list of allowable foot pairings, Russom allows xx/Ss, although he does not allow resolution at the second stress: *Old English Meter*, 21. Wolfgang Obst's Verstyp IIa includes many of my Type FF, together with one-stress CC, in a quite different system; he argues that resolution should not be suspended in the final position of a Sievers C Type, but does not distinguish between a verse with one initial unstressed syllable, and a verse with more than one. His equivalent to my x-S-xx (CC with suspended resolution) is therefore in the same group as my xx-S-S (FF with final resolution). Obst gives a brief English summary of his views on pages 111 to 114 of *Der Rhythmus des 'Beowulf': Eine Akzent und Takttheorie* (Heidelberg: Carl Winter 1987). A list of verses belonging to his Verstyp may be found beginning at page 126.

In calling for resolution in the Type FF, I am, of course, discounting Kaluza's Law, which attempts to explain phenomena on the assumption that Sievers is correct in allowing only five Types. In an FF Type with two stresses and resolution of the final position, a disyllabic word with a short first syllable is bound to follow a long stressed syllable; if this word order did not exist, the FF would scarcely be possible, restricted to those few instances where two stressed monosyllables end the verse. For a discussion of Kaluza's Law as modified by Bliss, see below.

6 In Appendix C of *The Metre of 'Beowulf,'* Bliss shows 296 examples of 1D1 (/ | / x x), 64 of 1D2 and 1D3 (/ | / \ x), and 66 of 1D4, 5 and 6 (/ | / x \). 1D1 (/ | \ x x) accounts for a further 101. One might well object to Bliss's classification of several types of compound as / x x. My own figures, based on linguistic rather than grammatical or positional stress, show the / | / x x forming a less impressive majority than Bliss's, with rather more of / | / \ x, and about the same number of / | / x \.

7 Or so I believe. Thomas Cable makes the suggestion in *The English Alliterative Tradition* (Philadelphia: University of Pennsylvania Press 1991). He notes that it is illogical to apply resolution to a half-stressed position in a verse such as *freowine folca*, adding that such a verse 'is simply type A with a disyllabic first dip that is heavier than usual but not so heavy as to break into two positions' (141–2). If this process were extended to the D* Type, then it would do damage to Cable's 'antepenultimate' rules, and make unnecessary his 'Clashing Stress' theory. I disagree with both of these concepts on separate grounds. I would extend Cable's insight to include half-stresses where resolution is not involved. As will be seen below, I agree with Cable's suggestion that *freowine folca* has a disyllabic first drop.

8 Most of these constraints have been well set out by Geoffrey Russom in *Old English Meter*.

9 While the 'traditional' course has been to label verses of the type under discussion as 'A3,' there has been a steady evolution in how such verses have been regarded by metrists, an evolution not without controversy, since Kuhn's Laws are not universally accepted. Sievers classified such verses as a subtype of Type A in which the first lift, often a finite verb, did not alliterate. For example, in the verse *Habbað we to þæm mæran* (270a), Sievers would consider *mæran*, which alliterates, to form the second lift, and *Habbað* to form the first, with a very long first drop containing four syllables. Kuhn, noting that A3 verses always occur in the on-verse, proposed that the stress of finite verbs was similar to that of particles, and depended on the position of the word in the clause ('Zur Worstellung und -Betonung im Altgermanischen,' *Beiträge zur Geschichte der deutschen Sprache und Literatur* 57 [1933]: 1–109). A verb in the first dip of the clause is normally unstressed. A verb displaced from the first dip acquires metrical stress through that displacement. In practical terms, that usually means that a verb in first place in the on-verse is unstressed, while a verb held over to the off-verse is stressed. In the sample verse given above, *Habbað* would be unstressed and

the only lift in the verse would be on the first syllable of *mæran*. Kuhn was
not as dogmatic about the application of his Laws as some of his followers
have been. A.J. Bliss makes use of the Laws in his theory of metre, and has
been influential in explaining them. He designates Sievers's Type A3 verses
as a1 or a2, a classification which maintains the link with the overall Type-
A profile (Bliss, *Metre of 'Beowulf,'* § 68–71). Recently, Calvin B. Kendall
has pointed out that on-verses with an initial finite verb or particle which
alliterates are syntactically identical with those verses where an initial verb
or particle does not alliterate; he proposes that the initial alliteration is extrametrical, and that the initial verb or particle should not bear metrical stress
(Kendall, *Metrical Grammar*, chs 2 and 3). The result of his proposal is that
a number of verses considered normal Type A by all of the metrists mentioned above become single-stress Type A3, a classification that Kendall
maintains.

10  *Beowulf* has a total of 939 FF Types, of which 420 in the on-verse have a
single stress. Of two-stress FF Types, 264 are in the on-verse, 255 are in the
off-verse.

11  Max Kaluza, 'Zur Betonungs- und Verslehre des Altenglischen,' in *Festschrift zum siebzigsten Geburtstage Oskar Schade*. (Königsberg: Hartung
1896), 101–34.

12  R.D. Fulk, *A History of Old English Meter* (Philadelphia: University of
Pennsylvania Press, 1992), § 174.

13  Six of the remaining seven have short-vocalic *þone*, one (1834b) has the
verb *bere*.

14  Short-vocalic forms are least frequent, with some, such as *fela*, of doubtful
status. Most short-vocalic endings belong to nouns and adjectives, which do
not often form the second lift of an FF Type. The 24 on-verses with the
pattern x-x-S-$\underline{S}$ use in the resolved second lift 10 verbals, 2 adverbs, 3
adjectives of indefinite quantity, 2 adjectives, and 7 nouns. However, 4 of
the nouns (*scipes* 896; *dæges* 1600; *Dena* 242; *gifa* 1930) are in the genitive
– always long-vocalic – following another noun. Of the remainder, one
(*guma* 20a) is an emendation, one (*Metod* 979a) is long, and one (*wine*
2047a) is short. It is a moot point whether short-vocalic examples are few
because the poet avoids them, or because opportunities to use them do not
arise.

15  That is, assuming that poets would prefer a four-part verse with one stress to
a three-part verse with two stresses. Although it is impossible to prove what
Old English practice was, maintaining the four-part standard would seem to
be less destructive of poetic rhythm. The existence of the one-stress FF (or
'A3') Type shows that one-stress four-position verses were tolerated; there is
no independent evidence for three-position verses.

16 When I say 'invokes suspension' I mean invokes it illogically. Bliss takes a verse such as *magodriht micel*, which consists of four positions, since *mago-* in first position must be resolved. The linguistic profile of the words is / \ | x x. However, the second word, *micel*, bears alliteration and may be stressable (though see my discussion below of Kendall's view of the status of words such as *micel*). He therefore notes the verse as metrically / \ | / x, with suspension of resolution in order to give ictus to *mi-*.

17 'Zu dem kurzstämmigen *swefan "schlafen"*, das er 12mal gebraucht, holt der Beowulfdichter sich das Partizip praesentis von dem langstämmigen Synonym *slæpan* (741. 1581. 2218), das er sonst überhaupt nicht gebraucht': Hans Kuhn, 'Westgermanisches in der Altnordischen Verskunst,' *Beiträge zur Geschichte der deutschen Sprache und Literatur* 63 (1939): 185. Kuhn is discussing the use of trisyllabic forms with short stems, but the observation is relevant to other forms.

18 The relevant verses are those given by Bliss in his Index to the Scansion of *Beowulf* (page 139) as 2A3b or 2A1b. They are listed below under the general groupings proposed in this paper, with 2A3b examples given first.

1. Verses with a finite verb unstressed through the operation of Kuhn's Laws: 284a, 303b, 994b, 2265b, 2460b; 2256b, 2457b, 2906b. In 2256b and 2457b, the two lifts occur in a participle with a long ending -*ynd* or -*end*, rather than in a two-element compound.

2. Adverb preceding a verb: 215b, 281b, 572b, 1065b, 2545b, 2551b, 2663b, 2956b, 3131b.

3. Adjective and noun, or two nouns forming a virtual compound: 629a, 817a, 1682a, 1896b, 1914b; 973a, 1457b, 2613b.

Noun with genitive noun: 657a, 1731b, 2035a, 2947a, 3000a; 120a. 1256a has an adjective with dative noun.

Verses with *cyning*: 619b, 1925b, 2110b, 2417b; 2158b.

4. Infinitive following a compound noun, usually its object, with auxiliary verb in an earlier verse: 252a, 786a, 1432b, 1964b, 2754b, 3019b, 3172a; 1672a, 1807b, 2972.

A similar construction with past participle replacing the infinitive: 406a, 643a, 1288b, 1310b; 3135b.

5. Verses ending in an indefinite pronominal adjective: 67a, 69a, 776a, 838b, 908b, 1015a, 1289b, 1510b, 2007b, 2334b, 2588a, 2959a, 2969b, 3081b; 1112b.

Remainder: 2174b has an adverb following two words with primary stress, which take precedence. 1834b and 2060b have a noun compound followed by a finite verb which is apparently not unstressed through the operation of Kuhn's Laws.

Excluded: I have not considered 390a, 1230b, and 1278b, which are traditional editorial emendations, and 1525b, 1869b, and 2241b, which are emendations by Bliss himself. Two verses seem to have been wrongly designated: 2016a and 2979a.

19  Kendall, whose interest is primarily in syntax, assumes that the Sievers Types are valid, and therefore that a particle or verb following a two-position stressable word is not in the first dip for the purposes of Kuhn's Laws, though he does acknowledge that the wording used by Kuhn could be interpreted otherwise:

'Kuhn, p. 9, seems to have considered a compound with clashing stress to be the equivalent of a single stressed word, although his statement is not entirely clear. However, the conclusion that it must be the equivalent of two stressed elements in the metrical grammar of *Beowulf* seems inescapable. See Campbell, "Verse Influences", p. 95; Bliss, "Auxiliary and Verbal", p. 165' (47, n9).

What Kendall calls 'a compound with clashing stress' is one consisting of two stressable positions. He is concerned to show that in a verse such as 1239a, *Bencþelu beredon*, the verb *beredon* is stressed because a compound with clashing stress, *bencþelu*, excludes it from the dip. On purely metrical grounds, however, *-þelu* must form the dip because of the general rule against forming a DD by resolving the second element of a compound. The verb is displaced not because the first word is a two-part compound, but because the second element of the compound consists of two short syllables. The only other example he gives of such a compound, *mearcstapa*, has a similar profile (though it is not used in the poem in verse-initial position in any case). Kendall does acknowledge that compound proper names may be followed by a verb in the dip, and assumes that proper names fall into a special class. In his Index of Verses, he shows a verse such as 994b, *Goldfag scinon*, as an A Type with suspended resolution on the verb. He does not explain why *Beowulf wæs breme* has the verb in the dip, and *Beowulf maðelode* (405a) does not. The difference may be, of course, that the copula is treated differently. It seems to me, however, that the reader must use his knowledge of metre rather than grammar to decide the point. If in 405a the word *Beowulf*, whose linguistic profile is / \ , is given the metrical status Ss, then the unstressed verb occupies four positions, giving the unmetrical verse profile Ss-xxxx. Of all Types, DD is most rigorously restricted to four positions. Seeing that a DD cannot be formed, the reader is free to resolve and stress the first two syllables of the verb, without any inconvenience to himself, since *Beowulf* will be given the same weight, / \ , in either case.

20  In practice, however, Sievers appears not to follow his own advice when

alliteration does not provide confirmation, especially in the off-verse. Bliss may therefore be supplying a rationale for Sievers's practice. I accept Kendall's argument that in such cases adverb and verb are essentially in a compound-like relationship (186).

21 'Compound-like relationship' is admittedly a clumsy expression, but I use it to avoid confusion with existing theories of metre or stress. The term 'quasicompound' might serve very well, but it has been used by Campbell and Kendall to describe word-groups which do not include all of those which I claim: both would classify an adverb-verb grouping such as that in *guman ut scufon* as a quasi-compound, but would exclude others (Campbell, *Old English Grammar*, § 94 n1; Kendall, *Metrical Grammar*, 185). Geoffrey Russom coins the useful terms 'linguistic compounding' and 'metrical compounding.' To illustrate the latter, he cites *leof leod-cyning* for the Pattern S/Ssx (*Old English Meter*, 76). Since I would label this half-line S-Sxx, it would be misleading to use his terms here.

22 Sievers, *Altgermanische Metrik*, § 23.3.

23 Ibid., § 23; Kendall, *Metrical Grammar*, 17.

24 Sievers, *Altgermanische Metrik*, § 27; Kendall, *Metrical Grammar*, 131ff.

25 Kendall points out (*Metrical Grammar*, 166) that the poet does not allow the sequence *\*wer won-sæli*, where a trisyllabic compound with a long stress on its second element follows a monosyllabic simplex, remarking that his objection seems to be to three long 'stress-worthy' syllables in a row. That the poet does allow *leof leod-cyning* suggests that the first syllable of *cyning* was considered short, whether or not it ever took stress without resolution. The reluctance of the poet to have three adjacent long stressable positions in four-position verses makes it unlikely that verses which I show as Ss-xx would have the final word resolved to provide a three-position verse with two stresses enclosing a stressable long syllable.

26 Campbell describes *feorh cyninges* and *fyll cyninges* as 'virtual compounds': *Old English Grammar*, § 91 n2. The name *Hreðel* in *Hreðel cyning*, 2430b, is unusual in having a short second syllable. If the verse is considered as a compound, however, the second syllable may be considered linguistically long by virtue of being followed by two consonants.

27 Hans Kuhn, 'Westgermanisches in der Altnordischen Verskunst,' 186ff. R.D. Fulk provides a discussion of the circumstances in which *cyning* is resolved or not in *A History of Old English Meter*, § 194 and 271–8. I agree with Kuhn that *ær* should be omitted from 1187a, leaving *umborwesendum* to form the verse on its own.

28 Kuhn points out that the poet uses the two-syllable nominative and accusative singular forms of *cyning* 40 times, compared with 10 for the three-syllable genitive and dative. In synonymous words, the ratio is 86 to 49.

Beowulfdichter muß also die Formen *cyninges* und *cyninge* ungern gebraucht haben' ('Westgermanisches,' 186). R.D. Fulk (*History*, 237 n2) also suggests reading 1004b as *sawolberende*.

29 Hans Kuhn, 'Altgermanische Verskunst,' 20ff.

# Computer Assistance in the Analysis of Old English Metre: Methods and Results – A Provisional Report

O.D. MACRAE-GIBSON AND

J.R. LISHMAN

## 1 Background

In 1986 Macrae-Gibson published an article[1] which examined closely the methodology and conclusions of A.J. Bliss's well-known book *The Metre of 'Beowulf,'*[2] and argued particularly that metrical types can be meaningfully grouped according to the proportions that occur in the three categories 'a-line with single alliteration,' 'a-line with double alliteration,' and 'b-line' (hereafter called simply 'the three categories'), as Bliss does, only if 'metrical types' becomes 'metrical-syntactic types,' for in some cases the distributions of types realized by different syntactic structures are strikingly different.

The article also raised the question whether the distributions found are peculiar to *Beowulf* or general in the poetry, as Bliss appeared to believe – rather strangely, if so, since S.K. Das[3] had much earlier presented an argument, which has been generally accepted, that Cynewulf's authorship was limited to the four signed poems, based in part on what he claimed to be distinctive features in these poems of this type of distribution. Das did not, however, make any use of statistical principles to establish whether the differences he found were significant, and although he considered syntax as well as metre he did not make properly systematic use of the combination. It would be desirable to put his conclusions on a sounder footing, and also to see whether such methods give interesting findings about other poems of the corpus.

Macrae-Gibson's intention to pursue this question was delayed in execution for some considerable time. Although he had made use of computer assistance with his analyses, it was clear that if the extended investigation was to be practical a good deal more use would be at least highly desirable, but he lacked at the time sufficient computing skills. This lack he spent some years in remedying (bringing himself in the course of his studies into a fortunate collaboration with his co-author, J.R. Lishman). Also intervening was a happy but time-consuming collaboration with Connie Hieatt, whose concern for the help the computer can give with the teaching of Old English is well known. It seems both fortunate and fitting that the conclusion of that collaboration in the publication of *Beginning Old English* should have allowed Macrae-Gibson enough time to prepare and present to her the present preliminary report on the possibilities of computer assistance in another of her fields of Old English interest.

Since publication of Macrae-Gibson's 1986 article there has been much work on Old English metre, not all favourable to Bliss, and some that has rejected even the general principle that the normal half-line is based on two metrical lifts.[4] On the latter point we observe only that argument based on modern investigation of the verse but ignoring the testimony of the medieval metrist Snorri Sturluson seems to us ill weighted; Snorri does not, of course, discuss Old English verse, but he does deal with what is accepted as its close relative, *fornyrðislag*, as well as with the more developed Skaldic metres. On the former, for the purposes of this study it is of scant importance whether Bliss's analyses well represent the rhythms with which the verse would have been spoken; if his types can be shown to be discriminately used by poets they must represent *something* of metrical importance, and can properly be used as part of an investigation into the extent to which practice differs among poets.

## 2 Can a Computer Read Old English Verse?

In such an investigation it is evident that the computer can give valuable help in the speedy assessment of the degree to which Blissian, or modified Blissian, analyses of two texts in fact demonstrate significant differences of practice, and we will return to this later. More interesting in computing terms is the possibility that the computer can to a useful extent take over the making of the analyses themselves. A great merit of Bliss's system is that it is in a quite high degree objective, and any objective method is in principle mechanizable. What is in computing terms an 'expert system' – that is, one that aims to come to the same conclusions that an expert in the field with time to give careful attention to the data would come to – is in principle a possibility. In practice the aim can seldom if ever be fully realized, and our work so far does not suggest that it can be in the present case, but we foresee that a success rate of at least 90 per cent may be attainable. There are then two approaches to the resultant output.

The first sees it as a preliminary stage, doing much of the routine analysis of obvious cases, leaving the investigator with the much shortened task of checking the output and adjusting the cases in which the computer has erred. The second makes a merit of the fact that even when the computer has, to the expert's eye, erred, it has done so on objective criteria. Though Bliss's system aims at objectivity, subjectivity of judgment can enter in some cases, and so of course can human error. The observations of an investigator with an interest in the outcome of the analysis can subconsciously skew data so as to conduce to a hoped-for outcome; this is a real problem and has produced spurious conclusions in more than one case. A computer, unless explicitly programmed to adjust its procedures in cases of uncertainty to favour a preconceived likely result, cannot fall into this trap. Erroneous analyses may blur the evidence so that genuine distinctions cannot be identified, but statistical principles, properly applied, cannot produce spurious distinctions, except to the extent that any distinctions detected by statistical methods may be spurious: the probability that they are so is low, and known.

We have so far based all our comparisons on unadjusted computer output, accepting that this will certainly include unsound analyses (or no analyses at all) of some lines. Quite apart from the argument in its favour advanced above, this method allows material to be surveyed very much more quickly than if it had first to be subjected to expert correction, allowing at least provisional conclusions to emerge. Whichever approach is taken to the output, the fact that the process is mechanized is normally an immense advantage at the stage of provisional conclusions, which frequently suggest that the original criteria of analysis were not quite right. The analyser program can then be modified and the analyses regenerated with comparatively small effort, whereas to redo a human analysis on modified criteria can often require labour little less than it took to make it in the first place. We are not yet at the stage of feeling impelled to modify some basic principles of analysis, but we quite expect to reach it.

A computer analysis of the metre of a line of verse evidently first requires an analysis of the language of the line. The field of computer analysis of natural language is now a large and active one. Analysis of syntax has been very successful, but the extraction of meaning has proved much more difficult because understanding language often requires knowledge of what is being written about. The problem is well exemplified in early work by Lindsay,[5] who quotes two examples, 'the pen is in the box' and 'the box is in the pen,' where the first pen is a writing instrument and the second a fenced enclosure. To understand the meaning of the words well enough to answer questions or translate into another language, the computer must store adequate knowledge about the referents of the words.

This is possible in limited domains. The inspiration to the field, Terry Winograd's famous program SHRDLU,[6] was able to respond correctly to complex sentences because it operated in a simple world of simulated blocks, of which it had full knowledge. A more recent review[7] reports successes in using natural language to interrogate databases, where the range of meanings is reduced by the context: in a geographical domain we may assume that a 'bank' is land beside water, not a financial institution. As far as we know, nobody has attempted natural-language processing of poetry.[8]

Our project represents a very special venture into this field, with abnormal distribution of difficulty. In normal natural-language processing, the identification of the words of the input is comparatively straightforward; the language will have a regular orthography and include relatively few homographs. In the processing of Old English it is a serious problem, since the language does not have a regular orthography and (given the allowances that must be made for this, and in view of its ready capacity to form compounds) has a much more extensive capacity for potential homography than we had appreciated at the start of the project. If one allows, for instance, for the possibility that a word with regular *e* may turn up with *æ* (thus *þægen*), the computer will identify the noun *wæl* as possibly representing instead the adverb *wel*. The obvious present plural *lufaþ* will be identified as possibly representing a compound *luf-aþ*, and so on.

One obvious way of evading this difficulty would be to use as data a full list of the word forms found in Old English poetry, which could be extracted from the published concordance,[9] with the grammatical status (and, what is also necessary, syllabic and stress structure) of each form determined by the investigator and added to the data. We have preferred to shirk this dull and laborious task and instead to use as data a list of the word roots found in the poetry, extracted chiefly from the *Grouped Frequency Word-List* of Madden and Magoun[10] (with the deplorably large number of omissions our edition proved to contain filled as discovered, chiefly from Bessinger's *Short Dictionary*).[11] To this are added tables of the regular affixes of the language, rules for the combination of elements, and rules for the modification of forms which occur when elements are combined. Such rules are regularly stated by grammars as phonetic rules, but these have of course been inferred from observation of textual forms, and can easily be reformatted as orthographic rules. Thus 'medial $\chi$ became a breathing between vowels ... the breathing was however lost early in OE'[12] readily becomes a rule that a form containing no character *h* can be interpreted as representing a root morpheme ending in *h* and a suffix morpheme beginning with a vowel character, with the addition that this vowel character need not be represented in the form (so that a form *feos* is correctly interpreted as representing *feoh* plus *es*). Other rules are added to allow for frequent modifications of base forms, as by the substitution of *y* or *i* for *ie*, representing what grammars describe as the phonetic process of monophthongization. We accept that such rules will create alternative analyses of many forms, as noted above, but hope that various devices such as those mentioned below will prevent more than a very few unsound analyses from yielding unsound final metrical categorizations.

## 3 Program Structures

All the programs used have been specially written in the language C. Its conciseness of expression makes it convenient for long and elaborate programs; its capacity in effect to pass characters, words, and phrases quickly from procedure to procedure, by passing numerical values acting as pointers to their storage locations in the computer memory, makes practical the complex examination of large amounts of text which the investigation demands. The analysis of words described above is realized by means of a recursive function which first calls a search through all forms in the data that can licitly occur at the beginning of a word to find one that can be matched against the 'head' of the presented form, that is, its characters taken from the left as far as necessary for the match. Then it calls itself on the 'tail' of the form (the remaining characters), but with new restrictions on licit forms depending on the first match: to take an obvious case, prefixes are not now licit. This proceeds until no match is found, or until the 'tail' becomes null (the search has reached the end of the word), in which case if the analysis appears to be a legitimate one (it must not, for instance, terminate in a root which can exist only in an inflected form) it is stored. The search then backtracks to the last point at which a successful match left unsearched possibilities, and resumes from there. Eventually all apparently legitimate analyses are stored. As an analysis proceeds, the program also generates a code representing the syllable structure of the word as analysed, with the positions of its main and any subordinate stress. If an analysis has made use of a match possibility that an expert would probably entertain only if no acceptable interpretation could be put on the word without it (as with the *æ* in *þægen*), the computer will also attach a negative score to the analysis. This will later be used to prevent the program from accepting the analysis unless all with a better score (if there are any such) prove to yield undesirable metre or syntax. A negative score is also attached to an analysis compounded of more than one root, on the basis that an expert identifying a form as a complete entity, or a regularly inflected form of a regular entity, would consider an alternative interpretation as a compound only if the simpler one would not fit.

Words are thus analysed in order through a half-line, as read from the main input data, which will consist of a section of the electronic text of the Anglo-Saxon Poetic Records as supplied by the Oxford Text Archive and, with the cooperation of Patricia Bethel, purged of the large number of errors it proved to contain. The program then examines in sequence all combinations of all analyses of all the words (in some cases cut-offs have to be imposed to prevent impossibly large numbers of such combinations from overburdening the computer, but fortunately this is rarely necessary). The program first ascertains where the metrical lifts would appear to fall, using the accepted principles that nouns and adjectives are normally stressed, that finite verbs and adverbs are not normally stressed at the beginning of their clauses but can be when displaced from there, that prepositions are regularly stressed when displaced from their normal 'preposed' positions, and so on. If the stressing thus arrived at is unsatisfactory (for instance, if the two stresses appear to fall on the last two syllables), a negative score for the whole sequence is added to the sum of the negative scores, if any, attached to the individual word analyses.

At this stage the program makes its very limited excursion into syntactic analysis, which as indicated above is the clearly successful part of normal natural-language computing. Full syntactic analysis of the structures of poetry, however – particularly in a language that, since it does not use syntactic punctuation, offers no reliable evidence even of sentence boundaries – would be quite beyond the range of the comparatively simple programs we have been able to create. Fortunately, a high proportion of the Old English poetic half-lines consist of self-contained syntactic units, and these will include the great majority of metric-syntactic entities which occur often enough for their distribution to lend itself to statistical examination. All the program at present does in this matter is to examine the grammar of the words forming the putative lifts, and in some cases of surrounding words, to see whether they could compose an acceptable syntactic unit. Even at this level the procedures are not yet fully developed; but, for instance, if two nouns provide the lifts, they are examined to see if they can agree in case, and therefore be coordinated, or whether one can be a genitive and therefore create a possessive structure, or whether one is preceded by a preposition and could therefore create an adjectival phrase qualifying the other. If none of these is possible a negative score is again added to any accumulated such score, so that if any more obviously satisfactory analysis of the half-line is available it will be preferred. Typical of ambiguities which can be resolved in this sort of way is *Beowulf* 3106a *ædre geæfned*, where an analysis as feminine plural noun ('blood-vessels,' as in the Paris Psalter, 138.11) plus uninflected past participial adjective can be negative-scored on the basis that the forms could not be in agreement, and so rejected in favour of the correct interpretation of *ædre* as adverb.[13]

Finally, the program examines the scores for the half-line analyses of the first and second half-lines, and chooses the best of those that also provide acceptable alliteration (if none do so, simply the best in themselves), recording whether the alliteration, if good, is double or single.

There is no excursion into semantic analysis at all. In most natural-language computing, semantic analysis is of the essence, since the object is normally to perform some action in response to a meaningful input or to re-express the meaning in a different language. Our program calls for no knowledge of meaning; fortunately the number of cases in which such knowledge is required to resolve an ambiguity affecting metrical-syntactic analysis is very small. Let us suppose the 'expert' whose analysis the program is emulating encounters in a newly discovered poem the half-line *lufaþ sworon*. He or she probably responds chiefly to the semantic congruence between *sworon* and *aþ* as the basis for concluding that the hitherto unrecorded compound *luf-aþ* does here exist. The program cannot do this. But it can be given the capacity to observe the syntactic unlikeliness of two apparently coordinated finite verbs, one present and one past, as well as the unusual metrical feature of a finite verb that provides the opening lift, a lift moreover which would seem to require resolution of the two opening syllables, leaving only two to complete the half-line. Any of these may be set to give a sufficient negative score to override that attached to the compound, and so lead the program by a different route to the same conclusion as the expert.

We have hardly begun the 'tuning' of the various negative scores by which we hope to reduce considerably the number of lines on which the expert would reject the computer's analysis. Meanwhile, however, for the reasons given above, we think that where our present, imperfect, analyses seem to demonstrate significant metrical-syntactic differences between poems, these differences are likely to be genuine.

## 4 The Metrical Analyses

Having by the means discussed above chosen a 'best analysis' of a poetic line, the program then performs a fuller analysis of the syllabic structure to obtain a Bliss-type coding of the metre. A coding of the syntax in a form like that proposed in Macrae-Gibson's 1986 article, but at the present stage of our work simplified, is created by conjoining the code letters chosen to represent the grammatical types of the lift-bearing words. Thus any half-line both of whose lifts fall on nouns will be coded HH. Should the distinction made in the 1986 article between this code and GH/HG,[14] and other such distinctions, prove to be important, our program holds enough information about the words as analysed to allow them to be recognized.

Bliss's actual codings are not convenient for a computerized application, because the same symbols can represent quite different things in different cases, and there is no automatic way to extend the system if a half-line is detected which does not exactly fit it. Thus an added (i) and (ii) usually represent, respectively, one and two unstressed syllables in the second dip, but in one case[15] in the first. One might also reasonably guess that an added (iii) would represent three such syllables if an abnormal line with three were encountered, but in fact it could not be so used because it is pre-empted to represent two syllables in the first dip where (i) and (ii) already refer to the second.[16] In another case (type 1A2) one and two syllables in the first dip are coded a(i) and b(i). In the computer form the numbers of unstressed syllables in the two dips of types A, B, and C are always represented by two figures, separated by a hyphen, within square brackets; in types D and E the number respectively after the second lift and between the lifts by a single figure within square brackets. Other distinctive features of the computer's codings are: (1) a prefixed arabic numeral 1 represents a clear break between words or phrases immediately after the first lift, 2 immediately before the second, 0 neither of these (this only partly coincides with Bliss's usage); (2) if the second lift is on a single short syllable this is indicated by an additional code *s*; (3) a clear secondary stress after the first lift is similarly coded #, after the second $; (4) the presence of an anacrusis is coded +.

If the analysis is performed in the full form summarized above, the result is, for many purposes, too many distinct entities with too few instances of each. To avoid this, the delicacy of the program can at choice be reduced, so as to omit the code for numbers of unstressed syllables, for short second lift, and for secondary stress. This can in some cases lump together types with different distributions. In type 2A in particular (type A with break immediately before the second lift), distribution can be significantly affected both by the length of the second lift and by the presence or absence of secondary stress.[17] However, such lumping together will not invalidate statistical conclusions, provided it is not done, consciously or unconsciously, in order to create groups that it is perceived from the actual test data will offer desired evidence. That risk apart, the earlier comment on the more general case of 'erroneous analysis' applies: while over-crude combination of groups may suppress what would be valid statistical evidence, it cannot create spurious evidence. Our provisional results have all been obtained with minimum delicacy; when the programs are more fully tuned we hope to be in a position to look at cases in which other distinctions are significant.

## 5 Comparison of Two Texts

This is done on two bases. The first, the more straightforward, simply ascertains for each metrical-syntactic entity found whether the distributions between the three categories in the two texts differ to an extent that suggests systematic difference of poetic practice, in the form of a probability that the differences could occur by mere random chance in the absence of any such systematic difference. The statistical mathematics of this are well known. To obtain a mathematically exact value for the probability is a complex operation, and an approximation known as the 'chi-square test,' quite close enough for most purposes, is normally used.[18] It ceases to be close enough when the number of instances becomes too small, and our program reports how many entities provided large enough samples for meaningful analysis, and which of these, if any, showed differences of distribution in different degrees unlikely to be due to chance.

Care is of course needed in the interpretation of the results. It is obvious enough that if ten entities have allowed analysis, and one of them shows a difference of distribution that might be expected by chance in one case in ten, there is no overall evidence that anything but chance has been at work. It is not so obvious, and is very difficult to calculate, just what accumulation of entities showing what individual odds against chance will yield overall evidence of what strength. Help can however be obtained empirically for any particular pair of texts by the following process. The lines of the texts are redistributed at random into two new texts of the same lengths as the original ones. These randomized texts are subjected to the same analysis and comparison as was performed on the original ones.[19] This is repeated enough times to give a clear picture of what might be expected by chance; if the original comparison showed greater differences than this, they are significant. To obtain a quantitative value for the degree of significance, however, and to allow the computer to be programmed to perform the repeated randomizings and comparisons (which are laborious when performed individually), it is essential to combine the evidence for all significantly different entities into a single overall value, a 'divergence score.' We have provisionally adopted the rather crude procedure of giving one point for a divergence reported as likely by chance less often than once in ten ('significant at the 0.1 level,' to use the normal statistical terminology), two points for, similarly, one in twenty ('the 0.05 level'), five points for one in fifty (0.02), and ten points for one in a hundred (0.01). These are probability values commonly used in statistics, for which criteria are therefore readily available in reference books. The points are then totalled to give the score. The computer reports the score for the original texts, and a 'median randomized score' from its repeated comparisons of the randomized ones, together with the ranges within which 90 per cent, 95 per cent, and 99 per cent of the randomized scores fell.

An alternative approach seeks to establish an overall index of the difference between two texts directly, combining the differences of all entities. Such a measure of the magnitude of the difference – which is of course a quite different thing from the statistical likelihood that the difference is significant – would obviously be useful in comparisons; also, it is clearly possible that such a difference could be statistically significant even if there were no single entity for which this was so. Now, as can be seen in Bliss's work and Macrae-Gibson's earlier development of it, the proportion of an entity's occurrences which fall into the three categories can be viewed as creating a point in two-coordinate space (two because, although there are three categories, once the proportions for two are known the third is determined, so there are only two 'degrees of freedom').[20] The separation of this point from the equivalent point for another text is an index of the difference of usage of the entity; a summation of the separations for all entities is an index of the overall difference. Clearly simple arithmetical summation, giving equal weight to separations representing entities with many and with few occurrences, is not sound; the most appropriate basis of weighting seems to us to be first to convert the number of occurrences in a text to a proportion of the total number of occurrences of all entities in that text (so that the two texts have equal weight, even though the reliability of points in the shorter will be less), and then to weight on the square root of the product (the 'harmonic mean') of the proportions for the two texts, giving a 'weighted mean separation' of the entity-points of the two texts. This procedure prevents a separation one of whose points is highly unreliable, because supported by very few instances, from having a large effect on the summation, however many instances there are in the other text. We know of no statistical theory that would allow us to calculate the probability that any summation of separations found by this method might be due to chance; but the same empirical method used for the other index of overall difference can be used here, giving a 'median randomized separation' and the ranges within which 90 per cent, 95 per cent, and 99 per cent of the randomized separations fell.

We are not yet clear how reliably and usefully this second index of overall difference does represent the magnitude of the metrical difference; in terms of statistical likelihood, it in most cases gives a similar indication to the first, as would be expected since both are based on the same facts about the same entities. Where the second index does not give a similar indication, it is not easy to give a confident interpretation of the findings. A merit of the first index is that one can identify from the files created by the analyser program the text lines in which the instances of the entities on whose differences it is based occur, and confirm from the texts themselves that the reported entities do indeed represent distinct types of half-line, which are indeed discriminately used in the texts being compared. The second index merely emerges from the 'black box' of the computer, with no equivalent means of confirming that it actually makes sense. Greater delicacy and precision in our methods may perhaps increase its utility at a later stage.

## 6 Some Provisional Findings

We looked first at the signed poems of Cynewulf, to see whether they in fact show authorial consistency in the distribution of types (a preliminary check omitted by Das). *Juliana* and *Elene*, as we expected, showed close similarity. The 'divergence score' (the first index of overall difference) was 1, representing a single entity whose differences of distribution, taken in isolation, would occur by chance less often than 1 in 10, in a total of 19 assessable entities; this is identical with the median randomized score. The 'weighted mean separation' (the second index) was 0.10, against a median randomized separation of 0.11. Very much the same similarity on the second index appeared between these poems, separately or together, and *The Fates of the Apostles*, but because of the shortness of this latter text there was only one assessable entity on which a divergence score could have been based, so the main conclusion here is that the samples are too small for reliable statistics.

To our surprise, comparison of *Christ II* with *Juliana* and/or *Elene* showed what appeared to be significant differences. Lines characteristically of the type *wintra for worulde* (*Elene* 4a) or *mærðum ond mihtum* (*Elene* 15a), with both lifts on nouns and the natural break neither immediately after the first nor immediately before the second, and so classified by the computer as 0AHH, appear predominantly as double-alliterated a-lines in *Elene* and *Juliana* (well over half in both cases), but about half as b-lines in *Christ II*. Lines of the type *Romwara cyning* (*Elene* 129b) or *heofonrices weard* (*Juliana* 212b), classified as 2EHH, are most frequently b-lines in these poems (well over half), but predominantly double-alliterated a-lines in *Christ II*. Statistically the differences are not striking. So much might be expected by chance around once in ten (putting the two indices together), whereas, as will appear below, some other pairs of poems go off our scale of improbability by chance. Yet the differences are there, and have caused us to treat only *Juliana* plus *Elene* as 'core Cynewulf' for the purpose of further comparisons.

We are not, however, proposing anything so hardy as that *Christ II*, despite the signature, is not by Cynewulf. Before coming to that conclusion one would have to be satisfied that poets never modify their metrical habits in response to different poetic contexts. The only way of investigating this possibility is, of course, to compare different sections of the same work (assuming that what appear to be distinct works were in fact composed by distinct poets – if not one can do nothing). We simply took the first and second halves of poems, arbitrarily, as 'different sections.' Of those we have surveyed, *Genesis A* shows the expected close similarity, as does *Exodus* (though it is rather short for reliable statistics). We were confident that *Beowulf* would do so too, since Macrae-Gibson's earlier article had to some extent already investigated the matter and concluded for consistency ('Metrical Entities,' 72 n30). But the fuller and faster searches now possible with computer assistance do not altogether support that conclusion. Both indices show a difference significant at the 0.05 level. This is chiefly due to the behaviour of one particular entity, which the computer classifies as 2AQH (adjective plus noun, break immediately before the second lift), characteristically realized by such half-lines as *laðan liges* (83a) and *ealde lafe* (1688a). As an a-line, this structure is predominantly double-alliterated in the first half of the poem, single in the second. One might wish to argue that the easy confidence of the young hero in the first part of the poem calls up a poetic mood in which nouns emphatically have their proper descriptors, but as sorrows and uncertainties grow such positivity weakens. At all events, it is clearly possible that literary forces of this sort may be at play as a poet's work proceeds. It may well be that the main value of the methods we are developing will be to discover differences which prompt such thoughts about Old English poetic craft, rather than to demonstrate just how different evidently different poems are.

The latter, however, they can also certainly do. As an example, we made the comparison also made by Das between 'core Cynewulf' and *Andreas*, which has, of course, at times been held to be by him. While on the second index the difference appears no greater than that between 'core Cynewulf' and *Christ II*, the first index indicated a difference that would occur by chance only once in a hundred times; the major differences are in the entities CHH (for example, *Elene* 140a *fræm dæges orde*; *Andreas* 444a *of brimes bosme*) and 2AHH (for example *Elene* 20a *Huna leode*; *Andreas* 3a *þeodes þegnas*), both of which are markedly commoner as double-alliterated a-lines in *Andreas* than in the genuine Cynewulf works.

We then compared *Beowulf* with two poems which have been held in different ways to imitate it, *Andreas* and *Exodus*. In the first case no fewer than six entities show differences of distribution significant at the 0.01 level; in the second only three, but out of many fewer assessable ones (reflecting that *Exodus* is much shorter than *Andreas*). In each case, both indices of overall difference lie far outside the 99 per cent range which is the most our present methods give, and the odds against chance difference are clearly enormous; the proposition that the distribution of metrical-syntactic entities between the three categories is a general feature of Old English poetic craft clearly cannot be sustained. Perhaps the most striking of the differences of practice which contribute to these values is in the entity analysed by the program as 2AHV, including in *Beowulf* such not-uncommon a-lines as *sund-wudu sohte* (208) and *Beowulf nemnað* (364), but very rare as an a-line in the other poems – even rarer if one doubts that, for instance, *garas trymedon* (*Exodus* 158a) is really an instance of the same entity. The much smaller difference between *Andreas* and 'core Cynewulf' than between *Andreas* and *Beowulf* suggests that, in respect of its metrical practice at any rate, *Andreas* is much more accurately called 'Cynewulfian' than 'Beowulfian.' This is the sort of question for which the absolute values of the second index of difference should be useful; the value is higher for *Andreas*/*Beowulf* than for *Andreas*/Cynewulf, but, as we are not yet clear what significance attaches to what particular figures, there would be no point in quoting them.

## 7 Conclusion

The provisional findings above are merely an indication of some of the types of conclusion that our methods should be capable of drawing (and of substantiating on clear and objective criteria), but we think they suffice to demonstrate that we have a research tool of considerable potential power, even in its present unfinished form. When we have improved its currently still clumsy and imperfect action, we shall hope to learn more of what can be done with it. One important possibility, on which we are working, is to improve the categorization of rhythmic types. In the reported findings, this follows the classical Sievers types, the very existence of which as significant entities has been challenged.[21] If there were in fact no correspondence between them and the rhythmic groupings actually significant in poetic usage no such findings could have been arrived at, but that does not mean that some other categorization would not give a better correspondence. Our programs would need only minor modification to work in terms of any categorization, and it is relatively easy to test any proposed categorization for internal consistency within its categories and significant difference among them; the difficulty lies in arriving at the best proposal. To examine all possible combinations of rhythmic (and, in fact, syntactic) features to determine what categorization would give the best correspondence is impossible by traditional methods, but computer capabilities change that, allowing at any rate a much wider range of combinations to be scanned. We shall hope to present findings based on such a scan at a later date.

Meanwhile, we end this preliminary report with a curiosity. We checked *Andreas* for consistency, as with other poems, by comparing its first and second halves. On the first index they differed no more than might have been expected. The second index showed a difference significant at the 0.01 level, apparently then created by a whole accumulation of entity differences none individually reaching even the 0.1 level of significance. We do not at present know what to make of this. For possible light on it we once more look hopefully to future improvements in the delicacy and precision of our methods.

Departments of Computing Science and English
University of Aberdeen

## NOTES

1  O.D. Macrae-Gibson, 'The Metrical Entities of Old English,' *Neuphilologische Mitteilungen* 87 (1986): 59–91.

2  A.J. Bliss, *The Metre of 'Beowulf,'* rev. ed. (1958; Oxford: Blackwell 1967).

3  S.K. Das, *Cynewulf and the Cynewulf Canon* (Calcutta: Calcutta University Press 1947).

4  Thus Wolfgang Obst, *Der Rhythmus des Beowulf* (Heidelberg: Carl Winter 1987), 26: 'Doch [i.e., despite widespread belief in it] ist weder die Grundannahme der Zweihebigkeit plausibel, noch sind die daraus gezogene Schlusse logisch zwingend.'

5  R.K. Lindsay, 'Machines which Understand Natural Language,' in E.A. Feigenbaum and J. Feldman, eds, *Computers and Thought* (New York: McGraw-Hill 1963).

6  Terry Winograd, *Understanding Natural Language* (New York: Academic Press 1972).

7  R. Weischedel, et al., 'Natural Language Processing,' in J.F. Traub, B.J. Grosz, B.W. Lampson, N.J. Nilsson, eds, *Annual Review of Computer Science 1989–90* (Palo Alto, Calif.: Annual Reviews Inc. 1990).

8  For those interested in the field of natural-language computing, P.H. Winston, in *Artificial Intelligence*, 3rd ed. (1977; Reading, Mass.: Addison-Wesley 1992), gives an elementary introduction to the technology, though his comments on the future of language understanding are more pessimistic in the latest than in the first edition; see particularly 597. G. Gazdar and C.S. Mellish, in *Natural Language Processing in Pop11* (Wokingham: Addison-Wesley 1989), show how to program parsers to cope with some of the richness of real language ('Pop11' is a particular programming language, but the

book has general application). H. Alshawi, in H. Alshawi, ed., *The Core Language Engine* (Cambridge, Mass.: Bradford Books, The MIT Press 1992), explains a project to build a useful translator program, although he reports few results.

9 J.B. Bessinger, Jr, ed., *A Concordance to the Anglo-Saxon Poetic Records*, programmed by Philip H. Smith, Jr (Ithaca, N.Y.: Cornell University Press 1978).

10 John F. Madden and Francis Magoun, Jr, *A Grouped-Frequency Word-List of Anglo-Saxon Poetry* (Cambridge, Mass.: Harvard University Press 1966).

11 J.B. Bessinger, Jr, *A Short Dictionary of Anglo-Saxon Poetry* (Toronto: University of Toronto Press 1960).

12 A. Campbell, *Old English Grammar* (Oxford: Clarendon Press 1959), § 461.

13 We have to admit that the other instances of *ædre* in *Beowulf*, in lines 77 and 354, cannot be disambiguated so simply.

14 Representing one noun as a genitive qualifier of the other.

15 His 1D*1, which always has two such syllables.

16 Type 2A2; also 2A1a, though here 2A1a(ii) does not occur.

17 Such distinctions are discussed on p. 71 of Macrae-Gibson 'Metrical Entities of Old English,' and we have constructed a program that will test for them in any particular case of doubt.

18 See, for example, Sidney Siegel, *Nonparametric Statistics for the Behavioral Sciences* (New York: McGraw-Hill 1956), 104–11.

19 To do this exactly as described would be very wasteful of processing, since each line would be identically analysed (though in a new position) each time. We randomize after analysis; the effect is the same.

20 As a further category, we have in fact also allowed for a-lines such as *Beowulf* 115 *Gewat ða neosian (syþðan niht becom)*, which may be seen as having two lifts, with alliteration on the second only, or as having only one; the space thus becomes three-coordinate. As there are few half-lines that fall into this category compared with those in the other three, the results on this basis do not diverge significantly from what is described here.

21 Geoffrey Russom, *Old English Meter and Linguistic Theory* (Cambridge: Cambridge University Press 1987), 20.

# The Case against
# a 'General Old English
# Poetic Dialect'

DAVID MEGGINSON

*Prosody*, and *Orthography*, are not parts of *Grammar*, but diffus'd, like the blood, and spirits through the whole.[1]

When Ben Jonson explicitly excludes prosody and orthography from his *English Grammar*, he admits the difficulty of describing these with the same accuracy and detail which he can apply to his (early Modern English) syntax and morphology. Old English prosody, too, often defies attempts at description: after more than a century of extensive study the details of Old English metre, for example, are still controversial, as demonstrated by the fact that scholars such as Constance B. Hieatt have devoted much of their critical energy to them, and by the very existence of this collection.

Curiously, there has been a movement over the past forty years to classify Jonson's other exclusion – orthography – as an element of Old English prosody. It is generally accepted that the spellings in Old English poetry are dialectally mixed: as Friedrich Klaeber asked in the introduction to his edition of *Beowulf*, 'how can this mixture of forms, early and late, West Saxon, Northumbrian, Mercian, Kentish, Saxon patois be accounted for?'[2] Since the 1950s, an increasing number of scholars have argued that there is no mixture of forms at all; rather, Old English poetry had its own dialect, independent of West Saxon, Northumbrian, Mercian, or Kentish (though able to draw on any of them) – in other words, that, just as the poems in Old English manuscripts show a metre and syntax distinct from those of prose, they also show a distinct orthography.

A theory like this – whose origins and proponents will be discussed shortly – immediately begs the question of the relationship between spelling and sound. The use of the term 'dialect' strongly implies that Old English poetry had a distinct *pronunciation*, not a distinct *orthography*; however, since the native speakers have been dead for a millennium, the orthography is all that survives. The relationship of spelling to sound is one which many scholars omit or gloss over: the rules which declare that the spelling <ælde> in a tenth-century manuscript, for example, is Anglian, while the spelling <ylde> is Southern[3] are based on shifts in pronunciation believed to have taken place in different dialect areas of England before the seventh century; the only self-evident difference between these two spellings, however, is that the former begins with the letter <æ> while the latter begins with the letter <y>; whether this difference in writing reflects the scribes' spoken dialects – rather than the scribes' educational backgrounds – is open to debate.

This point is no simple quibble: it has never been firmly established that an Anglo-Saxon scribe was expected to spell a word precisely as it was pronounced, or that a reader was expected to pronounce a word precisely as it was spelled; on the contrary, Alistair Campbell argues that by the eleventh century – when several important poetic codices, including the Junius Manuscript, the Nowell Codex, and the Paris Psalter, were copied – Old English orthography could be far removed from phonological developments: 'The eleventh century was a period of great change in the accented vowels, but these changes did not generally receive expression in the by then fairly stable Old English spelling' (*Old English Grammar*, § 329). This sort of standardization is not confined to the eleventh century. In his discussion of the tenth-century Kentish Gloss, as often elsewhere, Campbell makes extensive use of 'inverted spellings' to establish Kentish pronunciation (*Old English Grammar*, § 288 and *passim*), implying that the scribe was attempting (though occasionally failing) to follow a written standard different from his or her own pronunciation,[4] and elsewhere I suggest that the pronouns *he*, *heo*, and *hie* may have been falling together in some areas as early as the tenth century, despite the fact that scribes continued to distinguish them carefully in their writing.[5]

Another important demonstration of the gulf between spoken and written Old English appears in the writing of second- and third-person verb endings. It is often possible to tell whether the endings were syncopated or unsyncopated by examining the metre, as in the case of *Eftwyrd cymð*,[6] where the half-line is metrically deficient unless <cymð> is read as <cymeð>. Since our surviving manuscripts do not always contain the ending required by the metre, we must accept either that the Anglo-Saxon readers used the correct form instinctively when reading aloud (much as the reader of an early Modern English poem would with *-ed*), that our knowledge of Old English metre is seriously deficient, or that Anglo-Saxon scribes had no ear for poetry.

The result of all of this is that when a scribe writes an apparently non–West Saxon form like <aldor>,[7] <gefegon>,[8] or <weriges>,[9] it is by no means self-evident that that form was meant to be read aloud the way that it was written; it might just as easily have been intended to *look* different as it was to *sound* different. By extension, if there was a special orthography for Old English poetry, it might have been intended as a guide to pronunciation, or it might have been intended to enhance the appearance of the poem in the manuscript. This study will return to this question below; first, however, it is necessary to examine the origins and development of the theory of an Old English poetic dialect.

## 1 'A General Old English Poetic Dialect'

In 1953, the Clarendon Press published Kenneth Sisam's *Studies in the History of Old English Literature*. Among the many influential articles in this collection was one entitled 'Dialect Origins of the Earlier Old English Verse,' which concludes with the suggestion that there was: 'a general Old English poetic dialect, artificial, archaic, and perhaps mixed in its vocabulary, conservative in inflexions which affect the verse structure, and indifferent to non-structural irregularities, which were perhaps tolerated as part of the colouring of the language of verse.'[10] He arrives at this conclusion after considering the problems which editors face while attempting to discover the dialectal origins of poems, and the reasons why those problems are 'often reduced to the crude alternatives: Anglian or West Saxon?' ('Dialect Origins,' 121). Sisam goes on to attack the limitations of that choice, and after discussing several particular cases, offers his 'general Old English poetic dialect' as a third alternative.

Many editions of individual Old English poems have appeared since the 1953 publication of Sisam's *Studies*. The editions in the series from Methuen (now Exeter) and the University of Manchester, for example, and most individual editions from other publishers follow roughly the same format, including an introduction, edited text with apparatus, notes, and a glossary. The introductions themselves nearly always discuss the poem's manuscript context(s); sources, analogues, and historical context (where relevant); dialect; and date. This relatively fixed format, with its compulsory discussion of the poem's language, was fertile ground for Sisam's 'poetic dialect' theory. After classifying the spellings in their texts, editors were usually confronted with a mixture of forms from several different regional dialects, and Sisam's theory provided a simple and attractive alternative to the 'Anglian or West Saxon' choice. In the introduction to his 1978 edition of *Genesis*, A.N. Doane describes the effect which Sisam's theory had on his and the preceding generation of editors:

The confident standards which once placed the poem in a Northumbrian home in the late seventh or early eighth centuries have been hopelessly eroded. The loss of confidence in linguistic evidence in just the last quarter-century is shown by a comparison of the  linguistic apparatuses of Timmer's edition of *Genesis B* (1948) and Irving's of *Exodus* (1953), with that of Farrell's *Daniel* (1974); the latter offers only a few notes on the most out-standing forms 'made as a tentative guide to the reader,' while the earlier editions, though cautious about the earlier linguistic criteria, are able to come to rather elaborate and confident conclusions about the composition and homes of their poems. The circumstance which separates Timmer and Irving from Farrell is Kenneth Sisam's landmark study, 'Dialect Origins of the Earlier Old English Verse.'[11]

Doane himself provides a detailed list of spellings in *Genesis A*, grouping them into traditional dialectal classifications, but warns beforehand that 'all that can be done is the listing of the outstanding non-standard forms, with comment,' and concludes that 'the great mixture of forms, within a West-Saxon matrix, is merely the language of verse, and does not help to date or place the poem.'[12]

Donald Scragg is not nearly so restrained in his edition of *The Battle of Maldon*, where he mentions the poetic-dialect theory only to explain spellings for certain common poetic words: 'A few words display non-West Saxon spellings common in earlier poetry ... Because these are spellings particularly associated with poetry (in some cases, of words found only in poetry), they cannot be used as evidence of dialect origin or transmission history, though they do suggest an awareness of literary tradition in either author or scribe.'[13] Generally, however, the poetic-dialect theory has a more profound effect on the way in which editors approach the written forms in a poem. Peter Lucas, in his 1977 edition of *Exodus*, provides a detailed list of spellings from the poem and their traditional dialectal classification, but then concludes only that: 'It is exceedingly difficult to draw any firm conclusions from this linguistic information. One of the chief difficulties arises from the possibility that there was a general OE poetic *koiné* of a mixed dialect character and that poems were written or transmitted in this "literary dialect".'[14] Around the same time, R.E. Finnegan begins his discussion of spellings in *Christ and Satan* with the statement 'Kenneth Sisam answers a resounding "no" to the question "Do linguistic tests now available enable us to determine the dialect in which any longer piece of Old English poetry was composed"';[15] Arne Zettersten writes that 'there is some evidence indicating that there existed a "general Old English poetic dialect"'[16] before beginning a brief analysis of the poem's written forms; and Jane Roberts follows her analysis of orthography (including morphology) and vocabulary by writing that 'some forms can be described as Anglian, a few as Kentish, but, although it was once customary to regard such forms as proof of Anglian origins, the recognition of a poetic *koinê* entails that taken by themselves they are inconclusive.'[17]

Slightly earlier, in his 1974 edition of *Daniel and Azarias*, R.T. Farrell follows the same pattern, beginning the analysis of the spellings in *Daniel* with the warning that:

> Before entering on a discussion of the features of the language of *Daniel* it is necessary to outline some prevailing views on the language of OE poetry as a whole. Until recently, it was the common view that most early OE poetry was of Anglian origin, and remarks on the language often centred on ferreting out forms to support the view that an Anglian substratum existed. Dr Sisam has made a strong case against this approach in his study of the 'Dialect Origins of the Old English Verse' [*sic*].

He concludes, after five pages of analysis, that 'if Dr Sisam's postulation of a poetic dialect is accepted, little more than the identification and discussion of forms which seem out of place in standard OE seems possible.'[18]

Editors in the 1970s were clearly reluctant to use the orthography of their poems as evidence for dating or localizing texts, given the popularity of Sisam's poetic-dialect theory, but in this they were only following their predecessors of the 1960s. In his 1966 edition of *The Wanderer*, R.F. Leslie cites Sisam's study as justification for his own caution in using spelling for dating or localizing texts,[19] and in his 1964 edition of *The Phoenix*, N.F. Blake likewise paraphrases the poetic-dialect theory in a discussion of orthography: 'It is quite possible that there was in existence in Old English times a poetic language which was not closely related to any of the major dialects, but which contained elements otherwise characteristic of these dialects. The original poem might have been composed in this poetic language and thus it would be impossible to determine in what geographical area the poem was written.'[20]

In the second edition of his *Three Old English Elegies* (1966), R.F. Leslie also invokes the idea of a poetic dialect, writing that: 'Here and there occur linguistic forms foreign to this dialect; these are generally presumed to have survived from an earlier stage of their transmission, perhaps from the dialects of the poets. The confident assumption that much of the earlier poetry, including these poems, is of non-West-Saxon origin has been seriously undermined.'[21] He immediately quotes from Sisam's 'Dialect Origins' study, then begins a classification of the written forms in his poems. Leslie, however, does not seem to feel in any way restrained by Sisam's theory: despite his earlier statement, he goes on to claim on the basis of their spelling that the poems were originally Anglian (*Elegies*, 31–3).

On the other hand, Kenneth Brooks, in his 1961 edition of *Andreas and the Fates of the Apostles*, is somewhat more restrained, and concludes his classification of the written forms in those poems by writing that: 'It has been customary until recent years to assume that such a dialect mixture affords evidence of an Anglian original which later passed through a late West Saxon recension ... There seems to have been a general Old English poetic *koinē* of a mixed dialect character, to which an originally dialectally pure poem would become assimilated in transmission, and in which new poems would be written from the first.'[22]

Finally, in the same way, immediately after quoting from Sisam's study, I.L. Gordon qualifies her select use of orthography as evidence for the localization of a text by writing: 'Nor can the other Anglian forms in *The Seafarer* be regarded as evidence of an Anglian original, since the evidence of Old English poetry preserved in MSS of the late tenth or early eleventh centuries shows that there was a standard "classical" or literary language of poetry, which was predominantly West Saxon with a strong Anglian element.'[23]

Almost without critical scrutiny, the idea that Old English orthography can be grouped into a fifth poetic dialect, in addition to the four main regional Old English dialects, has become an important part of our understanding of Old English poetry and Anglo-Saxon culture. Although none of the editors quoted above makes an explicit case for orthography as an element of prosody, all strongly imply that either the spelling or the pronunciation it is supposed to represent is, somehow, an intrinsic part of Old English verse. This theory could have important implications: if the orthography were meant for visual appeal, then the manuscripts were clearly meant for private reading rather than public performance; if, on the other hand, the orthography were to function as a guide to pronunciation, then scholars might have recovered an important part of the lost art of the performance of Old English verse. In a recent study, Roberta Frank, after discussing shifts in the meanings of words in verse, writes: 'The late West-Saxon scribes who used two different spelling conventions for certain words in their copy-texts, one for poetry and another for prose, may have been signalling something similar. It is as if every Anglo-Saxon author were bilingual, "utriusque linguae peritus," competent in the separate dictions of poetry and prose.'[24]

Frank is not referring to Sisam's poetic dialect, but rather to two later studies concerned specifically with orthography, whose contents will be discussed below. The bilingualism which Frank proposes, however, seems to be exactly what many editors presume: that Old English scribes, for whatever reason, used one set of spelling conventions for prose and another for verse.

The problem is that both Frank and the editors who quote Sisam have a faith in the abilities of Old English scribes which Sisam apparently does not share. As a matter of fact, Sisam's poetic-dialect theory explicitly excludes orthography (and other scribal contributions) from the beginning:

> It is desirable then to confine attention to words and forms that are confirmed by the metre. The doubt will remain whether a poem preserved in one late manuscript has been interpolated or partly recomposed in a dialect different from the original; or whether the original itself contained things imitated from other dialects. But an inquiry that begins by accepting as original what is structural in the verse will not be overburdened with evidence. ("Dialect Origins," 123)

Sisam is interested only in what can be traced back to the author of a poem, and orthography is too easily subject to change in the copying process. On the same page, he argues that 'oral transmission at any point in the chain would eliminate non-structural [that is, orthographic] forms of the original, unless the reciter spoke the local dialect in which it was composed.' He does come back and suggest that 'non-structural irregularities' might 'perhaps' play a part in a poetic dialect (ibid., 138), but, presumably, only if the scribes have preserved them from the original author. In fact, after eliminating orthography and other 'non-structural forms' from consideration, Sisam actually examines only three types of evidence:

1 Verb endings of the second and third person present indicative, which can be shown to have been syncopated or unsyncopated by the metre (ibid., 126–32), a test originally proposed by Eduard Sievers.
2 Dialectal vocabulary.[25]
3 The cultural history of the different dialect areas, and the conditions in each that favoured the production of poetry (ibid., 132–8).

Even if, as seems likely, Sisam meant to include some aspects of orthography in the 'non-structural irregularities,' he presents no proof that archaic or dialectal spellings could be part of a general poetic dialect; rather, he examines an entirely different sort of evidence – the same kind that Ashley Amos classifies as evidence 'discernible through the medium of any scribal distortion.'[26] A few editors do use the poetic dialect theory as Sisam actually presented it – Rosemary Woolf, for example, in her second edition of *Juliana* (1966), attributes only 'the unsyncopated forms of the 2nd and 3rd per. sg. of the present tense of verbs' to Sisam[27] – but most of the editors examined for this paper (including all of those quoted earlier) presume that the poetic dialect theory applies to phonology or orthography rather than to vocabulary or morphology.[28]

Sisam's study shows little faith in the dialectal value of Old English orthography, and it provides, at best, little justification for the way most editors have used it. Why, then, has citing this study in discussions of orthography become such a common practice among editors? Certainly, editors tend to model their editions on those which have come before, so once a practice establishes itself, it is difficult to eliminate; furthermore, Sisam himself may have contributed slightly to the confusion by mentioning the linguistic form of *mece*, 'sword' in his section on dialectal vocabulary ('Dialect Origins,' 126–7). Finally, however, the explanation is more likely to be found in the writings of his contemporaries, Alistair Campbell and C.L. Wrenn, and of his predecessor, Otto Jespersen. Campbell's *Old English Grammar* has been the standard English-language reference work on Old English for several generations of scholars, and in it, he explicitly mentions this study: 'This verse is mostly preserved in copies dating from *c.* 1000, and while these are predominantly West-Saxon, they are extremely rich in dialectal forms of various kinds ... There seems to have been, in fact, a "general OE poetic dialect," mixed in vocabulary, phonology, and inflexion.'[29] While Sisam does discuss vocabulary and inflection, he is, at best, ambivalent, and at worst, suspicious, concerning the value of orthography, although orthography is precisely what Campbell is discussing in this section. However, Campbell's citation of Sisam, appearing near the beginning of a standard reference work, could not have failed to influence editors. There is even more evidence for the influence of Wrenn and Jespersen. Some of the editors who cite this study, including Brooks and Finnegan, refer to an Old English poetic *koiné*. The term is not Sisam's or Campbell's, but it does appear in Quirk and Wrenn's *An Old English Grammar* and in Wrenn's edition of *Beowulf*,[30] while Jespersen uses it even earlier in his book *Growth and Structure of the English Language*.[31] In their grammar, Quirk and Wrenn write that: 'in the later OE period it was Wessex that provided the dialect which became the cultural language of the whole of England, though somewhat influenced and modified by neighbouring dialects. It was in this literary or classical *koiné*, basically WS, that nearly all the earlier poetry was copied, and so preserved, at the time of the Benedictine Renaissance at the close of the tenth century and early in the eleventh' (*Old English Grammar*, 5). Wrenn adds a reference to Sisam's 'Dialect Origins' paper in later editions, but clearly the *koiné* is meant to account for apparently dialectal spellings in both poetry and prose[32] and thus cannot distinguish a specifically *poetic* dialect. The reference to Sisam in the later editions postdates the original discussion of the *koiné*.

The context in which these two grammars cite Sisam's study may have helped to create the impression that Sisam not only suggested but established that there was a special poetic orthography in Old English. Obviously, this is not what Sisam wrote, but it *is* what Jespersen suggested much earlier, in his own reaction against the then-dominant approach of the neo-grammarians:

> The language of poetry seems to have been to a certain extent identical all over England, a kind of more or less artificial dialect, absorbing forms and words from the different parts of the country where poetry was composed at all, in much the same way as Homer's language had originated in Greece. This hypothesis seems to me to offer a better explanation of the facts than the current theory, according to which the bulk of Old English poetry was written at first in Northumbrian dialect and later translated into West-Saxon with some of the old Anglian forms kept inadvertently – and translated to such an extent that no trace of the originals should have been preserved. (*Growth and Structure*, § 53)

In the same section, Jespersen suggests the idea of a 'poetical *koinê*' involving both 'forms and words,' but he does not present any evidence, and modestly suggests that 'the whole question should be taken up by a more competent hand than mine.' Sisam does take up the matter, but excludes orthography from his investigation.

It is clear that Sisam's 'general Old English poetic dialect' has been transmitted in at least two variants: the original, authorial version, which is somewhat limited in scope, focuses on the author, and excludes orthography; and the popular version, which is broadly based, focuses on the scribe, and emphasizes orthography. Sisam did not write the second variant, but his work inspired it to the point that it took his name; furthermore, since the second variant is so popular among editors of Old English poems, it obviously fills an important need. Editors cannot ignore orthography any more than they can ignore prosody – these are the 'blood and spirits' which circulate throughout the text – but any examination requires a good model to follow. The older, neo-grammatical model, which both Sisam and Jespersen criticize, has not proven especially successful for describing the spellings found in Old English poetic manuscripts; as a result, the popular version of the 'poetic dialect' deserves a serious examination. Is there a 'general Old English poetic dialect' that includes orthography? Or, more specifically, was orthography, as Frank suggests in passing, an element of Old English prosody?

## 2 'Poetic Potential'

As mentioned above, Roberta Frank's suggestion that Old English scribes were 'utriusque linguae peritus' – experienced in writing prose and verse as two different languages – was based not on Sisam's argument but on two later studies: E.G. Stanley's paper 'Spellings of the *Waldend* Group,'[33] and Angelika Lutz's 'Spellings of the *Waldend* Group – Again.'[34] Stanley demonstrates that certain words, like *waldend*, 'ruler, lord,' are more likely to appear in Anglian forms than others; Lutz analyses Stanley's evidence, and uses it to develop an alternative to Sisam's poetic dialect theory: 'the *a*-spelling in poetic texts should not be regarded as what Sisam called a "non-structural irregularity" that was "tolerated" by late Old English scribes, but as a characteristic feature of Old English poetry that they preserved deliberately, in the case of copies, and even applied intentionally, in the case of late West Saxon compositions' ('Spellings,' 55). Lutz is arguing that scribes wrote the Anglian forms deliberately when copying poetry, bringing her argument close to the popular version of Sisam's theory examined in the previous section. As evidence, she cites forms from the later poems in certain copies of the *Anglo-Saxon Chronicle*: these poems contain the Anglian form <waldend>, even though the surrounding prose contains the Southern (that is, West Saxon) form for *geweald*, 'power,' which is etymologically related (ibid., 56). Since the same scribe writes the Anglian form in the verse but the Southern, West Saxon form in the prose, Lutz concludes that the Anglian form <waldend> must be distinctly poetic.

Lutz breaks from both the original and popular versions of Sisam's poetic-dialect theory, however, when she presents her explanation for this distribution. According to Lutz, certain Old English words have 'poetic potential,' and those words alone are subject to special treatment in verse:

> *Waldend* would derive this poetic potential from its being an agent noun which, as such, was associated with the numerous poetic words for 'man', 'warrior', 'ruler' and the like. By contrast, *geweald*, being an abstract noun, would not have this specific poetic potential and would thus be spelled in the ordinary way, as would the verb. Spelling conventions of the kind observed in *w(e)aldend* should not be looked upon as 'non-structural irregularities' in the way Sisam meant, but should be considered a structural element of the written tradition and production of poetry in Standard Late West Saxon. (ibid., 62–3)

The poetic-potential theory shifts the emphasis from the poetic genre to the words themselves – orthography as a whole is not an element of prosody, since most words lack poetic potential, but certain words can change their written form under the influence of verse. This hypothesis would explain words like *mece*, 'sword,' *beadu-*, 'battle,' and *heaðu-*, 'battle,' all of which are especially common in poetry, and all of which appear exclusively or nearly exclusively in non–West Saxon forms.[35] A less obvious example is the common word *yldu*, 'age,' and the poetic word *ylde*, 'men,' both of which come from the same root and should ordinarily show the same root vowel.[36] The Exeter Book scribe, however, nearly always writes *yldu* – the prose word – in the expected West Saxon <y> form, but *always* writes *ylde* – the poetic word – in the Anglian <æ> form. Likewise, the first Junius scribe usually writes both *ealdor*, 'leader,' and *ealdor*, 'life,' in the Anglian form <aldor>. *ylde* and the two *ealdor*'s are all concrete and are all especially typical of verse,[37] and as a result they possess Lutz's 'poetic potential' and can be expected to appear frequently in non–West Saxon forms.

Unfortunately, there are serious problems with Lutz's theory. The greatest weakness lies in her evidence, as she admits: 'this hypothesis cannot be confirmed on the basis of the *Chronicle* material, since the *Chronicle* contains the agent noun *waldend* only in poetry and the abstract noun *geweald* only in prose' (ibid., 57). According to Stanley's data, which Lutz cites (ibid., 34), both the first part of the Junius Manuscript and all of the Exeter Book have <-a-> for *waldend* and <-ea-> for *geweald* consistently in their poems; as a result, the fact that *geweald* appears in the *Chronicle* prose is irrelevant, since this would also be the expected form in verse.

Secondly, not every scribe copying Old English poetry uses Anglian forms for the words that supposedly have poetic potential. According to Lutz's own data, most of the scribes copying poetry write Anglian <waldend> and Southern <wealdend> side by side, and some, like the scribe of the Paris Psalter, nearly always write the Southern (that is, non-poetic) form (ibid., 58–9). Lutz also attempts to argue from a broad statistical base that the Anglian forms are more common in verse, but 88 per cent (44 out of 51) of her prose examples come from copies of works written by a single author, Ælfric (ibid., 59), and many of the surviving copies of these works were produced a century or more after the Exeter Book and the Vercelli Book collections.[38] Other words with poetic potential fare even worse. While the first Junius Manuscript scribe, for example, writes mainly the Anglian (poetic) form <aldor> for *ealdor*, the same scribe writes *only* the West Saxon (prosaic) form <ylde> for *ylde*; exactly the opposite situation applies in the Exeter Book, where the scribe writes only the West Saxon (prose) form <ealdor> but the Anglian (poetic) form <ælde> for *ylde*. These two scribes agree only in that they give special treatment to some words with poetic potential; they do not agree, however, on the specific words that receive this treatment.

Lutz's argument does not work in reverse either. Presumably, if words with poetic potential tend to appear in Anglian forms, then words without poetic potential do not; however, individual scribes often give special treatment to other words. For example, the Exeter Book scribe nearly always writes *sawon* '(we, you, they) saw,' in the Anglian (poetic?) form <segon>, rather than the

West Saxon form <sawon>. It would be very difficult to argue that a common verb like *sawon* has any unusual 'poetic potential.'

The scribes who copied Old English verse may have allowed more Anglianisms on a broad level into their work, but they do not agree in their spelling of individual words. Furthermore, there is evidence that they sometimes even came into conflict with each other over questions of orthography. R.E. Finnegan notes that in the Junius Manuscript poem *Christ and Satan* a later scribe altered many of the original scribe's Anglian (poetic?) forms, including <waldend>, to West Saxon (prosaic?) forms:

> The Corrector's activity provides the stuff of a footnote to Sisam's hypothesis. Even if one grant the sometimes whimsical character of Old English scribal practice, it remains that the Corrector has a definite attitude toward the manuscript text, and that attitude is to change its dialect. Why? Is he a hack who does not recognize the poetic koine when he sees it? He may not have been a poet, but he was certainly literate and something of a linguist in the bargain, and he did exercise some care in working through a large collection of poetry. Was he preparing the manuscript for an exclusively West Saxon audience? But would they themselves not have recognized the poetic koine, and if so, why change it? (*Christ and Satan*, 59–60)

It is no wonder that modern scholars cannot agree about what constitutes a poetic dialect or poetic potential, when the Anglo-Saxon scribes themselves seem to have had no fixed idea.

### Conclusions

Jonson connected early Modern English prosody and orthography only by stating that both were beyond the scope of his *English Grammar*, and by comparing both to the vital fluids of life – both prosody, which affects the way a text is heard, and orthography, which affects the way it is seen, are fundamental to all other literary studies. As of yet, however, Old English prosody and orthography are still only half understood, and there has been a strong and recurring idea over the past century, from Jespersen on, that it might be possible to connect the two – to demonstrate that some of the peculiarities of orthography can be explained by the demands of the poetic genre. To prove the existence of a poetic, orthographic dialect, it would be necessary to discover a set of specific spellings common to verse but not to prose, and in this area, even the most promising words like Stanley's and Lutz's *waldend* eventually fail. The problem is that, while Old English poetry as a whole seems to deviate somewhat from the orthographic standards of late–West Saxon prose, the poems and scribes individually deviate far more from each other, leaving the idea of a common poetic orthography (or orthographic prosody) with little support.

The popular version of Sisam's poetic-dialect theory has become such an integral part of the critical idiom for Old English studies that, by 1990, Douglas Moffat could refer to it in the introduction to a critical edition without even citing Sisam's study (*Soul and Body*, 16). Alone, the fact that this popular version is a misinterpretation of Sisam's original study would not be enough to justify its abandonment – apparently, many editors have believed that it provides the best available model for discussing the orthography of their poems. But – a closer examination of the evidence suggests that, as far as orthography is concerned, there was no 'general Old English poetic dialect.'

University of Ottawa

## NOTES

1 Ben Jonson, *The English Grammar*, repr (1640; Mertson, England: The Scholar Press 1972), ch. 1(g).

2 Friedrich Klaeber, ed., *Beowulf and the Fight at Finnsburg* (Lexington, Mass.: D.C. Heath 1936), lxxxviii; see also Alistair Campbell, *Old English Grammar* (Oxford: Clarendon Press 1959), § 18.

3 Campbell, *Old English Grammar*, §§ 143, 193, 200.

4 Earlier in the grammar, however, Campbell seems to take the opposite view: 'there is a great diversity of spelling in Old English, arising not from inconsistency in the values of symbols, but from the diversity of sound' (ibid., § 48).

5 David Megginson, 'He (pl) and Other New Old English Pronouns,' *ANQ* NS 7 (1993): 6–13.

6 *Exodus* 540b. Citations of Old English verse are taken from G.P. Krapp and E.K. Dobbie, eds, *Anglo-Saxon Poetic Records* (New York: Columbia University Press 1932–42).

7 R.T. Farrell, ed., *Daniel and Azarias* (London: Methuen 1974), 14.

8 Peter J. Lucas, ed., *Exodus* (London: Methuen 1977), 37.

9 Kenneth R. Brooks, ed., *Andreas and the Fates of the Apostles* (Oxford: Clarendon Press 1961), xxxv.

10 Kenneth Sisam, 'Dialect Origins of the Earlier Old English Verse,' in his *Studies in the History of Old English Literature* (Oxford: Clarendon Press 1953), 138.

11 A.N. Doane, ed., *Genesis A: A New Edition* (Madison: University of Wisconsin Press 1978), 25.

12 Ibid., 27–34, 26, 34. Doane does, however, use spellings in an attempt to trace the poem's textual history (34–6).

13 Donald Scragg, ed., *The Battle of Maldon* (Manchester: Manchester University Press 1981), 23; Scragg cites Sisam's study in a note.

14 Lucas, *Exodus*, 36–9; Lucas's note: 'This view was cogently proposed by Sisam in his paper "Dialect Origins of the Earlier Old English Verse", *Studies* (1953), 119–39.'

15 Robert Emmett Finnegan, ed., *Christ and Satan* (Waterloo: Wilfrid Laurier University Press 1977), 56.

16 Arne Zettersten, ed., *Waldere* (Manchester: Manchester University Press 1979), 11.

17 Jane Roberts, ed., *The Guthlac Poems of the Exeter Book* (Oxford: Clarendon Press 1979), 71.

18 Farrell, ed., *Daniel* 11, 13–18.

19 R.F. Leslie, ed., *The Wanderer* (Manchester: Manchester University Press 1966), 45–7.

20 N.F. Blake, ed., *The Phoenix* (Manchester: Manchester University Press 1964), 4.

21 R.F. Leslie, ed., *Three Old English Elegies* (Manchester: Manchester University Press 1961), 31.

22 Brooks, ed., *Andreas*, xxxviii–xxxix.

23 I.L. Gordon, ed., *The Seafarer* (London: Methuen 1960), 32.

24 Roberta Frank, '"Mere" and "Sund": Two Sea-Changes in *Beowulf*,' in Phyllis Rugg Brown, Georgia Ronan Crampton, and Fred C. Robinson, eds, *Modes of Interpretation in Old English Literature: Essays in Honour of Stanley B. Greenfield* (Toronto: University of Toronto Press 1986), 156. The article is primarily concerned with semantics, and mentions orthography only in passing.

25 Sisam, 'Dialect Origins,' 126–32. Sisam relies on Richard Jordan, *Eigentümlichkeiten des anglischen Wortschatzes: Eine wortgeographische Untersuchung mit etymologischen Anmerkungen* (Heidelberg 1906). For more recent work on poetic vocabulary, see (for example) the brief discussion in H. Schabram, *Superbia. Studien zum altenglischen Wortschatz. Teil I: Die dialektale und zeitliche Verbreitung des Wortguts* (Munich: W. Fink 1965), 129, and Franz Wenisch, *Spezifisch anglisches Wortgut in den nordhumbrischen Interlinearglossierungen des Lukasevangeliums* (Heidelberg: Carl Winter 1979), 328, as well as M.S. Griffith, 'Poetic Language and the Paris Psalter: The Decay of the Old English Tradition,' in *Anglo-Saxon England* 20 (1991): 167–86.

26  Ashley Amos, *Linguistic Means of Determining the Dates of Old English Literary Texts* (Cambridge, Mass.: Medieval Academy of America 1980), 15.

27  Rosemary Woolf, ed., *Juliana* (London: Methuen 1966), 4. Likewise, T.P. Dunning and A.J. Bliss, eds, *The Wanderer* (London: Methuen 1969); P.A.O. Gradon, ed., *Cynewulf's 'Elene'* (London: Methuen 1958); and B.J. Timmer, ed., *Judith*, 2nd ed. (London: Methuen 1961).

28  Of the editions examined for this paper, representing a large number of those which have appeared since 1955, only the following do not refer to the poetic-dialect theory at all: Donald K. Fry, ed., *Finnsburh: Fragment and Episode* (London: Methuen 1974); Chadwick Buford Hilton, Jr, ed., *An Edition and Study of the Old English 'Seasons for Fasting'* (PhD diss, University of Tennessee 1983); and Edward Burroughs Irving, Jr, ed., *The Old English 'Exodus'* (New Haven: Archon Books 1970). In his edition of *The Old English Riming Poem* (Cambridge: D.S. Brewer 1983), 4, Duncan Macrae-Gibson writes 'all that can properly be said as to dialect is that it is consistent with the proposition that an educated poet in a comparatively late Old English period would have available to him a language including what were historically both WS and NWS features'; and Douglas Moffat writes in his edition of *The Old English 'Soul and Body'* (Wolfeboro, N.H.: D.S. Brewer 1990), 16, after classifying dialectal forms, that 'it seems unlikely that all these can be ascribed to poetic idiom'; neither, however, cites Sisam explicitly.

29  Campbell, *Old English Grammar*, § 18. Campbell's footnote: 'The phrase is K. Sisam's (*Studies in the history of OE literature*, p. 138), and his careful remarks on the poetical language are of the first importance.'

30  I wish to thank the membership of the computer discussion group *Ansaxnet* for their help with this point during discussions in 1991.

31  Randolph Quirk and C.L. Wrenn, *An Old English Grammar* (London: Methuen 1955); C.L. Wrenn, ed., *Beowulf with the Finnesburg Fragment* (London: Harrap Ltd 1953); Otto Jespersen, *Growth and Structure of the English Language*, 10th ed. (Oxford: Basil Blackwell 1938).

32  See also C.L. Wrenn, '"Standard" Old English,' in *Transactions of the Philological Society* (London 1933), 65–88.

33  E.G. Stanley, 'Spellings of the *Waldend* Group,' in E.B. Atwood and A.A. Hill, eds, *Studies in Language, Literature and Culture of the Middle Ages and Later* (Austin: University of Texas 1969).

34  Angelika Lutz, 'Spellings of the *Waldend* Group – Again,' *Anglo-Saxon England* 13 (1984).

35  Campbell, *Old English Grammar*, §§ 128 n2, 207.

36  <ie->, <y->, or <i-> in West-Saxon; <æ> or <e-> in Anglian or Kentish: ibid., §§ 143, 193, 200.

37 *ealdor*, 'leader' does appear frequently in prose, but generally in the compound *ealdorman* and not as a simplex.
38 The Paris Psalter manuscript, which is also late, has mainly the Southern, non-poetic form, as mentioned above; the Junius Manuscript, however, which does have only the Anglian form, is roughly contemporary with Ælfric.

# The Intonational Basis of Laȝamon's Verse

DOUGLAS MOFFAT

The purpose of this paper is to pursue a suggestion made some years ago by Carolynn Van Dyke Friedlander that the verses of Laȝamon's long line might be analysable from the point of view of intonation.[1] I will argue that underlying most of Laȝamon's half-lines is a common intonation pattern that serves as the basic 'prosodic contour' of his verse.[2] This intonation pattern closely resembles that of prose from the late Old English period through to the present day but contrasts with the dominant pattern of classical Old English verse. I will try to demonstrate that this pattern allows certain features that characterize Laȝamon's verse, particularly rhyme, to coexist with alliteration. While no method of metrical analysis will emerge from this paper, the examination of intonation should provide a linguistic basis for examining Laȝamon's combination of alliteration *and* rhyme into a larger whole, which might be better called a metrical conception rather than a system.

The problems posed by discussing intonation in older forms of English are not trivial and cannot be minimized. First of all, the study of intonation of living speakers, like many of the subdisciplines of linguistics, has sparked considerable disagreement among the experts, disagreement that, in the case of English intonation, has largely followed national lines, that is, American versus British.[3] However, even if intonationists were in substantial agreement with one another, the difficulties for the current study would not be significantly lessened. Intonationists study that part of language that is not written down, which is sometimes called the suprasegmentals or paralanguage. Intonationists are primarily interested in what is conveyed by audibly perceptible linguistic features like pitch, duration, and loudness, as well as gesture. In dealing with the older forms of English, of course, one can work *only* with what is written down.

In addition to this methodological challenge, the focus on Laȝamon's *Brut* presents many difficulties in regard to evidence. Certainly there is little shortage of controversy in the study of Old English verse metre. But it is not unreasonable to suggest that most of the 'facts' of Old English verse are agreed upon by all, and that the divergence between prosodists lies in the explanation of what these 'facts' mean, or perhaps which 'facts' to emphasize. For example, locating alliteration is unproblematical for the vast majority of Old English long lines, but explanations as to why alliteration occurs in just these locations can differ widely. No such 'factual' clarity greets the analyst of Laȝamon's work. In the *Brut* it is far from uncommon to find lines where even the location of alliteration is uncertain. Should we accept alliteration on usually insignificant function words if it is lacking on more significant words, especially if there is no rhyme to link the half-lines together? If rhyme links the half-lines together, how does it relate to any alliteration that may be present? Does it outweigh alliteration on function words, for example? Does off-rhyme carry the same weight as pure rhyme? What consideration, if any, should be given to inflectional rhyme found in the *Brut*?

In spite of these obstacles, I believe that a judicious application of intonational analysis can actually bring some measure of coherence to the perplexing array of metrical evidence one finds in Laȝamon's *Brut*.

It is generally accepted by intonationists that for 'well-executed, longer utterances' there is what Dwight Bolinger calls the favoured, typical, and 'unmarked' shape.[4] The existence of this shape has been known for a long time: it corresponds to what Daniel Jones, the famous English phoneticist, called Tune 1.[5] It is most frequently known now as 'the Hat Pattern,' a name given to it by the Dutch intonationists Cohen and T'Hart.[6] Figure 1 is a simplified version of Cohen and T'Hart's representation of 'the canonical pattern of the major class' of intonational contours in Dutch, that is, the Hat Pattern (ibid., 183). Their reason for the choice of name will become apparent. Although they studied Dutch intonation, Cohen and T'Hart claim, and the claim is widely accepted, that their findings apply to most European languages. They suggest that the English utterance 'I'm surprised to hear about it' conforms to the ideal Hat Pattern, with rise in pitch on the second syllable of 'surprised' and the fall in pitch on the monosyllabic 'hear.' Of course, as a rule we are not conscious of intonation patterns when we speak.

The Hat Pattern has a five-part structure, and, in fact, a five-part structure is typical of other intonation patterns as well. It will be useful to give these parts names and discuss them a little further. The leftward pitch obtrusion (b) is most frequently called the Head of the intonation pattern; the rightward obtrusion (d) is most frequently called the Nucleus.[7] The Head and Nucleus usually coincide with the lexically stressed syllables in what Cohen and T'Hart

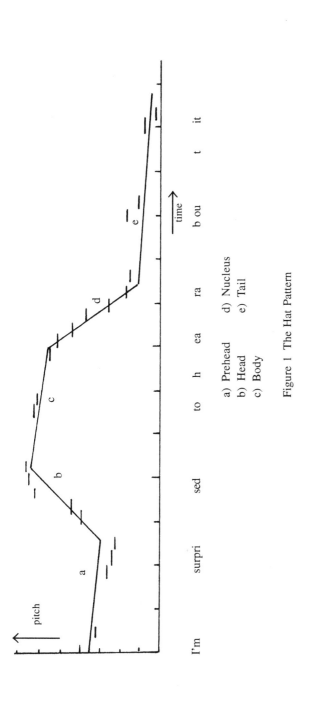

Figure 1 The Hat Pattern

a) Prehead    d) Nucleus
b) Head       e) Tail
c) Body

call the dominant words in the utterance, that is, the words the speaker chooses to emphasize. Change in pitch along with increases in loudness and duration usually combine to mark these syllables as prominent. Other dominant words can appear between them in the middle declination (c), which is sometimes called the Body. There is a strong tendency, probably present in all languages, for the Nucleus, the rightmost pitch obtrusion, to be the most prominent in any given utterance – 'last-heard-best-noted,' as Bolinger frequently says. This is an important point for my argument. Another important feature of the Nucleus and Head is their tendency to be separated from each other by less prominent syllables. That is, the linguistic phenomenon usually called clashing stress is generally avoided in intonation patterns.[8]

It remains to discuss the first and last parts of the pattern. The initial declination (a) is sometimes called Anacrusis, but I think the alternative (if ugly) term 'Prehead' is better for this discussion because it will prevent confusion with metrical anacrusis. The final declination (e) is usually called the Tail. Though less carefully studied than the other features of intonation, these two parts are crucial, along with pausing, for delimiting patterns. That is, they, along with pauses, act as boundary markers for intonation patterns. This usual role they play in intonation patterns is important to what follows in this paper. The Prehead is a common boundary marker of intonation patterns in general, not just the Hat Pattern.[9] That is, speakers tend not to leap immediately to a prominent syllable but rather to establish a gradually declining level of pitch from which to deviate in order to establish prominence in the desired place. (This can be true even when a prominent syllable is the first in an utterance.) The final syllable in the Tail also serves as a boundary marker in most languages. It achieves this status, whether it is stressed or not, by undergoing a degree of lengthening.

A crucial point must be stressed here in order to allow the linkage between the study of contemporary intonation and ancient forms of the English language. Intonationists regard the Hat Pattern not as a precise measurement of intonation but as a common standard against which they can compare the intonational nuances and deviations of living speakers. Cohen and T'Hart call it a 'descriptive device' ('Anatomy,' 187). Robert Ladd, who is clearly impatient with the Hat Pattern's imprecision, concedes that it is a useful generalization.[10] It is as a generalization that the Hat Pattern can be used in examining older forms of English, or, more precisely, it is because it is a generalization that it can be so used. Likewise, for the parts of the intonational pattern just outlined, it is only that which is most general about them that can be applied to forms of English no longer spoken. Trying to measure the nuances of Old or Middle English intonation against the Hat Pattern would be fruitless, if not ridiculous. But using it as a standard of speech intonation against which to place the rhythms of Old English verse, Ælfric's rhythmical prose, and, finally, Laȝamon's Early Middle English verse proves illuminating.

The Hat Pattern appears to underlie a good many of the 'well-executed, longer utterances' represented in the surviving documents written in prose; it was very likely the basic pattern in Old English speech, just as it is in present-day English. However, while it probably was the favoured, typical, and 'unmarked' intonation pattern for native speakers of Old English, as it is for us, it does not seem to have held that position in the verse. If we think of the five Old English verse types, the Sievers types, as representing the patterns of intonation demanded by Old English verse and look back to the Hat Pattern, important differences can be noted. In fact, there is a considerable degree of incompatibility.

| | |
|---|---|
| A | / x / x |
| B | x / x / |
| C | x / / x |
| D | / / \ x or / / x \ |
| E | / \ x / |

Figure 2 The Sievers Types

The fundamental difference is that each of the verse types is composed of four parts, while the Hat Pattern, as has just been pointed out, has five parts. This disjunction has been remarked upon in somewhat different terms in the past, especially by Thomas Cable in his *Meter and Melody of 'Beowulf'* where he claims that the *Beowulf* poet's avoidance of the 'five-position pattern' is fundamental to the poet's craft and should be so recognized even before the Sievers types are described.[11]

Because the verse types are four-part structures, they cannot be easily described by the Hat Pattern. In three of the verse types – A, D, and E – the poets were constrained to avoid a Prehead, which, as already mentioned, appears typically as a boundary marker of intonation patterns in speech. In three of the verse types – C, D, and E – clashing stress, which tends to be avoided in speech, is promoted, if not required. The tendency for the Hat Pattern to conclude with a final declination would seem to create difficulties for verse types B and E, as well as for the subspecies of D that ends with a half-lift, known to some as D2. The verse types D and E seem most at odds with the Hat Pattern; A, B, and C somewhat less so.

A further difficulty, which applies equally to all the verse types, arises from what would seem to be the tendency for maximum prominence to be located at the Head of an Old English verse rather than at the Nucleus, which is where it tends to fall in speech. In regard to clashing stress, Cable remarks that 'one may deduce from several independent arguments that the eighth-century *scop* intended for the first, not the second, of two clashing stresses to be prominent.'[12] One of these independent arguments has to do with alliteration:

> Of the 853 D verses by Pope's count, the 505 with single alliteration all alliterate on the first stress. Of the 1,118 C verses, 78 have double or crossed alliteration, and the rest alliterate without exception in the first foot. C and D verses do not alliterate on the second stress alone.
>
> Although stress, and not alliteration, is the basic element of Old English meter, alliteration is the most obvious clue to the pattern of stress. If one or both of two consecutive syllables within a verse can alliterate, but when only one does it is always the same one, then it is logical to assume that the stressed syllable which never alliterates alone is the less strongly stressed of the two. (ibid., 66)

I agree with the idea that 'alliteration is the most obvious clue to the pattern of stress' in Old English verse, and I think it reasonable to assume that 'stress' coincides with or is, indeed, identical with intonational prominence (ibid., 67). Therefore I think further evidence of the tendency to grant prominence to the Head rather than the Nucleus in the Old English verse is the constraint against postponed alliteration in the off-verse, that is, the second verse of the long line, a feature that affects all verse types. On-verses alliterating *x a* may well have intonational prominence on the Nucleus, but in the system as a whole this would be not the rule but the exception.

This is not to say that the intonation patterns suggested by the Sievers types could never occur in the speech of Anglo-Saxons, or in their prose writing. Rather, what is suggested is the high improbability that such four-part patterns would occur over and over again in the natural course of speech while the five-part Hat Pattern would be quite rigorously avoided. I am sure the Anglo-Saxons found their verse every bit as attractive as some of us do, and I am quite sure that most of them understood it much better than we do. But I also think that they could not have helped noticing the intonational peculiarities just outlined. Perhaps that was part of the attraction.

Understanding the intonational incompatibility of Old English verse with prose takes us some way toward explaining the contours of Ælfric's rhythmical prose as described by John Pope.[13] On the basis of both Pope's and Cable's analyses of Ælfric's rhythmical prose I think the claim can be made that Ælfric produced 'verses' that tend to coincide or fit comfortably with the intonational contour of the Hat Pattern rather than with the patterns of Old English verse.[14] In fact, Pope argues that Ælfric's earliest experiments with rhythmical prose more closely approximate the rhythms of Old English poetry than what he finally settled on as his style.[15] The two verse types most at odds with the Hat Pattern – D and E – are virtually absent from the rhythmical prose.[16] The C verse type with its clashing stress appears significantly less often than in Old English poetry. Types A and B do occur, but much more common is a verse type that seems to combine A and B: x / x / x. Cable, in his book *The English Alliterative Tradition*, follows Oakden in calling this five-part type B/A, but neither he nor I believe that B/A is actually a combination of those Old English verse types.[17] Clearly this five-part structure might correspond closely with the structure of the Hat Pattern, the three dips corresponding to the three declinations – Prehead, Body, and Tail – and the two lifts corresponding to the Head and Nucleus. In fact I think that the Hat Pattern is the favoured, typical, and 'unmarked' intonation pattern of Ælfric's rhythmical prose. To be sure, Ælfric achieves a degree of regularity by using alliteration, by tending toward two-stress verses in imitation of Old English verse, and by using some A and B verses. But I must agree with Mitchell against Clemoes when he says that he can 'find some of the alliteration' of Old English poetry in the rhythmical prose but 'none of the rhythm.'[18]

The influence of Old English rhythmical prose, be it Ælfric's or Wulfstan's, on Early Middle English alliterative writing cannot be clearly demonstrated. But comparison of the verse-types of Ælfric and Laȝamon reveals many similarities. As Cable amply demonstrates, in the *Brut* as in Ælfric, the five-part B/A 'verse' predominates; D's and E's are extremely rare; C's are much less common than in Old English verse.[19] The same is true of the Worcester *Soul's Address*, one of the other surviving examples of Early Middle English verse (*Alliterative Tradition*, 58). It would appear, then, that the same basic intonation pattern Ælfric relied on in writing his rhythmical prose is also fundamental to the *Brut*. What's more, I think Laȝamon's tendency to fall back on this intonation pattern also accounts for some of the important differences between his versification and what we find in the Old English rhythmical prose.

The last point of incompatibility between the Old English verse types and the Hat Pattern mentioned above was that the evidence of alliteration seemed to indicate that prominence was most likely to be found to the left rather than to the right in Old English verses – in intonational terms, on the Head rather than on the Nucleus – hence the avoidance of postponed alliteration. If Ælfric's typical intonation pattern was the Hat Pattern rather than one associated with classical Old English verse types, then it would be reasonable to expect postponed alliteration to be more common in his rhythmical prose than in the verse, because it could be assumed that prominence would more often be found on the Nucleus than in the verse, and that alliteration would be attracted to that position. And in fact postponed alliteration is much more common in the rhythmical prose than in the verse: Pope, relying on the figures of Brandeis, says that about 10 per cent of the off-verses in the rhythmical prose have postponed alliteration (*Homilies of Ælfric*, 123).

The figure for postponed alliteration in Laȝamon is strikingly higher than in Ælfric. Hilker, upon whose statistics I am relying, claims that while 23 per cent of the lines in the *Brut* alliterate in one of the usual Old English long-line patterns – $a \, x : a \, x, a \, a : a \, x, x \, a : a \, x$ – almost the same amount, 22 per cent, alliterate in an atypical way, and far and away the most common of these atypical patterns is $x \, a : x \, a$.[20] In the *Soul's Address*, I judge that about 15 per cent of the off-verses have postponed alliteration, so the doubling of the amount of postponed alliteration in Laȝamon compared to Ælfric may not seem startling; it could be argued that it results from a less sure grasp of the verse constraints. Nevertheless, a brilliant observation by Hilker on the alliterative pattern $x \, a : x \, a$ makes clear the significance of this increase: 'One can see the foundation for Laȝamon's frequent use of the alliterative structure x a : x a in the theory and in the use of end rhyme.'[21] That is, if one substitutes $r$ (a rhyming word) for $a$ (an alliterating word) one produces the fundamental structure of most of Laȝamon's rhyming lines, that is, $x \, r : x \, r$.

What Hilker seems to be suggesting with this insight is that there is a fundamental connection between Laȝamon's use of postponed alliteration and his use of rhyme. Unfortunately he does little more than mention it. However, this fundamental connection provides us with an opportunity to see the prosody of the poem as something more than a near-schizophrenic yoking of two incompatible metrical systems, which sort of analysis has usually resulted in the devaluing or disregarding of rhyme. It also points the way to something less heterogeneous than the amalgam of various prosodies, which fulfil different narrative functions, according to Arthur Glowka,[22] or provide variety, according to Elizabeth Salter.[23] Rather, there may be a single metrical or rhythmical conception, if not exactly a system, based on intonation in which alliteration and rhyme are both features.

As Salter notes, Laȝamon's heavy reliance on rhyme is the fundamental way in which he differs prosodically from Ælfric and other Old English homilists (ibid., 57). Pope's judgment is that neither pure rhyme nor off-rhyme is of any prosodical significance in Ælfric's rhythmical prose, though both are occasionally present (*Homilies of Ælfric*, 133). In the *Soul's Address*, pure rhyme and off-rhyme are more noticeable than in Ælfric; somewhat less than 10 per cent of the lines exhibit the former, while about 8 per cent have the latter. However, the figures for this work are much swelled by a number of repeated lines. For Laȝamon the figures are remarkably higher. Hilker finds 24 per cent of the lines in the *Brut* have pure rhyme and another 16 per cent, off-rhyme, either assonance or consonance, for a total of 40 per cent ('Der Vers,' 144). While it is true that some lines display rhyme in addition to alliteration, clearly the number of rhyming lines is very high.

The same intonational feature that would promote the appearance of postponed alliteration in Ælfric and in Laȝamon, that is, the tendency for intonational prominence to fall on the rightmost dominant word, also provides a favourable environment for the emergence of rhyme. Cohen and T'Hart found that the pitch obtrusions that marked prominence in the Hat Pattern usually coincided, not surprisingly, with the lexically stressed syllable of the dominant word, and typically the vowel of this syllable coincided with at least part of the pitch obtrusion ('Anatomy,' 184). And it is this syllable, of course, in the rightmost dominant word, that tends to bear rhyme. This is not to suggest that frequent use of the Hat Pattern of intonation caused Laȝamon to rhyme; it clearly did not, just as it does not cause us to. But this pattern of intonation provided linguistically congenial conditions for rhyme.

Moreover, it provided linguistic impetus for Laȝamon to try to overcome some of the difficulties inherent in writing rhyming verse in Middle English. Composing in rhyme was no easy feat, as Chaucer points out at the end of his 'Complaint to Venus': *Rym in Englissh hath such skarsete*. Although I have no figures to confirm it, my impression is that the inventory of rhyming pairs in the *Brut* is not that large and soon becomes quite predictable. One way in which Laȝamon may have tried to overcome this problem was to increase his reliance on off-rhyme. In the case of assonance, the same intonational prominence that promotes pure rhyme, coinciding with the vowel of the lexically stressed syllable, would have come into play. The fact that the pitch obtrusion marking this prominence is not restricted to the vowel alone, but can involve surrounding consonants, may have helped to make consonance an attractive possibility as well.

The tendency for the final syllable in the Tail of an utterance, whether stressed or unstressed, to receive some degree of lengthening because of its role as a boundary marker may also have enabled Laȝamon to overcome a special problem presented by his subject matter. The *Brut* is filled with non-English, polysyllabic names that must be worked into the verse in some way. Laȝamon frequently solves this difficulty by rhyming on the last syllable of these names, as he does in the following two lines: *and þus queð Androgeus Hærcne hiderward Iulius* (4432); *þis iherde Tennancius þe i Cornwale wes dux* (4485).[24]

Accepting the Hat Pattern as the favoured, typical, and 'unmarked' intonational pattern of Laȝamon's verses, then, provides a linguistic basis, or rationale, for the coexistence of rhyme and alliteration in the *Brut*. By bringing rhyme and alliteration together as components of one metrical conception I hope to render untenable the opinion that Laʒamon is an alliterative poet in any simple sense of the term.[25] That he not be considered an alliterative poet is crucial not only for our understanding of his prosody, but for our understanding as well of what he was trying to accomplish with his poem. I cannot agree with Norman Blake, who regards the *Brut* as a regularized, poeticized outgrowth of rhythmical prose of the Ælfrician sort. Bella Millett in her work on the *Katherine*-group has sufficiently demonstrated the inadequate oversimplification at the heart of Blake's argument. The Ælfrician/Wulfstanian model alone cannot account for what one finds in the *Katherine*-group alliterative prose ('Saints' Lives,' 30). Interestingly, P.J. Frankis points out that in passages where Laʒamon most likely relies on Ælfric as a source, neither rhythm nor metre mirrors the earlier writer in detail.[26] Nor can a reliance on Old English prose account for the appearance of Old English poetic diction in the *Brut* or for Laʒamon's use of rhyme. By refusing to look at Laʒamon's rhyme along with his alliteration I think we are refusing to look at Laʒamon.

E.G. Stanley has presented a very compelling case, in regard to diction and spelling in the Caligula text, for what he calls the poet's 'antiquarian sentiments.'[27] Laʒamon used, he concludes, 'an archaic, perhaps archaistic, idiom [that was] consciously, perhaps artificially derived from Anglo-Saxon poetry' (ibid., 34). We are not dealing, then, with an organic, natural development, which is the model Blake uses, but with an imperfect, if heartfelt, re-creation of a poetry from the distant past. I suggest that Laʒamon's approach to versification may resemble what Stanley has suggested for diction and spelling, an archaistic re-creation of what he thought was Old English classical verse. And what *did* he think?

Ælfric knew the Old English verse but chose to write prose. Laʒamon, on the other hand, chose to write verse, but he could not have known the Old English verse as a living tradition. The *Brut* has traditionally been dated to the end of the twelfth century, but the redating of the Caligula MS to *c.* 1275 has opened up the possibility that the poem was composed in the thirteenth century.[28] The unnatural, that is to say, artificial, rhythms of Old English verse would have been not only less re-creatable than its diction for Laʒamon but less perceptible as well. He would have seen the verse written down in the fashion of prose, looking on the page identical to Ælfric's. Perhaps his response was similar to Henry of Huntingdon's, who described the Old English poem *The Battle of Brunanburh*, as *quasi carminis modo proloquentes, et extraneis tam verbis quam figuris usi*, 'a kind of song using strange words and figures.'[29] Living no less than fifty and perhaps as many as a hundred years later, it is unlikely that Laȝamon could have seen into the mystery of Old English prosody with any greater clarity than Henry, even if he were equally struck by the diction. My question – unanswerable, of course – is, would rhyme have seemed to Laȝamon a contaminant of Old English verse? With occasional rhyme in the Old English rhythmical prose he might have known, and in rhythmical prose of later composition, with rhyme in his source (Wace's *Roman de Brut*), with rhyme becoming increasingly the mark of verse composition in English – especially if he is a thirteenth-century poet – why shouldn't Laȝamon have felt that Old English verse could have rhyme as well?

Steven Brehe's analysis of what he calls 'imitations of Old English verse in the *Brut*' seems to provide evidence that even when Laȝamon was most concerned to write in the style of an Old English poet he could resort to rhyme.[30] These imitative passages are characterized by verses that are independent clauses both shorter in length than the usual Laȝamon verses and beginning with stressed syllables, another atypical Laȝamon feature. They seem to imitate the Sievers type A verse and do not, therefore, represent the Hat Pattern. But even in some of these passages, rhyme appears, as in the last lines of the following two 'imitations':

Vðer lai wið-uten   & Octa wið-innen
Vðeres ferde   fusde to wale
ræsden to feondliche   þeines riche.                                    (9710–12)


bemen þer bleowen   bellen þer ringeden
cnihtes gunnen riden   wifmen forð gliden.                     (12219–20)

If Brehe is correct in designating these passages as imitative, then we must conclude that Laȝamon either did not know that Old English verse excluded rhyme as a typical feature or didn't care that it did. Regardless, this evidence also indicates that rhyme was fundamental to Laȝamon's own verse-making technique.

Stanley makes an instructive comparison in regard to Laȝamon's language: 'His antiquarian sentiments seem to have led him to the creation of an idiom in tune with his love for the English past: what Ben Jonson said of Spenser applies to Laȝamon, that he "in affecting the Ancients, writ no Language"' ('Laȝamon's Antiquarian Sentiments,' 33). In regard to prosody as well, Laȝamon's Anglo-Saxonism is analogous to Spenser's Medievalism. It is a stylistic choice that can reveal to us much about Laȝamon even if it tells us little about his supposed models. We study Spenser's Medievalism to learn about Elizabethan perceptions of an older time and primarily to learn about

144    Douglas Moffat

Spenser; we should take the same approach with Laȝamon's Anglo-Saxon-ism.[31]

*Middle English Dictionary*, Ann Arbor


NOTES

1 Carolynn Van Dyke Friedlander, 'Early Middle English Accentual Verse,' *Modern Philology* 76 (1978–9): 223. Friedlander's brief mention of intonation bears no relation to this argument. Bella Millett also raises the question of intonation in regard to Early Middle English prose in 'The Saints' Lives of the Katherine Group and the Alliterative Tradition,' *Journal of English and Germanic Philology* 87 (1988): 22 n19.

2 I have borrowed the term 'prosodic contour' from David Crystal, *The English Tone of Voice* (London 1975), 124: 'I should emphasize that my notion of "prosodic contour" is not merely a terminological switch from, say, "syllable stress pattern." By using this term, I have tried to suggest a whole new orientation, an emphasis away from the atomistic approach of the syllable and stress phoneme – or at least (anticipating the unsympathetic), towards a different kind of atomistic approach! The term relates to a model where the basic units are perceptually and semantically meaningful, where gradation in linguistic contrastivity is an important factor, and where the notion of exponence is sufficiently flexible to permit the same abstract metrical result to be achieved in a variety of different ways. In other words, I hope that the principles which are suggested here are sufficiently general to allow us to talk of a text as being *organized* as poetry.'

3 A brief overview of these disagreements can be found in D. Robert Ladd, Jr's *The Structure of Intonational Meaning* (Bloomington 1980), 1–33.

4 Dwight Bolinger, *Intonation and Its Parts* (Palo Alto 1985), 50.

5 See, for example, Daniel Jones, *An Outline of English Phonetics* 9th ed. (Cambridge 1972), 279 (par. 1021).

6 A. Cohen and J. T'Hart, 'On the Anatomy of Intonation,' *Lingua* 19 (1967): 177–92.

7 Ladd, *Structure*, 16, provides a useful chart for dealing with the differences in intonational terminology.

8 Bolinger, *Intonation*, 61.

9 Alan Cruttenden, *Intonation*, Cambridge Textbooks in Linguistics (Cambridge 1986), 39.

10 D. Robert Ladd Jr, 'Phonological Features of Intonational Peaks,' *Language* 59 (1983): 754.

11  Thomas Cable, *The Meter and Melody of 'Beowulf,'* Illinois Studies in Language and Literature 64 (Urbana 1974), 32.

12  Ibid., 66.

13  John Pope, *The Homilies of Ælfric: A Supplementary Collection,* Early English Text Society, OS 259 (Oxford 1967), 105–37.

14  Cable's analysis is in Thomas Cable, *The English Alliterative Tradition* University of Pennsylvania Press Middle Ages Series (Philadelphia: Pennsylvania University Press 1991).

15  Pope, *Homilies of Ælfric,* 113–17.

16  Ibid., 117; Cable, *Alliterative Tradition,* 42–5.

17  Cable, *Alliterative Tradition,* 43.

18  Bruce Mitchell, *Old English Syntax,* vol. 2 (Oxford 1985), 999.

19  Cable, *Alliterative Tradition,* 59.

20  Wilfried Hilker, 'Der Vers in Laȝamons "Brut": Untersuchungen zu seiner Struktur und Herkunft' (PhD diss., Westfälischen Wilhelms-Universität zu Münster 1965), 144.

21  Ibid., 129: 'Den Grund für Laȝamons häufige Anwendung der Stabstruktur x a x a kan mann im Prinzip und in der Verwandung des Endreims sehen.'

22  Arthur Glowka, 'Prosodic Decorum in Layamon's *Brut,*' *Poetica* 18 (1984): 40–53.

23  Elizabeth Salter, Derek Pearsall, and Nicolette Zeeman, eds, *English and International: Studies in the Literature, Art, and Patronage of Medieval England* (Cambridge 1988), 59–60.

24  G.L. Brook and R.F. Leslie, eds, *Laȝamon's 'Brut,'* 2 vols, Early English Text Society, OS 250 and 277 (Oxford 1963 and 1978).

25  That Laȝamon is not really an alliterative poet has been argued before. Angus McIntosh points out the inappropriateness of the label in his 'Early Middle English Alliterative Verse,' in David Lawton, ed., *Middle English Alliterative Poetry* (Woodbridge: D.S. Brewer 1982), 20–1.

26  P.J. Frankis, 'Laȝamon's English Sources,' in Mary Salu and Robert T. Farrell, eds, *J.R.R. Tolkien, Scholar and Storyteller: Essays in Memoriam,* (Ithaca 1979), 71.

27  E.G. Stanley, 'Laȝamon's Antiquarian Sentiments,' *Medium Aevum* 38 (1969): 23–37.

28  Françoise Le Saux reviews the arguments for dating in *Layamon's 'Brut': The Poem and Its Sources,* Arthurian Studies 19 (Cambridge 1989), 6–7. She prefers a composition date of *c.* 1216.

29  A.G. Rigg discusses Henry's translation of *Brunanburh* in 'Henry of Huntingdon's Metrical Experiments,' *Journal of Medieval Latin* 1 (1991): 60–72. The translation is Rigg's.

30  Steven Brehe, 'Lawman's *Brut* and Alliterative Tradition: An Investigation

of Metrics and Literary History,' (PhD diss., University of Minnesota 1990), 148–57.
31 I would like to thank Elizabeth Stevens Girsch for her very perceptive reading of an earlier draft of this paper, and the participants at the conference honouring Constance Hieatt for their comments and questions.

# Constraints on Resolution in *Beowulf*

GEOFFREY RUSSOM

In Old English poetry, a strong metrical position (or *arsis*) is sometimes occupied by two short syllables instead of a single long syllable, according to Eduard Sievers.[1] The short syllables are then said to be *resolved*. Metrists concerned with *Beowulf* have found it difficult to specify the conditions under which resolution takes place. Sievers makes some important observations, but his proposed rule has never achieved consensus.[2] Here I attempt to explain why resolution, though obligatory on some metrical positions, was discouraged or forbidden on others.

To determine the length of an Old English syllable, it is necessary to consider how consonants relate to the vocalic element or *nucleus*. Within a given syllable, consonants placed before the nucleus occupy the *onset* and consonants placed after the nucleus occupy the *coda*.[3] A syllable is *closed* if it has one or more consonants in the coda, as with *bæð* or the first syllable of *bin.dan* (where the point indicates the syllable boundary). A syllable is *open* if its coda contains no consonants, as with *sæ* or the first syllables of *he.re* and *læ.dan*. In Old English simplex words, a single consonant between vowels is always assigned to the onset of the following syllable, and the preceding syllable is then left open. The first of two intervocalic consonants usually closes the preceding syllable.[4] A short syllable is an open syllable with a short vowel, for example the initial syllable of *he.re*.[5] An open syllable is long if it contains a long vowel, as with *sæ* and the first syllable of *læ.dan*. All closed syllables are long.

Two adjacent short syllables do not necessarily constitute a resolvable sequence. Both syllables must lie within the same simplex word, and the first syllable must bear stress.[6] In recent work it has become clear that the obligatory presence of stress is a clue to the essential nature of resolution.

Resolved sequences and long syllables are equivalent because they are both minimal domains of stress assignment.[7] The following principles hold true for Old English (and for the cognate Germanic languages as well):

1 (a) Stress normally occurs on a long syllable, and may never occur on an isolated short syllable. Normal forms with initial stress are *bin.dan* and *læ.ran*.

(b) If the vowel of a word-final stressed syllable is short, that vowel will always be followed by one or more consonants, which will close the syllable and make it long. Examples of words with final stress are *sæ*, *scop*, *middangeard*, and *bī* (compare unstressed *be*).

(c) A resolvable sequence under full stress is equivalent to a long syllable. Thus **we.ro.des** is equivalent to *wor.des*, **we.rod** to *sæ*.

Stress is associated with length in many languages.[8] The characteristic feature of Germanic languages is 1(c), which allows a short syllable to become a stress domain by binding with a following syllable. Working within the framework of metrical phonology, Dresher and Lahiri represent the long stressed syllable and the resolvable sequence as equivalent entities from a purely linguistic point of view.[9] The resolved sequence under primary stress is in effect a long syllable of a higher order, and its treatment as monosyllabic by the poets is in no way artificial. It should be added, however, that resolved sequences are *marked*, or complex, in comparison with ordinary long syllables. Such sequences are often eliminated in Germanic languages by lengthening of stressed vowels in open syllables.[10]

There has been considerable agreement about the conditions under which a resolvable sequence must be assigned to a single (poetic) metrical position. In general, a resolvable sequence undergoes resolution if it is the first element of the verse with metrically significant stress. Only a handful of exceptions to this general rule are encountered, and those that appear to be genuine are of Sievers's type A3, in which the first syllable bearing significant stress is also the last.[11] There has been less agreement about the conditions under which a resolvable sequence must stand unresolved, occupying two metrical positions. A significant number of verses would conform to acceptable Sievers types with or without resolution, and until recently there have been no systematic procedures for choosing between the alternative scansions. During the past few years, however, three Old English scholars have introduced such procedures, showing that resolution was undesirable on the last arsis in certain verse types, and forbidden, or very nearly so, when the resolvable sequence was subordinated within a compound.[12]

Dresher and Lahiri are aware that short syllables sometimes stand unresolved on a subordinate arsis, and suggest that this had a basis in the natural language.[13] Shortening of root syllables with reduced stress does appear to provide such a basis. Old English unstressed vowels are short. Unstressed syllables can be long only if they are closed, and closed weak syllables can become open, hence short, through assimilation and geminate simplification.[14] The exact degree of subordination required for shortening has not been determined. Campbell suggests that a root vowel in the subordinate constituent of a compound proper name would always be shortened unless it was followed by a syllabic ending, but he does not discuss the possibility of occasional shortening in more prominent syllables.[15] For our purposes here, it is sufficient to observe that Old English syllables were often shortened due to subordination of their stress. Since it is motivated by a strong expectation of length, resolution should occur less often in subordinate constituents.

Within the word-foot theory,[16] a metrical constraint is explained if it can be derived from the following general principles of verse construction:

2 (a) Foot patterns correspond to Old English word patterns.
  (b) The verse contains two *word feet.*
  (c) Word feet are bound into verses and lines by alliteration, a metrical equivalent of the compound stress rule that binds smaller words into larger words.
  (d) The line contains two verses.

Principles 2(b) and 2(d) embody the familiar observation that Old English verses and lines have a binary structure. The principles of special interest here are 2(a) and 2(c), which link elements of poetic form to natural linguistic elements.

Principle 2(a) links the metrical positions of poetic feet to syllables in native Old English words. An *S position* (or *primary arsis*) is derived from long syllables with primary word stress. An *s position* (or *secondary arsis*) is derived from long syllables with secondary word stress. An *x position* (or *weak position*) is derived from weak syllables. Note that S and s positions are derived only from the unmarked type of Germanic stressed syllable, which is long. When applied to the native Old English vocabulary, these derivational procedures generate an inventory of nine feet corresponding to the nine basic word patterns:

3 Foot Pattern    Corresponding OE Word
  *x*             *ond*
  *xx*            *oðþe*
  *S*             *gōd*
  *Sx*            *dryhten*
  *Sxx*           *bealdode*
  *Ss*            *s ǣmann*
  *Ssx*           *s ǣmannes*
  *Sxs*           *middangeard*
  *Sxxs*          *sibbegedriht*

Old English words with short stressed syllables can constitute feet, but they have no fixed metrical interpretation, and are assigned to one or another of the patterns above.

The theory employed here is stricter than Sievers's theory in its regulation of unstressed syllables. Weak x positions of the foot are strictly enumerated. Each x is normally occupied by one syllable, with a few systematic exceptions due to elision.[17] All unstressed syllables of stressed words are subject to metrical constraints on verse form. Only unstressed *words* may be extrametrical, and bisyllabic unstressed words must lie wholly outside a foot if they are not included wholly within it. Each pairing of word feet counts as a distinct verse pattern, though patterns are grouped within the familiar Sievers types for the reader's convenience. The word-foot theory is justified by the simplicity of the equation '*foot* equals *word*,' not by a reduction in the number of types.[18]

Principle 2(c) represents alliteration as a metrical equivalent of compound stress. This artificial stress binds word feet into the larger constituents of the verse and the line just as compound stress binds smaller words into larger words. In linguistic compounding, primary stress is assigned to the root of the first constituent, and stress on the root of the second constituent is subordinated. Stress on the second root in a compound is further subordinated if that compound is integrated into a larger compound. Metrical compounding is strictly parallel. When a verse contains two S positions, alliteration is assigned to the first S, and the second S is metrically subordinated. Any s position within the domain of the alliterating S will be further subordinated. At the highest level of structure, principle 2(c) subordinates the second half of the line (the b-verse) to the first half (the a-verse).

Principles 2(a–d) make it possible to explain constraints on resolution in terms of a preference for the most natural assignment of syllables to (poetic) metrical positions. Ordinarily, a metrical position (S, s, or x) will be occupied by one syllable (the unmarked case in poetic metre as in metrical phonology). Because stress is associated with length, however, a resolvable sequence under primary stress will most naturally be treated as the equivalent of a single long syllable, especially on the first S of a verse pattern, which has the greatest metrical prominence.[19] To the extent that a resolvable sequence undergoes linguistic or metrical subordination, syllable count will prevail over length as the deciding factor, and the short stressed syllable of the sequence will stand unresolved on its own metrical position.

Natural matching of syllables to metrical positions is of course a unitary principle, but for application to particular cases it will be convenient to list the entailments of this principle as a set of explicit subrules:

4 (a) Within the word, resolution is most natural under primary stress, less natural under subordinate stress, and forbidden under zero stress.

(b) Within the foot, resolution is most natural on an S position, less natural on an s position, and forbidden on an x position.

(c) Alliteration on the most prominent S position makes resolution less natural on a subordinate S or s position within the same metrical domain.

(d) Resolution of a short syllable is less natural when the following syllable is long and the resolved sequence would therefore be equivalent to an 'ultralong' closed syllable containing a long vowel (Kaluza's Law).[20]

(e) On the most deeply subordinated s positions, both resolved sequences and ordinary long syllables are unnatural. Such s positions are most naturally occupied by a short stressed syllable (unresolved).

(f) When two or more naturalness constraints apply simultaneously, their effects are summed.

Let us consider how the principle of natural matching applies to Old English verses of type B, in which a light foot is followed by a compound foot. Simple examples are *Swā / giōmormōd* (*Beowulf* 2267a), a two-word expression of the x/Sxs pattern, and *hwæðer / collenferð* (*Beowulf* 2785a), a two-word expression of the xx/Sxs pattern.[21] Note that the word-foot scansions differ from those of Sievers in positing a secondary arsis (s position) rather than a second primary arsis.[22] In more complex variants of type B, the Sxs foot may be occupied by a word group rather than a compound word.[23] When this happens, the s position is sometimes occupied by a resolvable constituent, as for example in *þurh / rūmne sefan* 278a (x/Sxs). Such verses are unnatural by 4(b), since resolution occurs on a subordinate metrical position, but not by 4(a), since the resolvable sequence does not lie within the subordinated constituent of a compound. It is much more difficult to find simultaneous violations of 4(a–b). Most apparent examples have been otherwise explained by Terasawa. Verses like *æfter / māþðumgife* 1301a, for example, can be scanned without resolution as type C (xx/Ssx) if we disregard the epenthetic *-u-* of *maþðum-* and posit the monosyllabic form that corresponds to the spelling *maðm-*.[24] Unresolved short syllables are excluded from the verse-final s position of type B, but no special rule is required to explain this fact. Any stressed syllable placed at the end of a verse will be word-final, and word-final stressed syllables are never short in Germanic languages (compare 1[a–b]).

The paradigmatic type-C verse consists of an unstressed function word followed by an Ssx compound. Simple examples are *be / ȳðlāfe* 566a (x/Ssx) and *ofer / hronrāde* 10a (xx/Ssx). As in type B, the word-foot scansions have an s position where Sievers has a second primary arsis. Unlike the s position of type B, the s position of type C can be occupied by an unresolved stressed syllable. The unstressed syllable of the resolvable sequence then occupies its own verse-final x position, as for example in *þæt / healreced* 68a (x/Ssx), *būton / folcscare* 73a (xx/Ssx). Such an assignment of syllables to metrical positions is not represented as unnatural by 4(a–f), and examples are numerous, as expected. I found more than 470 in *Beowulf*.[25] Because short syllables stand unresolved so frequently on the s position of type C, a resolved sequence on the s position would go against strong audience expectation. Variants such as *Hē on / weg losade* 2096b (xx/Ssx) are accordingly rarer than the type-B variants represented by *þurh / rūmne sefan* (x/Sxs).[26] On the s position of type B, a resolved sequence in an unsubordinated constituent will not go against strong audience expectation because this arsis never contains an unresolved short syllable, for purely linguistic reasons, as we have observed. Fulk found a few verses like *under hēahrodore* (*Genesis*, 151a), a simultaneous violation of 4(a) and 4(b).[27] The three apparent examples in *Beowulf* can be otherwise explained, however. In *mid / ofermǣgene* 2917b, the secondary constituent of the compound should probably be interpreted as *-mǣgne*, with a type of syncopation attested by variant spellings of the same manuscript (compare *mǣgnes* in 670a). Syncopation seems equally probable in *sē þe / wæteregesan* 1260a (compare *egsan* 276a), *þæt hīo / lēodbealewa* 1946a (compare *balwon* 977a).[28]

The Ssx foot can also appear verse-finally in type Da (S/Ssx). As in type C, resolution of a secondary constituent on the secondary arsis is avoided.[29] The s position of a Da verse can be preceded by one or two alliterating S positions. In variants with single alliteration, the s position is usually occupied by a long stressed syllable. *Beowulf* contains 26 S/Ssx verses like *feorh / ūðgenge* 2123b, but no more than 7 like *bearn / Healfdenes* 469a.[30] In corresponding variants with double alliteration, subrule 4(e) applies to the deeply subordinated s position, which is most naturally occupied by an unresolved short syllable. As expected, the poet shows a distinct preference for variants with short s like *lēof / landfruma* 31a (23X in *Beowulf*), as opposed to those with long s like *wīs / wēlþungen* 1927a (3X).[31] S/Ssx variants with double alliteration and long s are rare partly because the order of feet can be reversed to produce an Ssx/S pattern (type E), which has a less deeply subordinated s position. In type-E variants like *māðmǣhta / mā* 1613a, for example, the long medial syllable of the compound occupies the subordinate arsis of the dominant foot rather than the subordinate arsis of the subordinate foot, and principle 4(e) does not apply. One can find 35 such variants in *Beowulf* to set beside the 3 like *wīs / wēlþungen*.[32] It is important to note that reversal displaces the compound foot from its usual location, incurring a cost in complexity.[33] This cost is evidently outweighed by the improved matching of syllables to metrical positions in variants like 1613a. There is no comparable incentive to reverse S/Ssx variants with short s. As expected, *Beowulf* contains few Ssx/S variants like *Sūð-Dena / folc* 463b.[34]

In *Beowulf,* a verse-initial Ssx compound is always followed by a monosyllable or resolvable disyllable, never by an unambiguously trochaic word. There are no verse patterns of the form *Ssx/Sx. The poet is relatively tolerant of variants with double alliteration and long s in the expanded Da pattern (Sx/Ssx) because these cannot undergo reversal. Examples like *sīde / sǣnǣssas* 223a (24X) are not much less common than those like *dēogol / dǣdhata* 275a (35X).[35] It is important to note, however, that the expanded variant with short s is often reversed to produce a type A2 variant of normal length. *Beowulf* contains 47 Ss/Sx verses like *morðbeala / māre* 136a, with the secondary constituent of the compound resolved on the relatively strong s position of the first foot.[36] Here simple variants of a complex type are reversed to produce complex variants of a simpler type, with consequent skewing of the statistics for each type considered individually. There would be no incentive for reversal if variants like *dēogol / dǣdhata* were naturally interpreted as Sx/Ss, with the usual number of metrical positions. Sx/Ss is a perfectly acceptable A2 pattern, but resolution on its deeply subordinated s must have been difficult to imagine, judging from the number of reversals like *morðbeala / māre.*

Although compounds like *morðbeala* could theoretically give rise to problems of scansion in the first foot, their metrical value is almost entirely predictable in *Beowulf.* All five variants like *Sūð-Dena / folc,* in which the compound must be scanned as Ssx, appear as b-verses. Variants like *morð-beala / māre,* in which the compound must be scanned as Ss, appear 45 out of 46 times as a-verses. These preferred locations are the most natural ones, as defined by the word-foot theory. According to rule 2(c), verses are bound into lines by metrical compounding, which makes the first of two constituents (here the a-verse) more prominent than the second (the b-verse). An s position in an a-verse therefore has greater prominence than the corresponding s position of a b-verse with the same metrical pattern.[37] The most prominent s positions, which provide suitable locations for resolved sequences, are s positions within the first foot of an a-verse. Any s position within the first foot of a b-verse will be metrically weaker, hence more suitable for occupation by an unresolved short syllable. This kind of asymmetry is obscured in type Da because double alliteration, which occurs only in a-verses, has an independent subordinating effect on an s position in the second foot.

Four representatives of the type-E pattern Ssx/S have a secondary constituent resolved on the s position (including two examples with an extrametrical syllable): *fæderæþelum / (on) fōn* 911a, *umborwesendum / ǣr* 1187a, *Hrēðsigora / (ne) gealp* 2583b, *wīgheafolan / bær* 2661b. Syncopation rather than resolved s might be assumed in verses 2650a and 2780b, which could then be scanned with underdotted vowels as *glēdegesa / grim* and *līgegesan / wæg.*

The somewhat greater tolerance for compounds like *wīgheafolan* in type E, as compared with type C, cannot be due to differing metrical prominence of the s positions. The s position in type C is quite prominent, being preceded by only one alliterating S, like the s position in type E. Recall, however, that avoidance of resolved s in type C is attributable in part to the high frequency of variants with unresolved s, which create a strong audience expectation. No such expectation would be created by the handful of E variants like *Sūð-Dena / folc*.

Although there are no clear cases of resolution on the s position of type Da, *Beowulf* provides two apparent examples of resolved s in type Db. No special problems are raised by *wōp / up āhafen* 128b, which scans as S/Sxs when divided at the major syntactic break. The only alliterating element is *wōp*, so the s position containing *-hafen* is not subject to 4(e). Because *-hafen* is not a subordinated constituent of a compound, the verse contravenes only 4(b), not 4(a). In type Db, as in type B, the verse-final s position is never occupied by an unresolved short syllable, for purely linguistic reasons. We would therefore expect to find resolved s more often in type Db than in type Da (S/Ssx), where unresolved s is so common, and resolved s goes against strong audience expectation. It is somewhat more difficult to explain *wōm / wundǫrbebodum* 1747a (S/Sxs, according to Klaeber's scansion, S/Sxxs, if the underdotted vowel is included). In this verse the element that undergoes resolution, *-bodum*, is the subordinated constituent of a compound, and the s position undergoes deep metrical subordination by the two alliterating elements that precede it. A theory that formulates constraints on resolution as stylistic preferences can allow for an occasional anomaly, and it may be necessary to do so here.[38]

In Sievers's theory, the metrical constant of the verse is its number of major stresses, which is asserted to be two.[39] Verses with a single stress are ruled out. Sievers must posit a medial stress in weak class II verb forms like *sweðrian* and *bealdode* because verses like *Swā / bealdode* 2177a would otherwise be too light.[40] On this hypothesis, 2177a would be included among the examples of type C with an unresolved secondary arsis, scanned here as x/Ssx. The motivation for Sievers's analysis is wholly internal to the five-types theory according to Fulk, who finds no independent linguistic evidence for stress on short medial syllables in simplex words.[41] Those who reject Sievers's metrical constant are under no obligation to accept his scansion of words like *sweðrian* and *bealdode*.

Within the framework employed here, the metrical constant of the verse is the number of word feet. Because the lexical status of major-category words is marked by stress in Old English, a verse of two word feet will often have two stresses. The two-stress verse of Sievers is captured as a special case.

Because Old English employs function words and compounds, some word feet will have no stress while others will have two stresses. A verse of two word feet may accordingly deviate from the norm of two stresses without violating the metrical constant, and no ad-hoc interpretation of linguistic material is required.[42] In the cases of present interest, we can represent the word foot corresponding to *sweðrian* and *bealdode* as Sxx, discarding the problematic assumption of medial stress. The Sxx representation is unavailable in the five-types system, which posits an undifferentiated thesis, but causes no problems in a theory that enumerates x positions. The last two syllables of Sxx words will never undergo resolution, since rule 4(a) requires some degree of stress on resolvable sequences.

We can now explain Fulk's observation that weak class II verbs seem to violate 4(d), Kaluza's Law, while obeying the rule of the coda.[43] In cases like *prēatedon / pearle* 560a, as Fulk points out, the short medial syllable of the verb must be resolved if it bears stress, since there is no reliably attested verse pattern of the form *Ssx/Sx. According to Kaluza's Law, however, the long inflectional syllable -*on* should block resolution. If the pattern of 560a is represented as Sxx/Sx, and there is no medial stress on the verb, resolution is impossible and Kaluza's Law simply does not apply.[44] Being inherently non-resolvable, Sxx words always fill three metrical positions at the end of the verse. Hence they cannot violate the rule of the coda.

The relative frequency of Old English verse patterns is restricted to the extent that they deviate from the norm of two stresses. Consider the distribution of verses in which the second foot is occupied by a compound like *healreced*, with a short medial syllable. The *Beowulf* poet employs such compounds in about 220 variants of type C, which have two stresses, but in only 79 comparable variants of types Da and expanded Da, which have three stresses.[45] In all of these variants the compound would be scanned like *bealdode* by Sievers. If Sievers's scansion were correct, C variants like *Swā / bealdode* 2177a and *Þenden / rēafode* 2985a would be expected to outnumber Da variants like *feorh / ealgian* 796b and *oftost / wīsode* 1663b. In fact the Da variants outnumber the C variants by 62 to 17.[46] This makes perfect sense if the C variants are scanned as x/Sxx and xx/Sxx and the Da variants are scanned as S/Sxx and Sx/Sxx. The C variants are then light, like xx/Sx verses of the restricted type A3, while the Da variants have normative weight, like the much more common Sx/Sx verses of type A1.[47] The Sxx hypothesis is also consistent with the distribution of trisyllabic forms verse-initially. Consider *nȳdwracu / nīþgrim* 193a and *drihtsele / drēorfāh* 485a, two ultraheavy Ss/Ss variants with the first s resolved. These are the only such variants in *Beowulf* to set beside the 46 like *morðbeala / māre* 136a (Ss/Sx), which are heavy but not ultraheavy. On the other hand, variants like *tryddode / tīrfæst* 922a, with a weak class II verb and a compound, are hardly less common than those like *sweðrian / syððan* 2702a, with a weak class II verb and a simplex.[48] This would be very surprising if variants like 922a had the ultraheavy Ss/Ss pattern. Analysed as Sxx/Ss, 922a has the same weight as common type D and E variants.

The primary objective of Dresher and Lahiri is to show that Old English has a coherent phonology, in the sense that all phonological rules operate on the same type of phonological structure (or 'metrical structure' in the linguist's sense). As the authors point out, a phonological system in which rules apply to persistent structures will be easier to learn and to use than a system in which each rule presupposes a different analysis of linguistic material.[49] The rules for Old English poetry seem to be coherent in the same sense. Rule 2(a) provides a foot for every native Old English word and confers on each metrical position essential characteristics of the corresponding syllable. When two prominent constituents occupy the same metrical domain, rule 2(c) always subordinates the second to the first. As we have seen, the degrees of subordination established within the line by 2(a) and 2(c) are respected by the subrules that determine what syllable length is appropriate for a given metrical position, 4(a–f). These degrees of subordination are also respected by the subrules that determine which metrical positions are appropriate for alliterating syllables.[50] On a given metrical position, the probability of alliteration, like the probability of resolution, is directly related to metrical prominence.[51] The persistence of poetic structure enabled Old English audiences to keep track of alliteration and resolution in a variety of patterns sanctioned by principles 2(a–d), just as the persistence of phonological structure enabled native speakers of Old English to keep track of stress and vowel length in a variety of word patterns, including compound patterns. We have observed interactions of some complexity among elements of the Old English poetic system, but the elements themselves, once isolated, turn out to be quite simple.[52]

Brown University

## NOTES

1 E. Sievers, *Altgermanische Metrik* (Halle: Niemeyer 1893), § 9.1. Jerzy Kuryłowicz noticed a very similar rule in Latin prosody of the older period, as exemplified by Plautus and Terence. See 'Latin and Germanic Metre,' *English and Germanic Studies* 2 (1948–9): 34–8, rpt in *Esquisses Linguistiques I* (Wroclaw: Zakład Narodowy imienia Ossolinskich 1960), 294–8.

2 In *Altgermanische Metrik* § 9.2, Sievers states that resolution is obligatory except when a stressed syllable immediately precedes. For recent criticism see David L. Hoover, *A New Theory of Old English Meter* (New York: Lang 1985) 136–7, and Robert D. Fulk, *A History of Old English Meter* (Philadelphia: University of Pennsylvania Press 1992), § 249. A major problem with Sievers's rule, as we shall see, is its failure to specify when resolution is forbidden.

3 These terms are now widely used in phonology. See, for example, Richard M. Hogg, ed., *The Cambridge History of the English Language,* vol. 1 (Cambridge: Cambridge University Press 1992), § 3.3.2.1. The nucleus and the coda are intimately related, since they both contribute to syllable length, which is of crucial importance for many phonological processes. Hogg uses the term *rhyme* for a higher-level constituent that includes the nucleus and coda.

4 Some exceptional cases involving intervocalic -*st*- are discussed as examples (98b–c) in Geoffrey Russom, *Old English Meter and Linguistic Theory* (Cambridge: Cambridge University Press 1987), § 10.2.

5 The medial consonant in words like OE *here* is linked to both the preceding and the following syllable by Seiichi Suzuki, in 'The Role of Syllable Structure in Old English Poetry,' *Lingua* 67 (1985): 97–119, who modifies a proposal in Roger Lass, 'Quantity, Resolution, and Syllable Geometry,' *Folia Linguistica Historica* 4 (1983): 151–80. Here I adopt the more traditional syllabification of B. Elan Dresher and Aditi Lahiri, 'The Germanic Foot: Metrical Coherence in Old English,' *Linguistic Inquiry* 22 (1991): 251–86. As Dresher and Lahiri point out (263 n12), representation of single intervocalic consonants as ambisyllabic makes it difficult to distinguish them from medial geminate consonants. Lass and Suzuki do not address the constraints that concern us here, those that exclude resolved sequences from certain metrical positions in acceptable verse patterns.

6 Resolution (called *Auflösung* by Sievers) should be distinguished from the elision of adjacent unstressed vowels that occurs a few times in *Beowulf*. See Russom, *Old English Meter*, § 1.8. Assignment of two non-elidable weak syllables to one metrical position (sometimes distinguished from *Auflösung* as *Verschleifung*) can be detected with assurance only in Norse skaldic poetry, and is based on actual contraction processes. See Hans Kuhn, *Das Dróttkvætt* (Heidelberg: Winter 1983), § 41.

7 This idea was first proposed by Kuryłowicz. See the reference cited in n1 above and 'Die sprachlichen Grundlagen der altgermanischen Metrik,' *Innsbrucker Beiträge zur Sprachwissenschaft* Vorträge 1 (Innsbruck: Institut für vergleichende Sprachwissenschaft 1970), 9.

8 For recent discussion see Dresher and Lahiri, 'Germanic Foot,' 270–5, and references cited there.

9  The defining concepts of metrical phonology are inspired by, yet distinct
   from, concepts employed in the study of poetic form. The term *foot*, for
   example, is used by phonologists to refer to a purely linguistic domain more
   inclusive than the syllable. The Germanic foot proposed by Dresher and
   Lahiri consists minimally of two *morae* (or *moras*), which are equivalent to
   one long syllable. 'Early Germanic,' the authors contend, 'did not require
   that these two moras be obtained from one syllable; if the stressed syllable
   of a word had only one mora, it was "resolved" – that is, bound together
   with the second syllable into a single metrical position' ('Germanic Foot,'
   251). The privileged form of the Germanic foot is trochaic, with a strong
   bimoraic constituent followed by a weak constituent. This corresponds to the
   privileged form of the Old English poetic foot (see Russom, *Old English
   Meter*, § 2.5). Employment of the Germanic foot to represent linguistic
   environments makes it possible for Dresher and Lahiri to explain high-vowel
   deletion and *j*-vocalization as well as stress assignment.
10 Since this change is linked to shortening of long vowels in 'ultralong' closed
   syllables, most stressed syllables then have exactly two morae. See Dresher
   and Lahiri, 'Germanic Foot,' 279–83.
11 See Russom, *Old English Meter*, § 4.8.
12 An 'antepenultimate rule' blocking resolution on the last arsis of types C
   and Da is proposed by Thomas Cable in *The English Alliterative Tradition*
   (Philadelphia: University of Pennsylvania Press 1991), 19, 25–6. A 'rule of
   the coda' with similar effects is tested against much data by Fulk (*History of
   Old English Meter*, chs 7–8). Here I draw on Fulk, since he is more particularly concerned with Old English problems. With regard to prohibited resolution on the last arsis of types B and Db, see Jun Terasawa, 'Metrical Constraints on Old English Compounds,' *Poetica* 31 (1989): 1–16.
13 Dresher and Lahiri, 'Germanic Foot,' 263.
14 Shortening of closed weak syllables occurs for example in *gyldene* (‹ *gyl-
   denne*), unstressed *þises* (vs. stressed *þisses*), *Æðered* (‹ *Æðelred*), *acuma*
   (‹ *acumba*): see Alistair Campbell, *Old English Grammar* (Oxford: Clarendon Press 1959), §§ 457, 484.
15 Ibid., §§ 87–92. The poetic evidence in § 90 n1, attributed by Campbell to
   'analogy,' raises problems for his sharp distinction between 'half-stress'
   (which allows for vowel length) and 'low stress' (which does not).
16 By 'word-foot theory' I mean the theory proposed in Russom, *Old English
   Meter*.
17 Cf n6 above.
18 The inventory of foot patterns in (3) is for normal verses. Very large compounds are excluded because they normally count as two feet rather than
   one. Such compounds can be employed as feet in hypermetrical verses,

however, e.g., in *mon on / middangearde* 2996a (Sx/Sxsx), *sǣton / suhter-gefǣderan* 1164a (Sx/Sxxsx). Thus principle 2(a) applies in its simplest and most general form, allowing every native Old English word to constitute a foot (see Russom, *Old English Meter*, § 6.6). I set aside the hypermetrical verses of *Beowulf* because their numbers are insufficient for statistical purposes.

19 An arsis acquires the highest degree of metrical prominence by subordinating an arsis to its right. The first and only arsis in type A3 is relatively weak, and sometimes contains an unresolved short syllable, e.g., in *Wæs mīn / fæder* 262a (xx/Sx). Cf 459a, 779a, 1514a, 1728a, 2048a. Resolution is obligatory on the first S of all other verse patterns. I have nothing to add here about optional resolution on the second S of type A and D variants (see Russom, *Old English Meter*, §§ 5.4.1, 5.4.3).

20 See Max Kaluza, *Englische Metrik in historischer Entwicklung* (Berlin: Emil Felber 1909), §§ 52 and 65. Translated by A.C. Dunstan as *A Short History of English Versification* (London: Allen 1911). The marked status of ultra-long syllables in Germanic languages often leads to their elimination through vowel shortening (cf n10 above). In *Beowulf*, ultralong sequences are resolved very seldom in subordinate constituents, but more often under primary word stress, which is more closely associated with length (Fulk, *History of Old English Meter*, § 179). As Fulk observes (§ 170), resolution in *Beowulf* shows sensitivity to the etymological length of inflectional syllables that were shortened quite early.

21 Old English verses, unless otherwise identified, are cited from Frederick Klaeber, ed., *Beowulf and the Fight at Finnsburg,* 3rd ed. rev. (Boston: D.C. Heath 1950). I use bold type to highlight resolvable sequences in the cited examples whether or not such sequences are resolved.

22 A secondary arsis has been posited in types B and C by other metrists on rhythmical grounds. See especially Robert P. Creed, 'A New Approach to the Rhythm of *Beowulf*,' *PMLA* 81 (1966): 23–33; Constance B. Hieatt, *Essentials of Old English* (New York: Thomas Y. Crowell Company 1968), 71–4.

23 The constraints on substitution of word groups for compounds are formulated in Russom, *Old English Meter*, ch. 8. It will not be necessary here to employ the special notation for heavy variants developed in that chapter.

24 Cf *māðþumfæt / mǣre* 2405a, *māððumsigla / fealo* 2757b, where the instances of *-u-* underdotted by Klaeber must be disregarded to avoid unmetrical patterns. Klaeber's criteria for underdotting metrically irrelevant vowels of the manuscript are explained in Appendix III of his *Beowulf* edition (274–8). The spelling *maðm-* is attested in *māðmǣhta / mā* 1613a, *māðmǣhta / wlonc* 2833b. It is more difficult to explain *nē þurh / inwitsearo*

1101a, but this is hardly a straightforward exception to Terasawa's rule, since it occurs in a triple compound. Conceivably the prominence of *-searo* relative to *-wit-* makes resolution more acceptable. For full discussion of apparent exceptions see Terasawa, 'Metrical Constraints,' 5–8. There are no exceptions, real or apparent, among type-B variants of the form x/Sxxs or xx/Sxxs. Nine or ten of these have resolution on the secondary arsis, but their resolved sequences obviously do not lie within subordinated constituents of compounds (294a, 591a, 800a, 1360a, ?1484a, 2397a, 2685a, 2808a; 879b, 1509b). The second foot in the queried example may reduce to Sxs by elision.

25  About half of these have a word group rather than a compound in the Ssx foot. Because it is the marked case, resolution attains high frequency only where linguistic and metrical strength coincide. Resolution on a secondary arsis is the exception rather than the rule even under primary word stress. In Norse skaldic poetry, an unresolved short syllable occupying the s of the Ssx foot is usually preceded by an 'ultralong' trimoraic syllable, and a long syllable in the secondary constituent is usually preceded by a syllable of two morae. See W.A. Craigie, 'On Some Points in Skaldic Metre,' *Arkiv for nordisk filologi* 16 (1900): 366. This is no more than a tendency, as noted by Kuhn (*Dróttkvætt*, § 17), though the expression 'Craigie's Law' is sometimes heard.

26  I counted 56 examples like *þurh / rūmne sefan*, but only 9 like *Hē on / weg losade* (the others, mostly with adjacent resolvable sequences, are 28b, 73b, 350b, 1154b, 1158b, 1603b, 2796b, 3128b). The rare C variants are restricted to the second half of the line, where they cannot be misconstrued as awkward variants of type Da with anacrusis (see Russom, *Old English Meter*, § 5.4.3). In *þæt ic þē / wēl herige* 1833b, the form *herige* probably had a medial glide rather than a medial vowel, and did not undergo resolution (compare the spelling *herge* in 3175b). In three other doubtful cases (164a, 1703a, 2309b), syncopation probably eliminated the resolvable sequence.

27  Fulk, *History of Old English Meter*, § 272. I have added the macron and bold type to Fulk's cited example.

28  Without syncopation, 1260a and 2917b would also violate Terasawa's rule against adjacent resolvable sequences in poetic compounds. See Terasawa, 'Old English *here-toga* and Its Germanic Equivalents: A Metrical and Lexical Study,' *Studies in Medieval English Language and Literature* 7 (1992): 35–51.

29  The one apparent example in *Beowulf, milts ungyfeðe* 2921b, can be scanned as type A1 (Sx/Sx), assuming unstressed *un-* (cf Campbell, *Old English Grammar*, § 75).

30 The Ssx compounds in these verses are proper names or ordinary prose
formations because poetic compounds would have to alliterate (see Russom,
*Old English Meter*, § 8.5). Like 2123b are 235a, 613a, 795a, 872a, 1971a;
164b, 529b, 621b, 631b, 957b, 1111b, 1383b, 1473b, 1498b, 1651b, 1769b,
1817b, 1999b, 2123b, 2177b, 2425b, 2483b, 2538b, 2681b, 2767b. This list
excludes 10 verses like *Wiht unhǣlo* 120b, which can be scanned as Sx/Sx
(type A1), assuming unstressed *un-*. Like 469a are 1319a, 2604a, 1020b,
?1230b, ?2241b, 2860b. Alternative scansions for the queried examples are
proposed by Alan J. Bliss in *The Metre of 'Beowulf,'* 2nd ed. rev. (Oxford:
Blackwell 1967), §§ 62, 77. The statistics cited in discussion of types D and
E are for two-word variants that have no resolved sequences on S positions.
This corpus provides clean contrasts with respect to the features of interest
(order of feet and type of linguistic material occupying the s position).
Verses containing Ssx simplexes with a long medial syllable are also excluded from the statistics because there are (I think) no contrasting Ssx
simplexes with a short medial syllable. See discussion of the Sxx foot below.

31 Like 31a are 54a, 57a, 160a, 288a, 322a, 551a, 554a, 692a, 742a, 936a,
1409a, 1845a, 1954a, 2025a, 2042a, 2090a, 2226a, 2271a, 2315a, 2368a,
2563a, 2827a. Like 1927a are 2582a and 2965a.

32 Like 1613a are 105a, 167a, 190a, 512a, 542a, 573a, 636a, 722a, 734a, 850a,
891a, 908a, 1042a, 1128a, 1160a, 1276a, 1278a, 1299a, 1429a, 1500a, 1567a,
1991a, 1993a, 2068a, 2393a, 2543a, 2650a, 2671a, 2695a, 2807a, 2843a,
2890a, 2904a, 3052a. The relatively greater metrical prominence of the s
position in type E is also demonstrated by the fact that it occasionally contains an alliterating syllable (e.g., in *synsnǣdum / swealh* 743a, *Gūð-Gēata /
lēod* 1538a). See Russom, *Old English Meter*, § 7.5.3.

33 See ibid., § 2.5.

34 Cf 623b, 783b, 1009b (with resolved second S), 2779b. A doubtful example
is 1584a, printed by Klaeber as *lāðlicu lāc*. The root vowel in *-lic-* is etymologically long, and the posited shortening probably has no metrical significance here. Cf n38 below.

35 Like 223a are 325a, 326a, 411a, 770a, 987a, 1002a, 1097a, 1512a, 1532a,
1565a, 1749a, 1865a, 1874a, 1886a, 2051a, 2065a, 2396a, 2646a, 2648a,
2725a, 2810a, 3031a, 3099a. Like 275a are 392a, 450a, 606a, 614a, 616a,
689a, 818a, 839a, 966a, 986a, 1212a, 1231a, 1298a, 1339a, 1348a, 1410a,
1468a, 1568a, 1678a, 1793a, 1969a, 2123a, 2205a, 2496a, 2545a, 2603a,
2649a, 2674a, 2689a, 2719a, 2760a, 2800a, 2811a, 2847a.

36 Variants like 136a appearing in the first half of the line are 76a, 156a, 208a,
222a, 226a, 430a, 622a, 640a, 753a, 1079a, 1116a, 1121a, 1122a, 1147a,
1177a, 1243a, 1284a, 1463a, 1470a, 1516a, 1619a, 1676a, 1722a, 1738a,
1778a, 1940a, 2046a, 2069a, 2077a, 2120a, 2133a, 2250a, 2265a, 2320a,

162    Geoffrey Russom

2357a, 2419a, 2429a, 2456a, 2535a, 2537a, 2584a, 2622a, 2742a, 3007a, 3149a. The only such variant to appear in the second half of the line is *holtwudu / sēce* 1369b.

37  See Russom, *Old English Meter*, § 7.5.

38  Resolution on a deeply subordinated s position after two alliterating elements also seems necessary in *sellice / sǣdracan* 1426a and *eahtodan / eorlscipe* 3173a, which would otherwise represent patterns of unparalleled length (see Russom, *Old English Meter*, § 2.5, rule 13b). In the very difficult *fyrdsearu / fūslicu* 232a, verse-final resolution would presuppose a short stressed medial syllable in *fūslicu*, but this syllable is only short because it has undergone stress reduction. If sufficient stress for resolution were retained, one would expect the length of underlying *-līc-* to be retained as well, making resolution impossible. The verse may originally have been *fyrdsearu / fūslic* according to E. Sievers, 'Zur Rhythmik des germanischen Alliterationsverses,' *Beiträge zur Geschichte der deutschen Sprache und Literatur* 10 (1885): 280. Fulk suspects transposition of an original *fūslicu / fyrdsearu*, which would be analogous to 1426a (*History of Old English Meter*, § 250).

39  Sievers, *Altgermanische Metrik*, § 8.1.

40  Ibid., § 78.5. If it is unstressed, moreover, the medial syllable of *bealdode* combines with the following unstressed syllable to form a single thesis when scanned according to Sievers's principles. *Swā / bealdode* then falls below the minimum of four metrical positions or *Glieder* (§ 8.1).

41  Fulk, *History of Old English Meter*, § 261. An influential discussion of medial stress is Karl Luick, *Historische Grammatik der englischen Sprache*, vol. 1 (Leipzig: C.H. Tauchniz 1921), §§ 312–15. It is important to note that Luick relates shortening of medial vowels in the forms of interest here to stress reduction (§ 313). Sievers's two-stress hypothesis is the only apparent basis for the claim that a light stress survived in open syllables after the shortening was completed (§ 314). For early doubts about Sievers's posited stress see Bliss, *Metre of 'Beowulf,'* 113–17 (Appendix A). Bliss goes too far, however, when he equates the long medial syllables of forms like *wīgendes* with unstressed syllables (cf Fulk § 214).

42  Sievers's principles of scansion change according to the verse type. In verses like *Swā / giōmormōd* 2267a (type B), and *ofer / hronrāde* 10a (type C), the secondary constituent of the compound is enumerated as a major stress; but in verses like *fromum / feohgiftum* 21a (type Da), and *hār / hilderinc* 1307a (type Db), the secondary constituent is not enumerated. An awareness of such problems is betrayed in Sievers's *Altgermanische Metrik*, § 9.3, where he notes the weakness of the second arsis in type C, supposedly a primary arsis. Another problem arises in type A3, where an occupant for a second primary arsis must be found among the non-alliterating function words of

variants like *ac hē him on / hēafde* 2973a. So far as I can see, Sievers's justification of the two-stress hypothesis is entirely ad hoc, and no legitimate
privilege is conferred on the linguistic presuppositions required to sustain it.

43 Fulk, *History of Old English Meter,* § 246.

44 This result is consistent with Fulk's finding that violations of Kaluza's Law
are 'so rare in *Beowulf* as to be negligible' (§ 183).

45 The count of Da and expanded Da verses includes the two-word variants
listed above and others with extrametrical words (712a, 764a, 1162a, 1554a,
1727a, 1790a, 2455a, 2462a, 2471a, 2591a, 2628a, 2751a; 1323b, 1840b).
The resulting figure is comparable to the figure for type C, which also includes variants with extrametrical words. Variants with resolved sequences
on S positions are excluded as before.

46 The count for light type C includes variants with extrametrical syllables, e.g.,
*Ful oft ge- / bēotedon,* 480a. The other examples are 96a, 144a, 536a, 630a,
1363a, 2766a, 2933a, 3159a, 3178a; 292b, 560b, 1819b, 2619b, 3103b. Like
796a are 971a, 2409a, 2668a, 2744a, 2805a, 3133a; 132b, 156b, 172b, 204b,
320b, 402b, 423b, 451b, 470b, 611b, 639b, 720b, 725b, 787b, 808b, 901b,
951b, 983b, 1204b, 1206b, 1212b, 1380b, 1391b, 1407b, 1413b, 1426b,
1444b, 1566b, 1687b, 1721b, 1795b, 1898b, 1916b, 2084b, 2085b, 2164b,
2168b, 2285b, 2383b, 2587b, 2605b, 2652b, 2655b, 2658b, 2767b, 2793b,
2897b, 3008b, 3027b, 3050b, 3104b, 3132b. Like 1663b are 3045a and
1125b. No variants with resolved sequences on S positions are included.

47 The much lower frequency of type A3 in *Beowulf* has often been noted. See
for example Sievers, 'Zur Rhythmik,' 290.

48 Like 922a are 1161a, 2085a, 2119a, 2132a, 3173a. Like 2702a are 560a,
1118a, 1137a, 2096a; 105b, 1699b.

49 Dresher and Lahiri, 'Germanic Foot,' 283.

50 Russom, *Old English Meter,* § 7.5, rules 50(a–d).

51 This type of coherence is regarded as unnecessary in Calvin B. Kendall, *The
Metrical Grammar of 'Beowulf,'* Cambridge Studies in Anglo-Saxon England 5 (Cambridge: Cambridge University Press 1991). 'Though alliteration
and metre are interdependent,' Kendall asserts, 'they are nevertheless distinct
systems, which are not entirely congruent with each other' (25).

52 I owe thanks to E.G. Stanley for useful advice.

# Translation and Transformation in *Andreas*

BRIAN SHAW

The traditional view of the literary merits of *Andreas* centres largely on the poem's ingenious typology. Among those who approach the work in this fashion are Thomas D. Hill, Penn Szittya, Joseph B. Trahern, Alvin Lee, James W. Earl, and, of course, Constance B. Hieatt.[1] While the contributions by such scholars to our appreciation of the poem cannot be overemphasized, these writers to some extent may unduly narrow our appreciation of the poet's art. Recently, some cautionary voices have been raised to suggest that poetry, even Old English hagiographical poetry, does not lend itself to any single line of investigation, though surely critical exploration of typological patterns is not meant to be exclusionary.

Among recent readers who have argued for a broader range of critical appreciation, Daniel G. Calder focuses on the problem of the use of the sources and of the very nature of typology itself:

> I have no quarrel with this approach to the poem. The explosion of typo-logical commentary has added immensely to our knowledge of Anglo-Saxon Christian poetry; the method has made what was once dark now bright. I can even agree that the *Andreas* poet made a special effort to expand the typological implications of his source so as to reinforce the pattern he found already there. But that is just the point – the basic typological equivalences in *Andreas* (and in most of the other Anglo-Saxon Saints' Lives) may also exist in the source. Indeed, they exist, strictly speaking, in all eternity. While the current research points to what is there, it does not truly *interpret* the poem. Identification of a typological system, however necessary, however applicable, should not be equated with analysis; discovery is not the same as understanding.[2]

As Calder suggests, the medieval poet can expand on what he finds, and the most apparent example would naturally be the typological patterns. But there are other patterns of thought inherent in the so-called source, and the *Andreas* poet's art is to see and to explore these marginal ideas. Thus while it is true that *Andreas* ultimately relies on a previous text[3] it is also clear that the poet does not merely translate: he adapts. The product may be a close rendition of its source while, at the same time, the process of composition allows the poet the freedom to create a work of artistic autonomy. Thus while the typology may inhere in the work, and while the work may reflect a doctrinal ethos,[4] yet the poem must also be judged on its own merits as it develops its own internal logic only suggested by the source.

While we may never recapture the exact version used by the poet, it is clear that he had before him a document composed in what must be for him a special language, for it is Latin, that unique language in which the poet would find recorded all of God's revelation. His task, then, must be to transmute this literate truth for a society whose foundation was originally oral and, thus, still very responsive to the authority of the spoken word.

To accomplish this task, the *Andreas* poet must be faithful to the spirit of the original and, simultaneously, rework the texture of the story to reinforce the idea of the validity of the spoken word, as Andrew's story moves from the Latin to the vernacular. In achieving this goal, the poet, I will argue, has carefully shifted the nuances of the Latin text so that the less-than-significant original references to concepts associated with speech echo throughout the recension to create what is essentially a newly focused version of the story. Thus the *Andreas* poet redefines the subtext of Andrew's story to make it the model of the ability of the word to rival the power of the letter. In this paper, I intend to examine some exemplary passages of *Andreas* in light of the version of the story presented in the source. It is not my purpose to be exhaustive but rather to select examples which seem to demonstrate aspects of the *Andreas* poet's ability to re-create a hagiographical story with a new emphasis on the way in which the saint's power is to be seen as primarily oral, until, by the time the real work of the conversion of Mermedonia begins, the saint is invisible and has become the disembodied voice speaking revealed truth.

From the beginning of the poem one senses an insistence on the oral transmission of truth. The source from which the *Andreas* poet worked probably contains nothing of the self-conscious narrator and begins with a submerged authorial voice: 'At that time all the apostles were gathered together and they divided the regions among themselves, casting lots to see which area each was to be assigned for preaching.'[5] Even if the poet consciously echoes *Beowulf* or simply uses a stock opening formula, he has selected a gambit that clearly calls attention to the fact that this story is preserved by words and that there is a separation between the words and the audience:

> HWÆT, we gefrunan   on fyrndagum
> twelfe under tunglum   tireadige hæleð,
> þeodnes þegnas.   No hira þrym alæg
> cam<p>rædenne,   þonne cumbol hneotan,
> syððan hie gedældon   swa him dryhten sylf,
> heofona heahcyning,   <h>lyt getæhte.                    (1–6)[6]

Two significant, if subtle, changes appear in the opening sequence of the poem. Most noticeable is the presence of an audience that hears about the events of the Christian heroes. Also significantly, God, rather than the mere chance of the lottery, controls the destiny made clear by God's word. The apostles thus seem less in control in the Old English, since they do not divide the regions among themselves but rather are dispatched by God's orders. While still warriors in the cause of right, their weapons have been replaced by words and they now bear true speech as they confront their enemies.[7] And the audience is about to hear retold an earlier story of yet another Christian warrior dispatched by God's word, a warrior whose weapon also was nothing more than the power inherent in the word, for the poem prefaces Andrew's mission with Matthew's role in promulgating the word. And in re-narrating, the poet has expanded particulars found in the source, again to validate the necessity of making the truth accessible through the act of hearing.

Matthew is associated with the word:

> se mid Iudeum ongan   godspell ærest
> wordum writan   wundorcræfte                              (12–13)

The source is silent on this point and merely presents Matthew directly among the Mermedonians. This added detail in the poem suggests the rationale that God might have had in sending Matthew specifically to the city of the cannibals. Just as he was the first to make Christian doctrine available to the Jews, an action essential for their salvation, so among the Mermedonians he will initiate the process of demonstrating the power of the word to save. It will not be until Andrew's arrival, however, that the power of the word will finally persuade and convert those who dwell in darkness.

But the Mermedonians also have their means of persuasion, and one that inverts and counterpoints what has been noted about Matthew. The poet makes it clear that the cannibals, in the way in which they treat their victims, present a double threat; they attack both the body (by blinding their victims as well as consuming their flesh) and, more hellishly, the spirit (through the magical drink that they concoct to deprive their victims of reason). These threats are intertwined, since Mermedonian cannibalism may very well be the anti-Eucharist[8] and the blindness, while physical, is certainly a familiar biblical trope for spiritual darkness. Additionally, the victims are mirrored as Mermedonians, denied normal human food and forced to eat hay and grass, an outward sign of the condition of the benighted beast without the words needed for reasoning. Denied reason and light, they become grotesque parodies of humanity, having the form but not the true essence.

While these essentials of cannibalism, blindness, and the diet of hay and grass are available from the source, the *Andreas* poet implies his own reading by altering the emphasis: four lines suffice to detail the blinding, but seven are devoted to the powerful narcotic that transforms the victim's mind. Both torments are horrific,[9] but the poet's emphasis on the denial of the rational enhances the real threat of evil. Malice may attack externally, but its real threat lies in depriving the mind of the words of wisdom with which the Christian warrior must always be armed.

Confronted by this double threat, Matthew may be an easy victim physically; but, remaining steadfast in God's true words, he preserves his soul from the drug's effects:

> Eadig ond onmod,   he mid elne forð
> wyrðode wordum   wuldres aldor,
> heofonrices weard,   halgan stefne
> of carcerne. (54–7)

The emphasis clearly is on the power of the word to overcome the treachery of the forces of evil. Matthew does not see his plight as horrible because he has been blinded and may be eaten; rather, he fears the Mermedonians for the seeming power of words that they now wield:

> Forgif me to are,   ælmihtig God,
> leoht on þissum life,   þy læs ic lungre scyle,
> ablended in burgum   æfter billhete,
> þurh hearmcwide   heorugrædigra,
> laðra leodsceaðena,   leng þrowian
> edwitspræce. (76–81)

Matthew realizes that the physical torments are ultimately insignificant, and this spiritual insight is exactly what enables him to escape the word-centred enmity of the Mermedonians. The source puts more emphasis on Matthew's fear of blindness and death (in fact omitting any reference to the hateful words of the Mermedonians) and Matthew merely prays that his sight be restored if he must die at the hands of his captors.[10] In the conflict of words and deeds, actions are decidedly secondary to the apostle's knowledge. Perhaps this dichotomy helps to account for the shift in tone from the source, where the hay and grass, the blindness, and the mind-altering drug seem more physical than the *Andreas* poet's version of the torments, a version which centres on how such suffering exacerbates the captive's fate by depriving him of his reason.[11]

In fact, as the poet manipulates elements of the source so that the evil of the Mermedonians focuses on their ability to dehumanize their victims by depriving them of their reason, it becomes particularly ironic that Matthew sees his torment as rendering him *Swa þa dumban neat* (66).[12] The images of fodder and cattle may very well recall Nebuchadnezzar, the perfect image of sin's ability to pervert the human intellect into the bestial as well as of God's punitive yet restorative power. If the poet intends Matthew to express his fear in a way reminiscent of the Old Testament king, then he has exploited another instance of the power of the word, since it is by articulating his pride that Nebuchadnezzar merits his punishment. Unlike Nebuchadnezzar, Matthew has the wisdom that allows him the proper use of words, in prayer, to assert his willingness to suffer whatever is allotted him. To the rightly ordered mind, God will be merciful and *Æfter þyssum wordum com  wuldres tacen* (88). God's words to Nebuchadnezzar take away a temporal kingdom; to Matthew, they promise an eternal one.

God's intercession on Matthew's behalf may initially seem disproportionate, for Matthew has, in fact, done little other than be captured and blinded. But it may be just that fact that has attracted the *Andreas* poet, for the insistence on the power of the word as a fit weapon against demonic foes is precisely the point he seems to make. The contrast through subtle shifts in nuance towards the celebration of the efficacy of the word has allowed Matthew to emerge as a model of a true Christian warrior, whose weapon is the speaking of truth. Just as Matthew had, in essence, translated the old dispensation to the new by offering the words of life to the Jews, so he will also serve as the prefiguration of Andrew's mission of translating the words of faith into the deeds of redemption. Even though Matthew is imprisoned and his enemies, prompted by the devil, momentarily gloat, their very words ring hollow, for demonic violence, founded in incorrect utterances, will be judged against the power that God has promised:

Oft hira [Mermedonians'] mod onwod

under dimscuan    deofles larum,
þonne hie unlædra    eaueðum gelyfdon.                    (140–2)

Now that the basic structure of the original narrative has established Matthew's danger, the story shifts to its main concern, the role that Andrew is to play both in rescuing his fellow saint and in converting the Mermedonians from adherence to the words of the devil to belief in God's commands. Matthew had taken the word to the Jews, apparently with some success; failure had met his efforts among the Mermedonians. Again we can see how the *Andreas* poet's conceptualization of his source seems to point him once again to a concern with God's word, both as the vehicle of primal creation and as the sole motivating force for action in the world. As in the previous portion of the translation, so in this, the poet's reading of his source as a primarily literary text to be fitted to the needs of an audience to hear rhetorical links seems to shape the translation. In contrast to the bare narrative of the source,[13] the *Andreas* narrative emphasizes the verbal quality of the Lord's commands. God is clearly the creator: *Þa wæs gemyndig    se ðe middangeard / gestaðelode    strangum mihtum* (161–2); but when He commands, the emphasis is clearly on the voice: *Þa sio stefn gewearð / gehered of heofenum* (167–8). And the divine thought is rendered as words: *modhord onleac, / weoruda drihten,    ond þus wordum cwæð* (172–3). It is, I think, not impossible that the poet's strategy of shifting attention to the divinity's association with and creation through the word (ideas likely either nonexistent or merely marginal in the poet's Latin text) demonstrates his ability to re-create an Andrew recognizable as the hero of the original legend and also identifiable as the warrior whose weapon has become the spoken word.

Thus, when the poet begins to shade Andrew's character, he must, naturally, follow the letter of the events laid out in the source. But, at the same time, he is free to manipulate the spirit of his story to give it the coloration desired. And, as with the presentation of Matthew, so with Andrew the poet resonates those ideas associated with the concept of the word. Even though saintly, Andrew lacks the ability intuitively to understand the significance of God's word. Andrew is not disobedient: he is merely ignorant about how to fulfil the divine mandate. In spite of God's assurance that Matthew will suffer death unless Andrew accomplishes the journey, the saint's answer is a denial of the power of God's word, for he says he cannot accomplish the voyage *swa ðu worde becwist* (193). The source simply has Andrew suggest that the journey is impossible and that the angel of the Lord be sent in his place. But God is not easily to be denied, and Andrew is again told that God's word is not to be trifled with, since even cities can be moved *gif hit worde becwið wuldres agend* (210). Given the insistence of the envelope pattern (with *worde* as a key element) within so short a space as seven lines, it is difficult to imagine how Andrew does not simply acquiesce at once to the divinely announced plan.

At this point in the action, after the word has been proclaimed, God ascends to Heaven and leaves Andrew to work out his own plan for enacting the command. For Andrew, the knowledge and the action must still be reconciled. In Andrew's first attempt at using the power of the word, it is made clear that the central conflict is between two sets of values, temporal and spiritual. It is evident, in Andrew's use of words with the sailors, that he comprehends the difference between the two values, imaged in the journey and the reward motif implicit in his equation of physical journey with spiritual reward. Andrew can offer only verbal assurance of God's pleasure, but that promise must be equally valid for the physical side of the journey:

> Wolde ic þe biddan,   þeh ic þe beaga lyt,
> sincweorðunga,   syllan meahte,
> þæt ðu us gebrohte   brante ceole,
> hea hornscipe,   ofer hwæles eðel
> on þære mægðe;   bið ðe meorð wið God,
> þæt ðu us on lade   liðe weorðe.                                        (271–6)

Christ the Helmsman tests this hypothesis (that the world is divided between those with physical treasure and those whose treasure is God's word) by pointing out two difficulties: first, Mermedonian hostility to strangers, and second, Andrew's lack of funds for the journey. Again, the *Andreas* poet subtly redefines the intellectual thrust of the source by using the potential inherent in the oral-formulaic tradition so that he is able to suggest by technique in a way totally foreign to the rhetorical patterns of the Latin version. The physical placing of Christ the Helmsman is of no real significance to the Latin text. An Old English audience would be attuned, however, to the subtle verbal manipulations that characterize the *Andreas* poet's presentation of the scene. In the first instance He speaks *of yðlide* (278) and subsequently *of nacan stefne* (291). Helping to unite the two ideas is the close similarity in the system used to describe Christ who is *engla scippend* (278) and *engla þeoden* (290). Assuredly, the poem suggests the protective quality of Christ, who creates and controls all things. But the control tends to expand away from the earthly realm and towards the eternal, since Christ is imaged in terms of the heavenly city inhabited by His creation, the angels. Andrew's physical goal, Mermedonia, is thus linked with the spiritual goal, heaven. In the subtle interplay of words, the poem links Andrew's speech to the

Helmsman (about not only the lack of money but also God's favour) with the spiritual voyage through obedience. In an ingenious way, Andrew's first test, the need to journey to Mermedonia, implies the larger concept of the voyage not as spatial but rather as spiritual. While Andrew is still only using words, he is nonetheless clearly indicating the link between the verbal and the physical as he gives a texture and shape to his request, a shape that involves the journey both to Mermedonia and to heaven.

Once the journey has been imagistically resolved, the saint faces his second problem, the lack of earthly treasure. Epithets suggestive of Christ's creative and protective aspect (such as *æðelinga helm* and *engla scippend* 277–8) can be replaced by a concept more focused on the redemptive aspect of Christ (*neregend fira* 291). Ironically, the notion of Christ as saviour of men immediately precedes the passage in which the sum to be paid for transportation is discussed, an irony heightened by Christ's physical position, *of nacan stefne*. Christ has, of course, 'paid' the fare of all for the voyage to heaven, though the saint may well not comprehend the full import of the metaphysical message.

The nexus of ideas inherent in the ship, the ark, and the church is too well established to be questioned,[14] and, of course, the *Andreas* poet here only picks up what is inherent in the story. But again, I would argue, the experiences of an aurally literate audience allow the poet to do more than merely translate in a pedestrian fashion. For example, building on the stock ideas of the ship and church metaphor, the poet evokes from the text a whole resonance of implications that the rhetorical structure of the source could never hope to encompass. Christ at the prow of the ship is surely the fulfilment of the Old Testament synagogue, a place from which those concerned with money changing were expelled. Now Christ, specifically imaged as the saviour, ironically challenges Andrew to produce the money for the voyage. In the source it is Christ who first broaches the problem of the money to be paid and, when Andrew admits his poverty, suggests that the saint had been foolish even to board the ship. In the *Andreas* poet's recension, it is Andrew who first notes that he has *beaga lyt* (271), but Christ seems to take the litotes rather too literally and attempts to bargain for the appropriate *gafulrædenne* (296) and *sceattas gescrifene* (297). This recension, then, takes a basic element of the story and forces the listener to hear in it a reiteration of the main thematic drive of the poem, the split between the physical and the spiritual aspects of the voyage.

The implication here seems to be that the word, the divine power of the command given that Andrew must go to Mermedonia, is to be weighed against physical destitution. Andrew may not have money, but he has direct communication with God, and surely that counts far more than the physical. Ironically, the lack of money can also endanger Andrew by making him rather like the Mermedonians themselves:

> Nafast þe to frofre   on faroðstræte
> hlafes wiste,   ne hlutterne
> drync to dugoðe?   Is se drohtað strang
> þam þe lagolade   lange cunnaþ.                    (311–13)

The journey may be difficult for those lacking the necessities, but they are not to be like the cannibals. From Andrew's point of view, they should remember that one does not live by bread alone. While the Mermedonians have taken a course of action, their choice is clearly wrong because exclusively physical. Andrew, on the other hand, can perceive the proper use of the material world and, in a sense, see through the material as just a metaphor for the real. To counter the Mermedonian threat with its magic potion, Andrew can rely on the word of God and can thus articulate, in answer to Christ's persistent question, the doctrine that stresses the word's superiority over the world. Andrew, in fact, returns to the original, evangelical mandate. Thus, while the question of food is raised in the source,[15] it is really only a passing issue. In the hands of the *Andreas* poet, the motif explores the dichotomy of the world and the spirit, an idea heightened in the Mermedonian response to the famine:

>                     He ðæt sylfa cwæð,
> fæder folca gehwæs,   ond us feran het
> geond ginne grund   gasta streonan.              (329–31)

And, surely, an audience trained to listen to the *scop*'s words with care would remember a very similar nexus of ideas associated with Matthew's torment and especially with his ability to escape the power that a diet of grass holds for transforming the human into the bestial.

Andrew's state is clearly not at all comparable to that of the Mermedonians. They have allied themselves with the devil and the drink that deprives one of reason. Andrew, to the contrary, has become one with the water of life, which, while it may demand physical hardship, is still eternal. When Andrew *wis on gewitte,   wordhord onleac* (316), he can rely on the biblical motif of Christ's use of the word to call together the disciples into a new social order based on the promulgation of the word of truth:

>                     We *h*is þegnas synd
> gecoren to cempum;   he is cyning on riht,

    wealdend ond wyrhta  wuldorþrymmes,
    an ece God  eallra gesceafta,
    swa he ealle befehð  anes cræfte,
    hefon ond eorðan,  halgum mihtum,
    sigora selost.                                    (323–9)

Perhaps as well as anywhere in *Andreas*, the poet here fuses the two cultural worlds, that of the Latin text and that of the Germanic recension, for the creation by divine fiat has been augmented by the implications of a loyal *duguþ* bound by its *beot* to proclaim the truth that encompasses all national identities.

In response to the fusion of cultures that unites a Germanic warrior to the bearer of the Christian word, the *Andreas* poet formulates a new role for the new concept of Christian warrior. Unlike the typically pagan warrior-thane relationship in which physical treasures are given and received, for Andrew the currency of the social bond has become the message that he bears. Just as God has chosen the apostles, so they must, in turn, call others. Just as Christ denied the wealth of the world in favour of the power of the word, so must the apostles do likewise. And Andrew makes this abundantly clear when he uses his voice to reiterate the divine word and directly recalls Christ's mandate to spread the word and His promise that all else, though secondary, will be provided (332–9).

By the very act of invoking Christ's words in response to the Helmsman's test, Andrew has achieved a new comprehension of the full meaning of the truth. Now the saint is able to experience at first hand the truth which he recalls about God's provision of all necessities. And the authorial voice clearly underscores the point that for Andrew and his men the promise and the fulfilment are one:

    Þa in ceol stigon  collenfyrhðe,
    ellenrofe;  æghwylcum wearð
    on merefaroðe  mod geblissod.             (349–51)

In fact, once the initial contact is made between Andrew and the Helmsman, their discourse serves to show the way in which the saint transmits the Lord's teaching in a series of questions and answers. These questions first reveal the truth to the saint about the Helmsman's perceived worldly virtues and thereafter lead incrementally to the final epiphany that the saint is again in the presence of the word made flesh. Among the various stages by which the truth is ultimately established, one of the most striking moments occurs in Andrew's recounting of the dramatic way in which Christ, during His ministry, chose to reveal truth in Jerusalem. There, Christ meets with disbelief and scorn, attacks not of the flesh but of the spirit. And these attacks are connected with the power of the word or with its demonic counterpart, the power of the lie:

> Us*i*c worde ongan
> þurh inwitðanc   ealdorsacerd
> herme hyspan;   hordlocan onspeon,
> wroht webbade.                                           (669–72)

And the lie that the priests in the temple tell concerns the very concept of the word made flesh, for they contend that Jesus is merely the knowable son of Mary and Joseph.

In addition to the actual revelation of the godhead, Christ performs a great miracle in which the stone of the temple is brought to life. While this event fits well with the typological readings of the poem, it also fits with the poem's dichotomy between words and deeds. While the version given in *Andreas* shortens and alters somewhat the emphasis of the story of the stone come to life, the thrust is clear. In the source, the stone attacks chiefly the falseness and misunderstanding of the priests. For the poet, the angelic miracle serves to reinforce the idea that Christ is indeed the word made flesh and is connected with the primal origin in which creation takes place through the power of the word. The priests misname things; Jesus has rightly named and ordered things, and continues to demonstrate how the word proclaims reality:

> Ge mon cigað
> Godes ece bearn   ond þone þe grund ond sund,
> heofon ond eorðan   ond hreo wægas,
> sealte sæstreamas   ond swegl uppe
> amearcode   mundum sinum.                                (746–50)

Christ stands at the centre of all things and must be rightly known; He is the creator whose word established the order of the world, made the original covenant with Abraham, and revealed the truth to the disciples and, if they would receive truth, to the priests themselves. But they prefer to deny the word of life and to worship stones. In a sense, they are the image of those whose belief is in the old law. But the poet's story deals insistently with the way in which the letter of the old law becomes the spirit of the new, just as the poet makes available in a new medium the truth of the word. Exposition must always be alive and must constantly rework the truth.

Thus the 'resurrection' of Abraham, Jacob, and Isaac, who come to refute the priests by announcing the divinity of Christ, serves as an image of the poet's art. From the story of the past can emerge the truth, in words, for each generation. The truth may be constant, but the proclamation of it is an ongoing process. The Latin source omits this material entirely, but the Greek version contains it, and in slightly more detail than the *Andreas* poet uses. It is clear that the text which the Old English author had in mind must have contained some version of the story of the awakening of the patriarchs. But perhaps the point that the *Andreas* poet adapted from his material is that the word has been proclaimed but must always be demonstrated in words. Christ has provided the proof that He is the word made flesh and that He has the power to make His own word incarnate in the three resurrected patriarchs, and the process of re-creating the truth is central to the truth itself. Thus Christ Himself provides the model of how the truth of the past must address itself to the needs of the present.

If the poet's conception is that the truth of the past must be retold for the needs of the present, then the original story suits his purpose well here: at this point the narrative voice again becomes dominant and informs us that Andrew continued to tell the Helmsman wondrous tales for the rest of the day, until sleep overcomes the saint and Christ transports him with his companions to shore. During the voyage, Andrew has been setting up the paradigm for the use of the word as the chief instrument by which the truth may be known and demonstrating the way in which that word made flesh has come to dwell in his heart through his comprehension of the truth. When Andrew is delivered safely to shore to face the test that will pit his faith against physical torments, he reaches an understanding of what he has been through. Paradoxically, Christ does not choose to reveal himself directly but rather through words. Though it is not really clear how Andrew knows, he is aware that the Helmsman was Christ Himself:

> Ic eow [i.e., the thanes] secgan mæg   soð orgete,
> þæt us gyrstandæge   on geofones stream
> ofer arwelan   æðeling ferede;
> in þam ceole wæs   cyninga wuldor,
> waldend werðeode.   Ic his word oncneow,
> þeh he his mægwlite   bemiðen hæfde.                    (851–6)

It is clear in the poet's use of the preterite that he means to imply that some-

how Andrew had already recognized Christ's word as genuinely divine, even
if the outward form of the speaker was disguised. On the other hand, the
source clearly indicates that Andrew's recognition of Christ comes only after
he has been set ashore:

> He [Andrew] was very surprised and hurriedly woke his disciples, saying,
> 'Get up, my brothers and children, get up quickly and let us bless the Lord
> Jesus Christ. Get up. See the great miracles He has done for us; know now
> for certain that the pilot in whose boat we come here and to whom we talked
> was the Lord Jesus Christ. He possessed our eyes so we shouldn't recognize
> Him, and therefore we did not.'                                      (23–4)

The source clearly distinguishes between Christ the person and His words,
and Andrew can easily recognize one without the other. The saint of the poem
seems to sense the very nature of the mystery of the unity of the word and
God.

The actual deeds of Andrew as he confronts the Mermedonians simply
display his now-legitimized power, for he is able to re-enact many miracles
to bring about the conversion of the cannibals. But the interesting part of the
hagiographic process is not really the litany of Andrew's miracles, but the
preparation of the saint to perform them. The poet has taken a scarcely
noticeable feature of the original version and built it into a compelling, artistic
substructure. In translating from the Latin, the poet has recast the slight
nuances about the efficacy of the word found in the source and given his own
reading of the text to heighten the focused and cogent way in which an oral
society might respond to the miracles as products of the word. In translating
from the language of the book to the language of the voice, the artist has, of
course, told the same story: but he also tells a different story, for his version
is also an examination of how the artistic translator may exploit the native,
oral tradition to create a more densely textured version for an audience
nurtured in a different aesthetic, one that demands close attention to the power
of the word. The poet has not just translated: he has transformed so that an
oral-poetic version coexists with a bookish version.

University of Western Ontario


NOTES

1 For example, one could cite: Thomas D. Hill, 'The Tropological Context of
  Heat and Cold Imagery in Anglo-Saxon Poetry,' *Neuphilologische Mittei-*

*lungen* 69 (1968): 522–32; Thomas D. Hill, 'Figural Narrative in *Andreas*: The Conversion of the Mermedonians,' *Neuphilologische Mitteilungen* 70 (1969): 261–73; Penn Szittya, 'The Living Stone and the Patriarchs: Typological Imagery in *Andreas*, Lines 706–810,' *Journal of English and Germanic Philology* 77 (1973): 167–74; Joseph B. Trahern, 'Joshua and Tobias in the Old English *Andreas*,' *Studia Neophilologica* 42 (1970): 330–2; Alvin A. Lee, *The Guest-Hall of Eden: Four Essays on the Design of Old English Poetry* (New Haven and London: Yale University Press 1972); James W. Earl, 'The Typological Structure of *Andreas*,' in John D. Niles, ed., *Old English Literature in Context* (Cambridge and Totowa, N.J.: D.S. Brewer and Rowman and Littlefield 1980); Constance B. Hieatt, 'The Harrowing of Mermedonia: Typological Patterns in the Old English *Andreas*,' *Neuphilologische Mitteilungen* 77 (1976): 49–62. This list is meant only to be illustrative of the substantial body of criticism in the typological/allegorical approach to *Andreas*.

2 Daniel G. Calder, 'Figurative Language and Its Contexts in *Andreas*: A Study in Medieval Expressionism,' in Phyllis Rugg Brown, Georgia Ronan Crampton, and Fred C. Robinson eds, *Modes of Interpretation in Old English Literature: Essays in Honour of Stanley B. Greenfield* (Toronto: University of Toronto Press 1986), 118ff.

3 The question of a source for *Andreas* is generally no longer a debated issue. It seems clear that we do not have a clear source for the work, though there are versions of the original that are close enough to *Andreas* to be most useful. The version that is nearest in most details is the Greek text, most readily available in translation as *Acts of Andrew and Matthias* in Rev. Alexander Roberts and James Donaldson, eds and tr., *The Ante-Nicene Fathers: Writings of the Fathers down to A.D. 325*, vol. 8 (Buffalo: The Christian Literature Company 1886). It is highly likely, though not absolutely certain, that the Old English poet would not have had access to the Greek version and would have relied on a Latin recension. The closest Latin version is to be found translated in Michael J.B. Allen and Daniel G. Calder, tr., *Sources and Analogues of Old English Poetry: The Major Latin Texts in Translation* (Cambridge and Totowa, N.J.: D.S. Brewer and Rowman and Littlefield 1976). The Greek and Latin texts, taken together, give a fairly close sense of what the poet must have had as a working version of the story. Since my argument relies on the general shape of the Latin and Greek versions rather than on a word-by-word comparison, I have, for the sake of convenience, relied on Allen and Calder's translation of the Latin version they deem closest to that which the *Andreas* poet would likely have had at his disposal.

4 One recent study has traced the way in which certain doctrinal shifts helped

shape the *Andreas* poet's manipulation of the material to reflect the concerns of the poet's time. See Robert Boenig, *Saint and Hero: Andreas and Medieval Doctrine* (Lewisburg, Pa: Bucknell University Press 1991).

5  Allen and Calder, tr., *Sources and Analogues*, 15. Unless otherwise noted, references to the source will be from this translation.

6  All quotations are from Kenneth R. Brooks, ed., *Andreas and the Fates of the Apostles* (Oxford: Clarendon Press 1961).

7  It is interesting to note that the later Old English prose recension of the Andrew story introduces the same element of a narrated event while keeping the idea of the casting of lots as central to the event: '*Her segð, þæt æfter þam þe Drihten Hælend Crist to heofonum astah, þæt þa apostoli wæron ætsomne; and hie sendon hlot him betweonum, hwider hyra gehwylc faran scolde to læranne.*' Charles Wycliffe Goodwin, ed., *The Anglo-Saxon Legends of St. Andrew and St. Veronica* (Cambridge: Deighton and MacMillan 1851), 2.

8  See, in particular, Boenig's *Saint and Hero*, which devotes a chapter to the topic of the Eucharist in *Andreas*.

9  The source fairly evenly divides emphasis between the physical and spiritual torments: 'Holding them by force, they would ruthlessly imprison them, pluck out their eyes and give them a harmful draught of poison to drink. This drink had been prepared through the evil spells of magic, so that all who took it lost their senses and were no longer in their right minds; thrust back in prison, they ate hay like oxen or cattle' (15).

10  The source here reads: 'I will not run away from your command. May it not be as I want, but as you do; for I am ready to suffer everything for your sake. Only most of all I pray you of your mercy that you grant me the light of my eyes so I may see how they tear my flesh' (16).

11  The source, as previously noted, is more physical, as it seems to relish the gory details of plucking out eyes and forcing the prisoners to eat hay. The poetic version is more suggestive, by far, in its focus on the details:

Swylc wæs þæs folces    freoðoleas tacen,
unlædra eafoð,    þæt hie eagena gesihð,
hette<n>d heorogrimme,    heafodgimmas,
aget<t>on gealgmode    gara ordum.
Syððan him geblendan    bitere tosomne
dryas þurh dwolcræft    drync unheorne,
se onwende gewit,    wera ingeþanc,
heortan <on> hreðre;    hyge wæs oncyrred,
þæt hie ne murndan    æfter mandreame,
hæleþ heorogrædige,    ac hie hig ond gærs
for meteleaste    meðe gedrehte.          (29–39)

12 In the source, the cattle image is part of the narrative voice. In the poetic
version, the image is transferred into Matthew's prayer (see lines 63–87).
13 The source reads: 'Then the Lord Jesus came down to a city in Greece and
taught His disciples there. He said to blessed Andrew, "Go down to the city
called Mermedonia and enter it, because wicked, evil men who drink men's
blood live there"' (17).
14 For a discussion of this typological convention see Jean Daniélou, *From
Shadows to Reality: Studies in the Biblical Typology of the Fathers*, tr. W.
Hibberd (London: Burns and Oates 1960).
15 '"Believe me, brother, I don't have gold or silver to pay you the fare, nor
even bread as provision." The Lord replied, "Brother, what's this you're
saying: you don't have gold or silver to give us for the crossing, nor even
provisions and supplies?"' (18).

# Speech and the Unspoken
# in *Hamðismál*

T.A. SHIPPEY

The *Hamðismál* has been regarded as structurally incomplete more often than any other poem of the *Edda*. In her edition of 1969 Ursula Dronke cites a string of adverse opinions, which use terms like 'fragmentary' or 'patchwork.'[1] In modern times, with 'reconstruction' out of favour and a general readiness to defend the integrity of ancient texts, these opinions have naturally been challenged; not least by Ursula Dronke herself, who makes out a strong case for the poem's 'artistic excellence,' building on several previous studies at once sympathetic and conservative.[2] Yet still the poem's admirers find it hard to repress the urge to expand the poem. Thus Dronke, between stanzas 5 and 6 of her edition, inserts an eight-line stanza from the *Guðrúnarhvǫt*, with the comment that this must have dropped out through some 'error of transmission,' since Hamthir's words in stanza 6 'could not have been provoked' merely by what we find in stanzas 4 and 5 (*Heroic Poems*, 185). Her argument is a sensible and compelling one, but there are others almost equally so. Sophus Bugge inserted the same stanza as Dronke in his ground-breaking edition of 1876,[3] but went on to include a dozen further lines in his text, with twice as many more strongly urged in the footnotes. While Lee Hollander's translation of 1962 rejects most of these insertions, it nevertheless keeps some of the popular *Guðrúnarhvǫt* stanza and adds several more lines suggested by Svend Grundtvig, with one particularly well-motivated and persuasive one from Hugo Gering.[4]

My point is not to say that this expansive urge is right or wrong, but that it is widespread among both the poem's admirers and its detractors. There must be something in the poem, then, to provoke it: something, indeed, perhaps felt as strongly in ancient times as in modern. While the issue of the *Hamðismál*'s relationship with chapter 42 of the *Vǫlsunga Saga* and section

50 of Snorri's *Skaldskaparmál* is naturally much vexed,[5] a possible explanation for both works would indeed be that their authors knew the poem much
as we have it – the latter cites a phrase from it and the former half of stanza
30 – but that neither could refrain from trying to expand, explain, and
reinterpret the poem in ways analogous to those of modern scholars. Even
the scribe of the Codex Regius himself, it could be argued, shared this
anxiety over the poem's completeness. Just as Hollander adds the 'stage
directions' '(Hamthir said)' or '(Sǫrli said)' to stanzas 13, 15, 28, and 27,
respectively, so the Codex Regius MS adds the line *Hitt qvað þá Hamðir,
inn hugomstóri*, 'Hamthir then spoke, proud in valour,' to stanza 26: only to
have this rejected by Dronke, Hollander, and most others, as an evident error
based on the assumption that stanza 27 (definitely addressed to Hamthir)
must answer stanza 26 (the scribe thought, addressed to Sǫrli). One can
agree at least that many problems in the poem have been caused by uncertainty over who says what. It is however the purpose of this article to argue
that the expansions of medieval writers and modern scholars alike are caused
by unfamiliarity with an ancient and elliptical mode of speech: a mode
which, surprisingly, we are perhaps better placed to understand now than at
any time since the far-off composition of 'the old Hamthir-lay,' *Hamðismál
inn forno* itself.

What has made the difference is the analytic method created by 'pragmatic
linguistics.' Credit for this should be given in the first instance to H.P. Grice,
whose article of 1975, 'Logic and Conversation,' proved extraordinarily
fruitful.[6] It has been followed by many studies, notable among them Geoffrey
Leech's *The Principles of Pragmatics* (1983) and Penelope Brown and
Stephen C. Levinson's *Politeness: Some Universals in Language Usage*, of
1978 (so pre-Leech) but with a second edition of 1987.[7] I have discussed the
ways in which their insights might be applied to heroic poetry elsewhere,[8] but
for the purpose of considering *Hamðismál* only two major ideas are necessary: that of the 'implicature,' taken from Grice, and that of the 'Face
Threatening Act,' or FTA, taken from Brown and Levinson.

Grice's basic and most fruitful idea was this. All conversations, he
proposed, even unsuccessful or confrontational ones, had at bottom a 'Co-
operative Principle,' which he stated as the general rule: 'Make your conversational contribution such as is required, at the stage at which it occurs, by
the accepted purpose or direction of the talk exchange in which you are
engaged.' This principle he then embodied in four maxims, which I give in
abbreviated form as follows:

1 Quantity (a)  Make your contribution as informative as is required.
          (b)  Do not make your contribution more informative than is
             required.

2 Quality   Do not say either (a) what you believe to be false or (b) that for
which you lack adequate evidence.
3 Relation   Be relevant.
4 Manner   Avoid (a) obscurity (b) ambiguity, and be (c) brief (d) orderly.

No speakers of course follow all these rules all the time (not even philosophers of language). Almost all listeners, however, become accustomed to
allowing for 'performance errors' – as when some enthusiastic faculty
member tells his listeners far more about his subject (or theirs) than could
possibly be required. This is a breach of Maxim 1(b), but one caused by self-
centredness or inattention.

Much more serious are breaches of the Co-operative Principle carried out
knowingly. Just because the Co-operative Principle is so generally accepted
as a basis for conversation, if a listener realizes that a speaker is consciously
flouting it, then that listener will assume the flouting has been done for a
purpose; it becomes the listener's job to work out what that purpose is. In
Grice's terms, an 'implicature' has been created: not an implication (something which has been implied), but an implicature (something which is to be
implied). Very commonly, of course, as Leech points out, the speaker's
hidden motive is politeness, a reluctance to put something into words which
nevertheless cannot be entirely suppressed. Implicatures are, however, also
very commonly used aggressively, to create a reproof or a threat for which
the speaker does not wish to take responsibility. And at this point one may
introduce the idea of the FTA or 'Face Threatening Act,' the speech-act
which threatens to disturb the 'face' or positive self-image of the addressee,
and so directly threaten the basis of the Co-operative Principle. In their book
Brown and Levinson consider FTAs in exhaustive and multicultural detail.
Yet their book is after all titled *Politeness*, and challengingly subtitled *Some
Universals in Language Usage*. In view of what they themselves say about
cross-cultural or subcultural differences, one may wonder quite how far
'politeness' and 'co-operation' remain as universals for members of a heroic
society like that of the *Hamðismál*. Even if some aspects are universal, or at
least common to Norse society and our own, there is room for discrepant
reaction to implicatures and FTAs to create just the kind of uncertainty and
compulsive expansion which we see in modern editions and, perhaps,
medieval sagas.

As a test of the theory, one may begin with those implicatures in the poem
which, because of some ingrained cultural continuity, have never caused
modern European commentators any trouble. In stanza 24 Hamthir speaks;
and his words, in Gricean terms, are almost ludicrously irregular. Hamthir and
his brother Sǫrli, urged on to avenge their sister Svanhildr, have broken into
the hall of the Gothic king Iǫrmunrekkr. There one brother cuts off the king's

feet, the other his hands, and throws them in the fire; and Hamthir says (these are the last four lines of eight):

| 'Fœtr sér þú þína, | 'You see your feet - |
|---|---|
| hǫndom sér þú þínom, | You see your hands |
| Iǫrmunrekkr, orpit | Iǫrmunrekkr, flung |
| í eld heitan.' | into the hot fire.' |

One can hardly imagine much more of a breach of Grice's maxim 1(b), 'Do not make your contribution more informative than is required'! *Of course* Iǫrmunrekkr has seen his hands and feet cut off and thrown in the fire. He is hardly likely not to have noticed! Hamthir's four lines contribute *no information at all* to Iǫrmunrekkr or to the conversation.[9] Yet no commentator has bothered to remark on this. All have realized that one has to take these on-their-own-redundant four lines together with the four lines immediately preceding:

| 'Æstir, Iǫrmunrekkr, | 'You were longing, Iǫrmunrekkr, |
|---|---|
| okkarrar kvámo, | for us to come, |
| brœðra sammœðra, | brothers born of the same mother, |
| innan borgar þinnar.' | into your fortress.' |

What Hamthir says in these four lines is true (as we can tell from stanza 21), and so obeys Grice's maxim 2. It may well also obey maxim 3, 'be relevant,' for after all people often forget previous feelings and need to be reminded of them. Nevertheless, the real force of Hamthir's speech at this point lies not in his rule-obeying first four lines, nor in his rule-defying last four, but in the 'implicature' created by the evident gap between them. What he is really saying – and I repeat that all commentators seem to have grasped this without difficulty – is in effect:

a) 'You were longing for us to come into your fortress.
b) ['Well, we have,
c) ['but the results are not what you wanted. For proof of which ...]
d) 'you see your feet, you see your hands, flung into the hot fire.'

Hamthir's speech is a contemptuous taunt, contrasting Iǫrmunrekkr's previous estimation of his own power and the brothers' weakness with the true state now proven. The complete redundancy of its last four lines to any truly 'co-operative' conversation acts only to generate an aggressive implicature of extreme degree but familiar type. The lines say, not 'Do you see your feet?' but 'Do you see your mistake?'

In much the same way, no commentator has paused for long over the force of lines 7 and 8 of stanza 14.[10] In this encounter, Hamthir and Sǫrli, near the

start of their quest for revenge, meet their half-brother Erpr. The details of
their conversation are discussed below; but at what seems to be the end of it,
after a provocative remark from Erpr, we get the lines:

| Kóðo harðan miǫk | Very bold, they said, |
|---|---|
| hornung vera. | the bastard was. |

We are told that the brothers say this in unison, which seems hardly likely,
and we are not told whom they say it to: presumably each other, not Erpr.
Nevertheless, the lines present no difficulty. All modern Anglophone commentators are perfectly familiar with the conversational tactics being employed, laborious though it might be to spell them out. It is notoriously an
extreme Face Threatening Act to discuss someone in front of them without
acknowledging the person's presence; that is what the brothers do in speaking
to each other rather than replying to Erpr. The use of the word *hornungr* or
'bastard' has been a standard insult from ancient times to now, even when the
insult is not factually true, as may well be the case here.[11] Nor is there any
problem in interpreting the brothers' apparent compliment – 'he is very bold'
– as an insult. In an unmistakably insulting frame an apparent compliment (in
order to 'be relevant' and obey Grice's maxim 3) must be taken as a further
and deeper insult. The brothers are not being simply sarcastic, for Erpr clearly
is 'very bold' at this moment. What they mean is that he is very bold *for a
bastard* (courage being the birthright of the *goðbornir* or 'god-descended' like
themselves); and that this inappropriate boldness must be put in its place.
Remarks of this kind are common practice in modern barrooms.

Yet if stanzas like 24 and the end of 14 remain easily comprehensible,
because their conversational tactics happen to have remained familiar, one has
to go only a little farther up the ladder of implicatures and FTAs to find
problems arising. Take, for instance, the first conversation of the *Hamðismál*
(there are four in all),[12] that between Guthrun and her sons, Hamthir and Sǫrli.
This is a *hvǫt* or 'whetting,' and there is indeed a specific Old Norse verb for
what Guthrun is doing, *eggja*, 'to incite' or 'egg on.' English has no similarly
precise verb or noun in common use, and the scene, along with the revenge-
cult it derives from, is no longer culturally familiar. Just the same, the
opening of Guthrun's speech at least can be explained in the terms already
used. Guthrun says to her two sons (stanza 3):

| 'Syster var ykkor | 'Your sister |
|---|---|
| Svanhildr um heitin, | was called Svanhildr, |
| sú er Iǫrmunrekkr | whom Iǫrmunrekkr |
| ióm um traddi | trampled with his chargers |

| hvítom ok svǫrtom | white and black |
| á hervegi, | on the common highway, |
| grám, gangtǫmom | with the gray, smooth-paced |
| Gotna hrossom.' | horses of the Goths.' |

The last four lines of this are evidently redundant, but the redundancy produces no decisive implicature; it seems to be part of the repetitive and appositional style of heroic poetry. The first four lines, however, form another
unmistakable example of the aggressive implicature. Just as with stanza 24,
what the speaker says here can convey *no direct information at all* to her
hearers. 'Your sister was called Svanhildr': they know that! 'Iǫrmunrekkr had
her trampled': they know that too. Why is their mother telling them known
facts as if they were an unknown history? Since she is unlikely (maxim 1[b])
to be speaking merely pointlessly, it is the brothers' duty to search for an
implicature: in this case, obviously, the unspoken questions, 'Have you
forgotten? If you haven't forgotten, why have you done nothing? Do you need
to be reminded?'

In this circumstance, Guthrun's next two remarks are equally unmistakable
(stanza 4):

| 'Eptir er ykr þrungit, | 'You have been crushed back, |
| þióðkonunga – | you kings of nations – |
| lifið einir ér | only you remain |
| þátta ættar minnar.' | of the strands of my race.' |

One notes that the latter two lines, like *harðan miǫk* in stanza 14, could be
construed in other circumstances as a compliment or a statement of affection.
In its aggressive frame, though, the remark has to be taken as further
aggression. Guthrun is saying, in effect and in logical rather than scornful
order:

a) You have forgotten your sister,
b) and you are the only ones I have left, so
c) the true royal race is much reduced.

The implicature of these statements is very obviously not d) the pair of you
are all I have left, and so are precious to me, but d) the pair of you are
degenerate from your ancestors, who would never have needed these reminders.

Guthrun goes on with a stanza, 5, which is self-pitying, a play for sympathy, and a switch in tactics. But we come now to the issue of whether, at this
point, one needs to supply a stanza from the *Guðrúnarhvǫt*, as suggested by
both Bugge and Dronke. In the stanza which they would insert, Guthrun goes

on, as it were, from (c) above, to say openly: 'You have not grown like [your uncles Gunnarr and Họgni] ... You would have sought to avenge [Svan-hildr's] death, if you had had the spirit of my brothers ...' It is quite true that this stanza from another poem does follow on with perfect logic from what Guthrun has said in the *Hamðismál*. But since the logic is so perfect, and so perfectly obvious, do the words actually need to be said? Implicatures work by silence. The aggression in them comes often from their contemptuous assumption that what is said is obvious, would not need saying except to a fool. In such a case there is something to be gained by leaving *out* the obvious conclusion to a train of thought. It would be characteristic, too, for a later reworker like the poet of the *Guðrúnarhvọt* to feel an urge to put it *in* – finding the implicature at the edge of speech, as it were, too teasing to suppress. This expansive urge is then naturally felt and duplicated by modern scholars. But while the inserted stanza does indeed focus and put into words the train of thought created by the stanzas which are there, we should realize that all it does is to verbalize an implicature. It adds nothing new.[13]

Hamthir's reply to his mother then steps up at least one level of difficulty. His speech in stanzas 6–9 contains a strong element of description, more even than stanza 3 already quoted, but can be paraphrased as: 'You would once upon a time have praised your brothers little, when they murdered your husband Sigurthr. As for your revenge on Atli, it hurt you more than him.' He closes with four lines not present in the *Guðrúnarhvọt* (which has taken over much of this speech) and described by Dronke as 'cynically sententious' (*Heroic Poems*, 151):

| | |
|---|---|
| 'Svá skyldi hverr ọðrom | 'One should encompass |
| veria til aldrlaga | another's death |
| sverði sárbeito | with wound-cutting sword |
| at sér né stríddit.' | without hurting oneself.' |

It is notable that this speech says nothing about Svanhildr, the subject they are discussing. It is also strongly marked by litotes: 'You would once have praised Họgni's prowess little' means 'You were once bitterly hurt by Họgni's prowess and had every reason to lament it.' When Hamthir describes Sigurthr's death to his mother, he is of course also telling her something she knows much better than he does. Is he not once again deliberately flouting the spirit of Grice's maxims 3 ('be relevant,' that is, stick to Svanhildr), 4(a) ('avoid obscurity,' that is, do not talk in understatements and general maxims), and 1(b) ('do not tell your listener what she knows already')? If so, implicatures should be generated, and clearly they are: though it is less absolutely clear than before *what* they are.

As a response to Guthrun's speech, Hamthir's implies, by its contradictions:
a) You have been praising your dead relatives.
b) You seem to have forgotten what they cost you.
c) I will remind you, in detail.
The implicature of that reminder, if it is to be relevant to Svanhildr, must then be something like:
d) If Sǫrli and I have taken no action, it is because we remember the cost of revenge, which you have forgotten. So we can tell that past disasters will be repeated. That is why we have not avenged Svanhildr.
But by this stage Hamthir could be seen to imply many things. He could be rejecting his mother's plea for sympathy – you did it to yourself. He could be answering her Face Threatening Act with a Face Rehabilitating Act – we are not afraid, we are wise. His move into sententiousness could be taken as 'cynical' or as resigned – for, of course, one thing he does *not* say is 'we refuse to go.' Sǫrli at this point indeed breaks in with a comment on the increasingly complex and unproductive nature of the implied accusations being made:

| 'Vilkat ek við móður | 'I will not argue |
|---|---|
| málom skipta. | with my mother. |
| Orz þikkir enn vant | Each of you thinks |
| ykro hváro.' | there is more to be said.' |

His censure of his brother for bandying words (unmanly by tradition), turns to direct censure of his mother, and to a statement that the pattern now *will* be repeated: they will do her wishes, and she will lose the last two remaining of her blood-relatives. Not said, but hanging unspoken, is the thought that if she had not wanted them both dead she should not have called them cowards.

Yet it is neither this conversation nor the one in Iǫrmunrekkr's hall which shows most clearly the poem's reliance on 'pragmatic' decoding. Those two demonstrate that *Hamðismál* does work through gaps and silences, and also indicate reassuringly that some of the tactics used have remained familiar enough for modern readers to grasp them. What has caused consistent trouble to all commentators, however, is the conversation in stanzas 12–14 between Hamthir and Sǫrli on the one hand, and their paternal half-brother Erpr on the other. Even the order of speeches is disputed. The manuscript's stanzas 12, 13, and 14 have commonly since Bugge been rearranged as 13, 14, 12. The reasons for this are compelling: MS stanza 13 (new order 12) appears to open with a meeting, which should be the start of the conversation. MS stanza 12 (new order 14) ends with the word *hornungr*, 'bastard,' after which one would expect words to turn to blows. Nevertheless, even after reordering, the way the characters speak to each other, especially Erpr, has seemed opaque and indeed infuriating to more than one modern critic.

If one accepts the 'Bugge Shift,' the conversation between Hamthir and Sǫrli (sons of Guthrun and Iónakr) and Erpr (son of Iónakr and a woman not named) goes as follows:

1 Erpr: Can I help you? or, I want to help you. [This statement is completely absent from the poem as it stands. It can be inferred only from what follows.]

2 Hamthir, or Sǫrli, or both together: 'How will this brown pigmy help us?' [Direct speech, no speaker named.]

3 Erpr, here *inn sundrmæðri*, 'son of a different mother': 'He said that he would give help to his kinsmen as one foot to another.' [Indirect speech: strictly speaking, coloured indirect speech – indirect speech which nevertheless preserves within it some of the exact words of the speaker.][14]

4 Hamthir and/or Sǫrli again, again in direct speech: 'How can a foot help a foot, or a hand grown from the body's flesh help a hand?'

5 Erpr, in direct speech for the first time, indeed signalled as *kvað ... eino sinni*, 'spoke a single speech':

| | |
|---|---|
| 'Illt er blauðom hal | 'No good comes |
| brautir kenna.' | of showing a coward the way.' |

6 The lines already quoted from Hamthir and Sǫrli, this time in indirect speech, and seemingly spoken jointly: 'Very bold, they said, the bastard was.'

After this, if one still accepts the 'Bugge shift,' the two brothers kill the third and continue on their way.

Whatever else one thinks of it, this conversation is very strongly marked – more so than any of the others in the poem – by the tactics of the Face Threatening Act, their effect exaggerated by the skilful and deliberate way in which the poet moves in and out of direct speech. The only speech of the six indicated which might *not* contain an FTA is the one the poet does not give. Presumably Erpr must have offered his two half-brothers help, or they would not ask 'How?'; and offers of help are unlikely to contain any FTA directly.[15] But the poet with characteristic economy forces us to infer the offer from the refusal. Speech 2, meanwhile, must be a refusal of sorts, though it contains no direct 'No.' It is however an FTA on at least three levels. First, the brothers do not talk to Erpr directly, but to each other as if he were not there. Second, they use the term *iarpskammr*, 'brown pigmy,' in their terms a double insult. Third, they doubt his ability to help. The multiple nature of this FTA ought to make Erpr either retreat or retaliate. Only the fact that it has not been said directly to him leaves some faint loophole for continued co-operation, which Erpr attempts to take. Yet his next remark has become significantly 'non-Gricean.' Its simile – he would help his kinsmen *sem fótr ǫðrom*, 'as one foot another' – is obscure, and so in breach of maxim 4(a). What he says is also highly elliptical, so breaching maxim 1(a). It was indeed at this point that Hugo Gering suggested that another line was needed: Hamthir and Sǫrli's reply mentions feet *and hands*, Erpr's speech only feet.[16] Surely something has dropped out? But what is missing may be more significant than a mere verbal variation.

What Erpr is doing here is to cite a proverb. *Hamðismál* is insistently proverbial. Hamthir has already broken into a traditional sententiousness in stanza 8. In stanza 14 Erpr again speaks proverbially. Sǫrli uses maxims in stanzas 26 and 27, and Hamthir – if it is Hamthir – all but ends the poem with one in stanza 30. Since all three speakers in this scene use and value proverbs, it makes sense to suggest that Erpr is here offering his brothers one – or rather, offering his half-brothers half of one. This is again a Face Threatening Act. An ellipsis demands an implicature. It may also, if it tests a hearer's understanding, represent a challenge. Few things are more irritating than the lifted eyebrow of superior knowledge. Yet if the listeners here were to complete the proverb and pass the test, both the FTA of speech 3, Erpr's, and that of speech 2, Hamthir and Sǫrli's, would be wiped out. For the proverb Erpr alludes to, in full form, would be something like: 'Brother helps brother, as one foot helps another.'[17] The true force of the insult to Erpr in speech 2, this suggests, was not what was said – *iarpskammr*, etc., – but what was *not* said. Specifically, he was not greeted as *bróðir*, 'brother.'[18] In his speech 3, then, Erpr offers a choice. Complete my proverb; pass the test of knowledge; use the word 'brother' to me; accept my offer of kinship and my offer of help; and I will treat the FTA of your last speech as a misunderstanding, while there will be no FTA to you in what I have just said. Or, fail to understand the proverb, in which case what I have just said becomes retrospectively an FTA, designed to expose your stupidity.

The two sons of Guthrun fail this test, merely repeating Erpr's words interrogatively. Erpr then speaks for the last time, entirely proverbially: 'It is no good showing a coward the way.' The force of this remains by no means clear. Carl Wesle, indeed, was forced by it into a by-no-means-unreasonable expostulation against the post-Bugge reading of the whole scene. How can Erpr call the other two cowards, he protests: 'the reproach of cowardice just at this moment, when the brothers have committed themselves to the endlessly dangerous, foolhardy deed of vengeance is the most senseless that one can imagine.' No, Wesle concluded, Erpr could not have said that to their faces at that point. He must have said it to himself, the words 'are a monologue.'

He did so before he knew the others had made their minds up, while still wondering whether they *were* cowards. This stanza should then return to its manuscript place before speeches 1–4, and the killing of Erpr be motivated (as indeed in *Vǫlsunga saga* and *Skaldskaparmál*) only by the 'foot and hand' proverb. As for that proverb itself, it contains 'no trace of scorn and derision,' while Erpr's refusal to see 'the contemptuous tone' of the others' question, Wesle argues, is 'an especially fine stroke.'[19]

Wesle's reinterpretation, still followed by H. Reuschel in her specifically proverbial study of 1939 (see note 17 above) is I believe unacceptable, but it does pose one very pointed question: how can anyone possibly call Hamthir and Sǫrli cowards? The answer, I suggest, is as follows. Erpr has not exactly called Hamthir and Sǫrli cowards. Instead, he has stated a proverb, and invited the others, in accordance with Grice's maxim 3, to ponder its relevance. In modern English culture the further unspoken statement would be: 'If the cap fits, wear it:' that is, if *you* consider my remark applicable to yourselves, do so, but if you do not, then assume nothing has been said. What does seem relevant to Hamthir and Sǫrli is the words about 'showing the way.' This has again been taken as a literal statement – Hamthir and Sǫrli need Erpr as a guide![20] But obviously Erpr has been 'showing them the way' in a non-literal fashion: a way towards co-operation, the annulment of verbal FTAs, ultimate success. He did that with his first, cunning proverb depending on the unspoken word *bróðir*. When they failed to recognize and complete it, they rejected his guidance. He now has to answer their FTA with one of his own.[21] And that will in its turn lead literally to 'no good' for Erpr, indeed to his death. What Erpr is saying in his proverb, then, is:

    a) I gave you a chance but you didn't take it.
    b) It was a weakness in you not to take it.
    c) That weakness will now rebound on me.

Hamthir and Sǫrli are hardly *blauðir*, 'cowards,' but then Erpr is probably not a *hornungr* or 'bastard.' FTAs are in approximate balance. The whole conversation has been dominated by Erpr, first trying to steer it positively, then accepting and accentuating the others' negation. Hamthir and Sǫrli's final remark, as has been said above, is in its sarcasm and its refusal to acknowledge another's presence a mere barroom commonplace, devoid of wit.

The killing of Erpr at this point is disastrous, as is noted in all versions of the story. Hamthir and Sǫrli needed Erpr, not for them to kill Iǫrmunrekkr, but for them to do so *and escape*.[22] This again is signalled by a speech-failure, in this case Hamthir's speech of stanza 24, quoted on page 184 above. Having mutilated Iǫrmunrekkr, Hamthir stops to taunt him. And Iǫrmunrekkr, for almost the only time in the poem, replies like someone who has paid attention to Professor Grice! He speaks relevantly, clearly, truthfully, and saying neither too much nor too little:[23]

| | |
|---|---|
| 'Grýtið ér á gumna, | 'Stone the men, |
| allz geirar né bíta, | since spears will not pierce them, |
| eggiar né iárn, | neither swords nor steel, |
| Iónakrs sono.' | the sons of Iónakr.' |

His advice is taken, and both Hamthir and Sǫrli are killed. What exactly is the mistake that Hamthir and Sǫrli have made? They broke a taboo to do with stones, says the *Vǫlsunga saga*.[24] They did not follow their mother's instructions, suggests Snorri in the *Skaldskaparmál*.[25] The answer of the *Hamðismál*, surely, is that Hamthir in particular *talked too much*. That is the point of the one phrase in the poem repeated by all three authorities, in stanza 28:

| | |
|---|---|
| 'Af væri nú hǫfuð, | 'Off would be the head now, |
| ef Erpr lifði' | if Erpr were living.' |

In saying this, Hamthir – Snorri and *Vǫlsunga* both ascribe the saying to Hamthir, though the poem does not – accepts that if they had taken Erpr with them, he would have acted instead of talking. Untaunted, Iǫrmunrekkr would not have spoken or had the chance to speak, and they would have fought their way out, invulnerable to iron, as they fought their way in. And the next word in Hamthir's speech is *bróðir*:

| | |
|---|---|
| 'bróðir okkarr inn bǫðfrœkni | 'our battle-brave brother, |
| er vit á braut vágom' | whom we killed on the road.' |

He has finally supplied the missing word from Erpr's test proverb, understood his brother's implicature – and learnt the value of silence. The point is rubbed in by the brief, and to the scribe of the Codex Regius, seemingly baffling stanzas from Sǫrli, 26 and 27, each of which ends in a proverb: 27 with the straightforward 'a man lacks much when he lacks a brain,' 26 with the metaphorical 'bold counsels come often from a bleeding bag' (that is, Iǫrmunrekkr, the 'bag' opened by Hamthir's taunts). The proverbs say 'You were a fool to open the bag of speech.'

*Hamðismál* continues to offer problems of similar nature almost to its last line. Is it Sǫrli who says both stanzas 26 and 27? Is it Hamthir who says 28? Does Sǫrli speak in stanzas 29–30 or is it Hamthir who continues? Is stanza 29 (in different metre from the rest of the poem) an interpolation? However, enough has perhaps been said here to make out this larger proposition. *Ham-*

*ðismál* has been viewed convincingly as a poem about hands and feet, about co-operation;[26] and as a poem about the *sammæðrir* and the *sundrmæðr*, about the strains of blood and marriage.[27] I would suggest that it is also a poem about the art of speech. Its position, to modern ears, is paradoxical. It appears not to value plain-spokenness. Its major hero, Erpr, is a master of the art of obscure and proverbial statements, which continually set listeners problems of interpretation. Erpr would appear to be valued also in the end for not permitting speech; while Sǫrli, the wiser of the two full brothers, scorns speech both at the end, when he rebukes Hamthir for his fatal taunt, and at the beginning, when he censures both Hamthir and Guthrun for talking too much, *Orz þikkir enn vant ykro hváro*, 'each of you thinks there is more to be said.' Both Guthrun and Hamthir precipitate disaster by talking.

Yet, at the same time, more than half the poem (124 lines out of 220) consists of speech, and all the named characters (except Iǫrmunrekkr) feel strongly the fascination of riddling talk. While words are dispraised as mere talk, cheap talk, they are also in an obvious way vital: once said, they cannot be withdrawn. Perhaps one should conclude in the end that to the poet (and his culture) words were intrinsically dangerous, threatening, and challenging. Because of this, on the one hand saying nothing was strongly prized, along with the maxim that 'deeds speak louder than words.'[28] On the other, the most valued of the arts of speech was to create meaning without saying it, exploiting strong cultural awareness of something like Grice's maxims, but in a way which can only be tenuously attached to a 'Co-operative Principle.' The heroes of the poem, one might also say, show a fierce attachment to Grice's maxims 2 and 1(b) ('be truthful' and 'do not say more than necessary'). They operate on the very edge of 1(a) ('say as much as is necessary'); and demand the utmost from their listeners in finding the implicatures from Maxim 3 ('be relevant'). As for the final catch-all Maxim about avoiding ambiguity and obscurity, the heroes have no feeling for that at all. The obscure and understated is their natural mode. Those who cannot cope with that disqualify themselves *ipso facto* as potential heroes. The tragedy of *Hamðismál* is not just that Hamthir is a poor speaker, a man who talks too much, but that he is a poor listener – he and Sǫrli are condemned to death not when they react to Guthrun but when they fail to understand Erpr's deliberately incomplete proverb. If they had understood it, the ultimately fatal taunt would not have been uttered.

One weakness in the general argument of this paper is simply that it does not seem to have been put before. In this view, the medieval and native-speaker readers of the *Hamðismál* who wrote *Vǫlsunga saga* and the *Skaldskaparmál* did not understand the poem, for (among other things) neither of them realizes that the point of *Af væri hǫfuð* is to prevent the command of stoning.[29] The Codex Regius scribe meanwhile failed to identify the course of the central conversation, and attributed stanzas to the wrong speakers. As for nineteenth- and twentieth-century critics, their urge is overpoweringly to fill in the gaps: the gaps in which, I suggest, the poem's implicatures expand. Views as idiosyncratic as this demand some overall explanation to commend themselves.

If one may be offered, I would propose this. For many centuries, including those of the *Vǫlsunga saga* and the *Skaldskaparmál*, educated people have been taught to value the arts of literacy, which include argumentative fullness and verbal clarity. They have at the same time been taught to ignore or dispraise the arts of speech, which may rely on facial expression, tone of voice, gesture, or even significant non-response. These arts have, of course, continued to be practised. But not till the advent of tape-recorder and video-camera could they be replayed, reviewed, and analysed. If 'the old lay of Hamthir' was indeed known to Torf-Einarr, Jarl of the Orkneys, *c.* 890, and survived in some form or other all the way through to Lübeck in 1560 (see Dronke, *Heroic Poems,* 1: 214–17, 221–4), then it may perhaps preserve for us some indication of the complexity and power of pre-literary art. In such a view it is not boastful to claim a 'new reading,' but salutary to think how much effort it takes to achieve an 'old hearing.' The poet of the *Hamðismál* was at home in modes to which modern philosophers of language are only starting to reach out.

Saint Louis University


NOTES

1 Ursula Dronke, ed., *The Poetic Edda: Vol. 1, The Heroic Poems* (Oxford: Clarendon Press 1969), 168. All subsequent quotations and translations are from this edition.

2 Ibid., 168–92 *passim.* See also Caroline Brady, 'The Date and Metre of the *Hamðismál,*' *Journal of English and Germanic Philology* 38 (1939): 201–16, and A.J. Brodeur and Caroline Brady, '*Sundrmœðri – sammœðra,*' *Scandinavian Studies* 16 (1940–1): 113–28.

3 Sophus Bugge, '*Hamðismál*: aus den Vorarbeiten zu einer neuen Ausgabe der sogennanten Sæmundar Edda,' *Zeitschrift für Deutsche Philologie* 7 (1876): 377–406, 454.

4 Lee M. Hollander, tr., *The Poetic Edda,* 2nd ed. (Austin: University of Texas Press 1962), 316–21.

5 Dronke, *Heroic Poems,* 1: 177–80, summarizes a long scholarly debate.

6 H.P. Grice, 'Logic and Conversation,' in Peter Cole and Jerry L. Morgan, eds, *Speech Acts*, Syntax and Semantics 3 (New York: Academic Press 1975), 41–58, repr. in H. Paul Grice, *Studies in the Way of Words* (Cambridge, Mass., and London: Harvard University Press 1989), 22–40.

7 Geoffrey Leech, *The Principles of Pragmatics* (London and New York: Longman 1983) and Penelope Brown and Stephen C. Levinson, *Politeness: Some Universals in Language Usage,* 2nd ed. (Cambridge: Cambridge University Press 1987).

8 T.A. Shippey, 'Principles of Conversation in Beowulfian Speech,' in John M. Sinclair, et al., eds, *Techniques of Description: Spoken and Written Discourse (A Festschrift for Malcolm Coulthard)* (London and New York: Routledge 1993), 109–26.

9 They do, of course, contribute information to the poem, in which the event is only announced in dialogue and after the fact. Nevertheless, as one imagines the scene, Hamthir is still saying what is shockingly obvious.

10 Once, that is, the force of the word *hornungr* was grasped. Bugge, reluctant to see the speech as an FTA, ascribes it to Erpr, '*Hamðismál*,' 401.

11 Both *Skaldskaparmál* and *Vǫlsunga saga* see all three as full brothers, children of Guthrun and Iónakr. Even if Erpr is 'the child of a different mother,' as in *Hamðismál*, it is not impossible that his mother was also a wife of Iónakr. In the poem, a critical if unstated point is of course that Erpr has no blood relationship to Svanhildr through either his father or his mother: he is offering a generous extension of his kinship duties.

12 I do not discuss the third, in stanzas 19–22, in which the arrival of the two brothers is reported to Iǫrmunrekkr, and a female figure appears to try to dissuade them.

13 Except the names of Guthrun's brothers and her reference to the Hunnish kings. However, in view of her remark about her relatives there can be little doubt whom she means by the *þióðkonungar*. Hamthir would not need prompting to bring in the references to Gunnarr, Hǫgni, and Atli in stanzas 6–8. On the other hand, since he does mention them, a gap-filler (like, perhaps, the poet of the *Guðrúnarhvǫt*) would find it easy to 'reconstruct' the disputed stanza by spelling out the implicature of Guthrun, amplified by the response of Hamthir. See Dronke, *Heroic Poems*, 1: 185, for the opposed view.

14 See Norman Page, *Speech in the English Novel* (London: Longman 1973) ch. 2, 'Methods of Speech-presentation,' 32ff.

15 Though it is possible, in some societies, that the very act of offering help may be felt as intrusive or insulting: see Brown and Levinson, *Politeness*, 14, on the negative reactions of Apache culture to modern American 'positive politeness.'

16  See Hollander, *Poetic Edda*, 319. Hollander gives no original reference for Gering's suggestion.

17  See H. Reuschel, 'Wie ein Fuss dem Anderen: zum Aufbau des *Hamðismál*,' *Beiträge zur Geschichte der Deutschen Sprache und Literatur* 63 (1939): 237–50.

18  This is in direct contrast to the similar scene between half-brothers in the *Hlǫðskviða*. Here Angantýr greets his half-brother as *bróðir* in the second line of his first speech. Compromise is, however, destroyed by Gizurr's use of the word *hornungr* eight stanzas later.

19  See Carl Wesle, 'Die Sage von Ermenrichs Tod,' *Beiträge zur Geschichte der Deutschen Sprache und Literatur* 46 (1921–2), 248–65, esp. 254–6. In 262–3 Wesle is obliged by the logic of his position to argue against any parallel with the *Hlǫðskviða*. The translations from Wesle's German are my own.

20  Wesle considers this idea but rejects it, 'Die Sage,' 254.

21  In my article, 'Principles of Conversation,' cited in note 8 above, I suggest that in the Beowulfian society it is a point of honour to answer any FTA in kind and with a similar degree of severity.

22  Reuschel, in the article cited twice already, points out that our three major Old Norse sources for this story offer between them four conditions for a successful revenge on Iǫrmunrekkr, such as killing him in his sleep, not breaking a taboo on not molesting stones, etc. *Hamðismál* is the only account in which the two full brothers 'fall, because they do not understand the clever answer of their half-brother Erpr.'

23  The only redundancies are the variations of *geirar* by *eggiar né iárn* and of *gumna* by *Iónakrs sono* – ascribable, as with those in Guthrun's stanza 3, to the appositional nature of the poetic style.

24  See *Vǫlsunga saga*, ch. 42 in Guthni Jónsson, ed., *Fornaldar sögur Norður-landa*, vol. 1 (Reykjavik: Islendingasagnaútgáfan 1976), 217–18.

25  See Arni Björnsson, ed., *Snorra Edda* (Reykjavik: Skálholt h.f. 1975), 170–1.

26  See Reuschel, 'Wie ein Fuss dem Anderen.'

27  See Brodeur and Brady, *Sundrmæðri*.

28  I do not find this maxim in so many words in the collection of *Íslenzkir Málshættir* edited by Bjarni Vilhjálmsson and Oskar Halldórsson (Reykjavik: Almenna Bókafélagið 1966), though there are several maxims praising silence and cautioning against speech. It does exist in Old English: see Ælfric, 'On the Old and New Testament,' lines 1257–8, in S.J. Crawford, ed., *The Old English Heptateuch*, Early English Text Society, OS 160 (London: Oxford University Press 1922), 74, *weorc sprecað swiþor þonne þa nacodan word.*

29 As Dronke points out, *Heroic Poems*, 177, in both Snorri and *Vǫlsunga* the command to stone the brothers, from Iǫrmunrekkr or from Othinn, comes only *after* Hamthir's cry, whereas the cry should surely be a vain response to it.

# Heroic Aspects of
# the Exeter Book Riddles

ERIC GERALD STANLEY

Late twentieth-century readers of individual poets or of single works or groups of works of poetry will distrust generalizations about poetry as a whole. If it were not for that distrust I might have turned to Anglo-Saxon riddling in a generalizing spirit, like that of Socrates in the Platonic dialogue *Alcibiades*, assuming that we understand exactly what Plato, probably pseudo-Plato, means when he reports Socrates as saying of Homer that 'he speaks in riddles' (in the usual translation of the verb *ainíssomai*):[1]

> He, like almost every other poet, speaks in riddles. For poetry as a whole is by nature inclined to riddling, and it is not every man who can apprehend it. And furthermore, besides having this natural tendency, when it gets hold of a grudging person who [in his poetry] wishes not to show forth to us his own wisdom but to conceal it as much as possible, we find it an extraordinarily difficult matter whatever this or that one of them may mean.

The etymology of Greek *ainíssomai*, in the words of an etymologist of Greek, Chantraine, '"dire des paroles significatives", donc difficiles à comprendre' and *aínigma* 'obscure utterance, riddle,' is itself obscure, and any statement gravid with significativeness will have the reader or audience guessing, whether through authorial intention or not. Though in some Old English poetry, as often throughout the history of poetry, obscurity, and therefore a reader's puzzlement, may be an unintentional result of the use of figurative language, or, as Socrates seems to allege, the result of the essential indirection of almost all poetry, the Anglo-Saxon poets do not appear to have produced deliberate obscurity, except for riddles. I do not mean to puzzle anyone by using in the title the word *aspect*, but it may be wondered if its sense here goes beyond a specious seeming, that is, beyond an assumed heroic manner, to reveal what lies deep within: an heroic world of thought and feeling, the conception of heroes expressed in the only language fit for heroes. The double-edgedness of the word *aspect* is consonant with one of the earlier and best writers on the riddles of the Anglo-Saxons in Latin and in the vernacular, Adolf Ebert, commenting on the originality of the Exeter Book Riddles: 'A characteristic, entirely national style of [poetic] art rules them.'[2] The 'entirely national style of art' is my main subject.

The Anglo-Saxons, without sharing our idea of literature as an art, would probably have understood poetic form; they might even, like early Anglo-Saxonists, have thought of it in terms of song. If they understood poetic kinds at all, they would certainly have understood that the riddle is a poetic kind, and the intellectuals in any Anglo-Saxon centre which might have produced a compilation like the Exeter Book would have seen the relationship between the vernacular and the Latin riddles as clearly as did Ebert. For whatever reason, they included one Latin riddle among more than ninety in Old English.

Even in a paper on heroic aspects, the Latin *Riddle 90*[3] deserves a place. It is the only Latin poem in the whole of the Exeter Book. A wolf and a lamb, and more wolves, are prominent in the five lines of the riddle. The mere mention of wolf sent an early hunt of scholars in wild pursuit of Cynewulf, and, as a better poet says, *Baldely þay blw prys* in self-deluding celebration. It is an odd poem, reminiscent of wolf and lamb in Isaiah's famous chapter 11, important for Christ's descent from Jesse:[4] 'The woolfe shal dwel with the lambe.'

| | |
|---|---|
| Mirum uidetur mihi,   lupus ab agno tenetur | It seems wonderful to me: a wolf is held by a lamb! |
| obcubuit agnus *rupi*   et capit uiscera lupi. | The lamb lay resting on a rock and seizes the wolf's guts. |
| Dum starem et misarem,   uidi gloriam magna*m*: | While I stood and marvelled I saw a great glory: |
| dui lupi stantes   et tertium tribul*antes*: | two wolves standing and oppressing a third: |
| Quattuor pedes habebant,   cum septem oculis uidebant. | they had four feet, they saw with seven eyes. |

Prophetic books are easily exploited for number symbolism. Verse 2 of the same chapter of Isaiah introduces the Seven Gifts of the Holy Spirit: 'the spirit of wisdom, and vnderstanding, the spirit of counsel, and strength, the spirit of knowlege, and pietie, and the spirit of the feare of our Lord.' That these could be the seven eyes of the last line of the riddle may be explained in the light, or darkness, of Apocalypse 5:6: 'a Lambe standing as it were slaine, hauing seuen hornes & seuen eies: which are the seuen spirites of God, sent into al the earth.' That connection was first made by an early commentator on the riddle, Henry Morley:[5]

> The marvel of the Lamb that overcame the wolf and tore its bowels out is of the Lamb of God who overcame the devil and destroyed his power, ...
>     The great glory then seen was of "the lamb that had been slain," the Divine appointment of the agony of one of the three Persons of the Trinity. The four feet were the four Gospels; and the seven eyes refer to the Book of Revelation, where the seven eyes are the seven Spirits of God sent forth into all the earth.

Morley goes on to suggest tentatively in a footnote: 'the two wolves might be the Old and the New Testament troubling the devil, and having the four Gospels upon which their teaching stands.' If in this riddle the wolves stand for the Persons of the Trinity, as Morley suggests, Father and Holy Ghost appointing the Son's agony, then Father and Son provide the Trinity's total of four feet (line 5a), whereas the Third Person has the seven eyes of the Spirit, so that in the last line as in the preceding line the great glory is the Trinity. The devil is not infrequently given the appellation 'wolf,' for example, in John 10:1–16, especially verse 12 on the good Pastor of his flock of sheep: 'and the woulfe raueneth, and disperseth the sheepe.' The Father and the Son as virtuous wolves are not easily found in patristic writings; and I hope that someone learned in Patristics will give me what has eluded me. At the same time, I hope that it will be from some obvious source, so that I shall not have that uneasy Swiftian sense of

> As learn'd Commentators view
> In *Homer* more than *Homer* knew,[6]

which overcomes me from time to time as I read the writings of those of my Anglo-Saxonist colleagues who are learned in Patristics. I mention the Latin riddle only because the heroic reader of Anglo-Saxon verse might feel that when he or she comes to the wolf a good Wodenism is in sight: that feeling cannot last long for a riddle the solution of which I believe to be, probably on insufficient grounds, 'The Trinity.'

The last riddle of the Exeter Book, No. 95 in the numbering of the Anglo-Saxon Poetic Records, may show that in this poetic genre vernacular poets had some self-awareness, especially if the right solution were 'riddle'

(Trautmann) or 'riddle book' (Pinsker and Ziegler);[7] but that is far from certain. Perhaps it is natural for a bookish reader to wish that the collection should be rounded off with a riddle on riddling, even if the reader despises bookishness, at least in others:[8] 'one might suspect it to be a kind of monkish colophon to the collection,' says Wyatt who regards this riddle as 'a poor composition and not worth further discussion,' while pointing to the textual problems and the uncertainty of the solution; 'the ultimate in meta-linguistic level-switching and a programme for research,' says Barley in an anthropological and structural reading of the poem which fails to come to grips with the Old English text of the riddle, while turning its 'composer' into the prototype of an incoherent academic. The solution 'riddle' or 'riddle book' is based on the last sentence of the poem, which indeed forms a good end to any collection of *enigmata*, and a good beginning therefore to any discussion of them:

> Þeah nu ælda bearn,
> londbuendra,   lastas mine
> swiþe secað,   ic swaþe hwilum
> mine bemiþe   monna gehwylcum.

Though the children of men, dwellers on earth, do greatly seek my tracks, I conceal my path, time and again, from everyone of mankind.

I agree with Kevin Crossley-Holland's comment:[9] 'It would be pleasant to think that the poet or poets who composed the *Exeter Book* riddle collection rounded it off with a riddle about a riddle, but neither this nor the other proposals [Crossley-Holland gives 'Moon' and 'Wandering Singer'] are very convincing.' While I suggest, tentatively, a solution for the Latin riddle, I remain quite unsure what the solution of *Riddle 95* might be, and the reason is not that I think it 'a poor riddle ... a poor composition.' I simply cannot solve it though I should like to; and I suspect the wish that the solution may provide a fitting conclusion to the collection. The last sentence could with greater probability form the end of a riddle the solution of which is some kind of written word, such as a sacred text, and in a very full discussion by Helga Göbel it is plausibly included among Old English *Schriftwesenrätsel*.[10] The first six lines of the riddle remain difficult to reconcile with the last seven; yet in the manuscript the great capitals IC of the first word of the riddle and no

break or capitalization elsewhere would make it an act of interpretation to see this riddle as two riddles, the second beginning with *nu*, not a very likely opening word.[11] *Riddle 47* 'bookmoth' is written continuously with *Riddle 48* 'a sacramental vessel' ('chrismal,' 'paten,' or 'chalice' are likely solutions). *Riddle 68* is written as if a single riddle with the incomplete *Riddle 69*, and many editors and commentators take the manuscript unit to be a single riddle.[12]

In *Riddle 95* a few words are characteristic of Old English 'heroic' poetry: *indryhten* (line 1) 'noble,' *eorl* (line 1) 'man' (often rendered, by etymologizing translators, 'earl'), and *in burgum* (line 6) 'in the dwellings' or 'in the cities.' I doubt if *ricum ond heanum* 'with the mighty and the humble' goes back to the heroic age or even to poetry celebrating an heroic age. This poetic phrase is found also in *Riddle 32* line 13, *Guthlac* line 995, and (in a different order) *Judith* line 234. It is to be compared with *wlanc ond hean*[13] in *Meters 17* line 6 and *The Whale* line 43 as well as some prose uses such as *ægðer ge welige ge heane* Paris Psalter 48:2: always, the mighty or proud in contrast with the humble. In the riddles and perhaps elsewhere that kind of pairing of antonymic adjectives (used absolutely) may stand for 'everybody, all and sundry,' comparable with such verse uses as Middle English *blak and broun* (the sense, probably, 'fair and dark'). The phrase *ofer eorþan* 'on earth, throughout the world' (line 10), like *on eorþan*, is very common, and could be *super terram* and the like, frequent in the psalms. This is not a great number of locutions to be perhaps related to heroic verse. Even *indryhten* and its noun *indryhto*, though confined to verse, do not occur in heroic poetry or, unless it were in this riddle, even in secular poems, for *The Wanderer* and *The Seafarer* would hardly be regarded as secular now: in *The Seafarer* the noun *indryhto* comes at line 82 in the religious part of the poem, and in *The Wanderer* the adjectival *indryhten þeaw* 'noble practice' comes at line 12 in a moral precept. Such words merely show our uncertainty when trying to understand connotations in the Old English poetic lexis.

There are in other riddles more certain heroic aspects than are to be found in the riddles so far mentioned, especially in riddles on martial subjects (or connected with hunting): 'shield' or 'chopping block,' 5; 'horn,' 14; 'ballista?' 17; 'sword' or 'falcon,' 20; 'bow,' 23; 'mail-shirt,' 35 (and Leiden Riddle); 'battering ram,' 53; ('shield,' 'gallows'?) 'scabbard,' 'sword-rack,' 55; 'sword, dagger, shield, helmet,' or (more generally) a weapon made of iron, 71; 'lance or spear' (or 'bow and incendiary arrow'?), 73; and 'horn,' 80 and 93. Secondly, some locutions recall a warrior society, especially as used in some of the riddles on martial themes.

*Riddle 17* well exemplifies a poetic diction that seems to recall the heroic world to which such martial language had its first application, a world in which that diction may have achieved its greatest justness. The solution is most often given as 'ballista,' but 'fortress' has also been suggested.[14] Like many other Old English riddles, *Riddle 17* is a good example of riddling by parts, and that it has no universally accepted solution is not detrimental to using it as an example of a style describing an object enigmatically rather than as part of a straightforward battle-piece:

> Ic eom mundbora     minre heorde,
> eodorwirum fæst,     innan gefylled
> dryhtgestreona.     Dægtidum oft
> spæte sperebrogan.     Sped biþ þy mare
> 5     fylle minre.     Freo þæt bihealdeð
> hu me of hrife fleogað     hyldepilas.
> Hwilum ic sweartum     swelgan onginne
> brunum beadowæpnum,     bitrum ordum,
> eglum attorsperum.     Is min innað til,
> 10     wombhord wlitig,     wloncum deore.
> Men gemunan     þæt me þurh muþ fareð.

I am the protector of my flock, secure by means of wire-enclosures, filled within with noble treasure. By day I often spew forth spear-terror. My success is all the greater for my being full. My lord beholds how the warlike darts fly from my belly. At times I endeavour to swallow battle-weapons, black and brown(?), bitter points, hideous poison-spears. My inwards are good, the treasure in my belly beautiful, precious to the proud. People remember what passes through my mouth.

The vocabulary is that of heroic poetry, especially in its compounds. In the opening, *mundbora*, which occurs more often in verse than in prose, but is not confined to verse. Bosworth-Toller and Toller's *Supplement* have a fairly full set of references, without including the use in the riddle: I., 'protector, patron, guardian, advocate' applied to the protection of human beings; II., 'a guardian' (of things), for which the only use quoted is that at *Beowulf* line 2779, referring to the dragon as the guardian of the treasure:[15]

>                 Bill ær gescod
> – ecg wæs iren –     ealdhlafordes
> þam ðara maðma     mundbora wæs
> 2780     longe hwile,     ligegesan wæg
> hatne for horde,     hioroweallende
> middelnihtum,     oð þæt he morðre swealt.

The sword of the aged lord, its blade was of steel, had injured the one that for a long time had been the guardian of those treasures and had, because of that hoard, brought hot fire-terror, fiercely surging forth in the middle of the night, until he died in the slaughter.

Not only is the dragon's guardianship unusual, being almost uniquely of things rather than the protection or patronage of human beings, but the guardian himself is unusual, uniquely a dragon, and not a human being, nor an angel, nor God: for dragons are no daily occurrence even in heroic story.[16] If a more workaday use of *mundbora* is sought, it is to be found in the legal texts of Archbishop Wulfstan's composition, for example VIII Æthelred 33:[17]

> And gif man gehadodne oððe ælþeodigne man þurh ænig þinc forræde æt feo oððe æt feore, oððe hine bænde oððe hine beate oððe gebismrige on ænige wisan, þonne sceal him cyngc beon for mæg & for mundboran, buton he elles oðerne hæbbe.

> And if for any reason one wrongfully deprive a man in holy orders or a foreigner of property or of life, or binds him or beats him or insults him in any way, then the king is to discharge for him the function of a kinsman and protector, unless he otherwise has another (protector).

Presumably, this is an ordinary secular sense. It is not impossible that it was a legal concept in origin, though the fact that the word occurs only in Wulfstan's legal formulations makes that less likely. The word occurs most often in religious contexts. A good example is Wulfstan's own use in a homily in which Christ addresses Moses:[18]

> Ic eow wille rædan & swyþe araeran & freondscipe cyðan mid rihtan ge-trywþan, wealdan eow blisse & micelre lisse, habban eow to þegnan & beon eow for mundboran, gif ge me gehyrað, swa swa me licað.

> I will counsel you and greatly exalt you and show friendship with true faith, to bring to you bliss and great joy, to have you as my retainers and to discharge the function of protector to you, if you obey me, as is my pleasure.

The editor's note on the homily is of interest in connection with *mundbora*:

> Wulfstan adjusts the lesson [of Leviticus chapter 26] to an English audience and substitutes English ideas of social relations for Hebrew, as in *heretoga, mund-bora, þegnan*. It cannot be said definitely that the translation [of Leviticus] reflects his experience with drawing up legal codes, but such phrases as these, as well as *on griðe & on friðe* and *under mines munde*, suggest that it does.

There is a lesson here: 'English social relations,' not those of the Bible; but English social relations of which period? Certainly not the 'English social relations' of the heroic age. Perhaps not independent of Old English usage, Old Saxon *mundboro* is used nine times in *Heliand*, always with reference to God (usually Christ).[19] In Old English and in Old High German the word is found in glossaries rendering a variety of Latin words, usually *patronus* or *protector* 'protector, guardian,' or *suffragator* 'advocate, intercessor.'[20]

To return to *Riddle 17*, we cannot recapture the connotations of the first lexical item in it: *mundbora minre heorde*, presumably 'guardian of my flock,' perhaps 'guardian of my family.' Two senses of *heord* given in Bosworth-Toller seem relevant: 'I. a company of domestic animals of one kind kept together under the charge of one or more persons'; and the sense to which that dictionary assigns the use in this riddle, 'III. the family under the care of its head.' The word is rare in verse; and whether the phrase refers to the keeping of live-stock or of a family, there is not much that is heroic about it. In fact, the opening of the riddle exploits the essential uncertainty of interpretation: What kind of creature is the speaker, animal or human, or an inanimate thing? In what relationship does he or she or it stand to others mentioned in the riddle?

Another significant word is *dryhtgestreon* 'noble treasure' (line 3). The word is *hapax legomenon*, but *dryht-* compounds are poetic, and *dryhtmaðm* with the same sense and also *hapax legomenon* occurs at *Beowulf* line 2843, in a context in which the fleeting nature of life on earth is made explicit with reference to the two that died in the battle, Beowulf and the dragon:

> Biowulfe wearð
> dryhtmaðma dæl,   deaðe forgolden;
> hæfde æghwæðer   ende gefered
> 2845 lænan lifes.

The share of noble treasures came to Beowulf, paid for by death;[21] each of the two had reached the end of transitory life.

The world of *Beowulf* may be heroic, but this moral reflection in the hero's hour of death is not specifically heroic.

The weaponry is expressed in the riddle in compounds, all of them *hapax legomena* except that *hildepil* occurs also in *Riddle 15* line 28: *sperebroga* 'spear-terror' (line 4), *hyldepilas* 'javelins of war' (line 6), *beadowæpen* 'battle-weapons' (line 8), and *attorsperu* 'poisonous (*or* deadly) spears' (line 9). It is easy to find similar compounds in the verse texts; but the very fact that so many warlike compounds occur nowhere else in such Old English poetry as used to be regarded as secular or Christian epic makes me wonder at the evocative art of the Anglo-Saxon vernacular enigmatists, who in easy playfulness recall an heroic world to which they belong only bookishly, like the Anglo-Saxonists and Germanists of this century and the last.

How is *wombhord* (line 10) to be regarded? It lacks an heroic aspect. The first element, *wamb-* 'belly,' does not form many compounds in the language, only *wambadl* 'belly-disease,' *wambseoc* 'belly-sick,' and *þyrelwomb* 'with belly pierced.' The first two occur in the Leechdoms and describe various, strictly medical, conditions which make the stomach turn or the guts rot.[22] The third, *þyrelwomb*, occurs at the damaged end of *Riddle 81* line 11 the solution of which is 'weathercock,' that is, a pierced thing stuck on a pole, perhaps simply keeping watch over the neighbourhood rather than functioning to indicate the direction of the wind by turning.[23] The weathercock is described anatomically and as suffering in inclement weather, without a hint of heroism. The use of *wombhord* in *Riddle 17* is a little more glorious:

> Is min innað til,
> 10   wombhord wlitig,   wloncum deore.
> Men gemunan   þæt me þurh muþ fareð.

My inwards are good, the treasure in my belly beautiful, precious to the proud. People remember what passes through my mouth.

Such riddles as have martial solutions, or perhaps solutions connected with hunting, are more vigorously heroic in lexis. Yet *Riddle 5* begins *Ic eom anhaga* 'I am a recluse,' which to early readers might have recalled Sts Cuthbert and Guthlac rather than 'shield' or 'chopping block,'[24] the solution of the riddle. The word *anhaga* is mainly poetic, but certainly not heroic. What follows that opening is, however, heroic in tone and sense:

> Ic eom anhaga,   iserne wund,
> bille gebennad,   beadoweorca sæd,
> ecgum werig.   Oft ic seo
> frecne feohtan.   Frofre ne wene,
> 5   þæt me geoc cyme   guðgewinnes
> ær ic mid ældum   eal forwurde.
> Ac mec hnossiað   homera lafe,
> heardecg heoroscearp,   *hond*weorc smiþa,
> bitað in burgum.   Ic abidan sceal
> 10   laþran gemotes:   næfre læcecynn
> on folcstede   findan meahte,
> þara þe mid wyrtum   wunde gehælde;

> ac me ecga dolg   eacen weorðað
> þurh deaðslege   dagum ond nihtum.

> I am a recluse, wounded by weapons of steel, gashed by the blade, sated
> with deeds of battle, weary of weapon-edges. Often I see warfare, fierce
> combat. I look to no succour, that help will come to me in warlike strife
> before I perish utterly among men.[25] What is left by hammers, hard of edge,
> sword-sharp, the products of the hands of smiths strike down on me, bite me
> in the dwellings. I must experience a very hostile encounter:[26] I could never
> find a school of physicians in the dwelling-place of the people, such as
> might with simples heal the wounds, but my slashes from weapon-edges
> increase in size with every death-blow, day in, day out.

It has been said,[27] 'Trautmann's solution, "chopping block," is ruled out by
ll. 3b–4a [*Oft ic seo frecne feohtan*].' But that may be taking too literally the
view, uttered in prosopopœia as is usual in the riddles, of the lone stand of
the chopping block when the butchering weapons hail down, as if in war.
This riddle is designed to mislead the would-be solver, as are many other
riddles, especially riddles in which those lacking innocence see explicit sex,
though that is not the true solution.[28] Of course, *Riddle 5* is not an obscene
riddle; if 'chopping block' is the right solution, it is a riddle on a household
implement, described in the language of weaponry, to mislead the solver,
regardless of whether an Anglo-Saxon reared on heroic poetry and its
Christian reflex, or an Anglo-Saxonist unable to shake off a bookish preoccu-
pation with a long-lost Anglo-Saxon heroic age.

There is not time to deal with many other riddles as fully, but a few details
may be mentioned. The subject with which *Riddle 14* opens is solved as
'horn,' described at line 13a as *freolic fyrdsceorp* 'noble ornament of war.'
The horn's varied activities, ten of them introduced by *hwilum* 'at times,'
include not only a summons to wine, but also (twice) the warlike call to arms:
*hwilum ic to hilde hleoþre bonne ‖ wilgehleþan* 'at times with voice I
summon willing comrades to battle,' lines 4–5a; *hwilum wraþþum sceal ‖
stefne minre forstolen hreddan, ‖ flyman feondsceaþan* 'at times with my
voice I rescue stolen property from fierce enemies, put to flight the hostile
ravagers,' lines 17b–19a.

*Riddle 80* is, according to all the more recent editors, another riddle with
the solution 'horn' (with perhaps the single-line *Riddle 79* its first line,[29]
though I ignore it here):

> Ic eom æþelinges   eaxlgestealla,
> fyrdrinces gefara,   frean minum leof,

cyninges geselda.　Cwen mec hwilum
hwitloccedu　hond on legeð,
5　eorles dohtor,　þeah hio æþelu sy.
Hæbbe me in bosme　þæt on bearwe geweox.
Hwilum ic on wloncum　wicge ride,
herges on ende.　Heard is min tunge.
Oft ic woðboran　wordleana sum
10　agyfe æfter giedde.　Good is min wise,
ond ic sylfa salo.　Saga hwæt ic hatte.

I am a prince's comrade, a warrior's companion, dear to my lord, a king's retainer. At times a queen with fair locks, a nobleman's daughter, lays hands on me, noble though she is. I have in my breast that which grew in the grove. At times I ride on a proud horse, in the van of the army. My tongue [? i.e. mouthpiece] is hard. I often give to a singer some reward for (his) words in accord with his song. My melody [or nature] is good, and my own person dark.[30] Say what I am called.

The horn is used by a prince, a king even, in the army as he goes forward into battle on his horse. A queen too touches it, though it is dark and she noble and fair, as she hands round the drinking horn, like Wealhtheow in *Beowulf* lines 612b–24, and like the queen in *Maxims I* lines 84b–92.[31] The end of the riddle appears to refer to the horn accompanying a singer, or coming in at the end of a song or at the end of sections of it. This is truly a picture of heroic life in hall and in the field.

The badly damaged *Riddle 93* is also on the subject 'horn,' but extended into the scribal sphere of an inkhorn, the origin of which is traced from the antler of the deer that had the wolf as its foe (lines 28–9).[32] In the scene in which the deer is slain, up to line 24a, there are aspects of the life of courtiers who hunt, and who inflict suffering on the hunted deer from whose point of view the scene is described. Unlike *Riddle 80, Riddle 93* is, however, basically unheroic.

*Riddle 20* is generally solved as 'sword,' though another solution, 'falcon,' has recently found favour again.[33] Anglo-Saxon falconry is a technical subject of some difficulty. The occurrence of *hafoc* 'hawk' at *Beowulf* line 2263 has played a role in dating that poem, but little is known of Anglo-Saxon austringers and their practices: did they keep falcons in mew (if we can so interpret *on heaþore* line 13a), or lead them forth jessed and varvelled (if we can so interpret *on ‖ bende legde* lines 29b–30a, literally 'laid bonds upon'), perhaps while borne by a rider?[34] The warlike language found in a few places seems to carry a Christian connotation, difficult to reconcile with the solution 'falcon,' in one word, *gæstberend* 'soul-bearer, human being' of lines 8b–9a: *Oft ic gæstberend ‖ cwelle compwæpnum* 'I often kill soul-bearers with weapons of war.' Two other occurrences of *gæstberend* 'soul-bearer' in the strictly religious contexts of *Christ C* line 1599 and *The Gifts of Men* line 2, both unambiguously referring to human beings endowed with a soul, may not be sufficient to rule out entirely the possibility of *gæst, gast* carrying the sense of 'vital principle' or *anima* of animals or humans. Both the native *feorh* 'life, soul' and the Latin etymologies might allow a riddling use of *gæstberend* for such members of the animal kingdom as fall victim to falconry.[35] Three of the heroic and martial compounds in *Riddle 20* are found nowhere else: *compwæpen* 'war-weapon' (line 9); *radwerig* 'weary of riding' (line 14), this adjective better suited to the falcon[36] on its lord's glove as he rides than to the sword, perhaps tired of being carried by its lord as he advances towards battle (on foot); *orlegfrom* 'active in war' (line 15).

The opening word of *Riddle 23* has been used, inconclusively, for dating the composition: *agof* reversed for *boga* 'bow,' with <f> and <b> confused, perhaps because of the date of the relevant sound-change, no later than the eighth century, leading to the differentiation of the consonant, a plosive initially, from its allophone, a fricative post-vocalically.[37] The half-line *on gewin sceapen* comes both in this riddle, line 2b, and in *Riddle 20*, 'sword' or 'falcon' (line 1b). The sense has been given as 'shaped for conflict,' and it has been suggested, by the very scholar who revived the solution 'falcon' and rejected the generally accepted solution 'sword,' that this sense is 'from the heroic language of weapon manufacture,' without commenting on the other interpretation 'shaped amid combat.'[38] No 'heroic language of weapon manufacture' is known to me in Old English, and a glance at the concordance[39] shows that both accusative *on gewin(n)* and dative *on/in gewinne* or plural *on gewinnum* occur, and that the dative phrase is used, singular and plural, in the versified psalms of the Paris Psalter, 87:15, not as part of any heroic language, but to render *in laboribus* 'in labours,' and twice in *The Battle of Maldon*, lines 248 and 302, 'in battle,' not 'into' or 'for battle.' The accusative occurs only in the two riddles. But Bosworth-Toller gives the two uses in these riddles, s.v. *scippan*, III.a., assigning the sense to the verb 'to destine, adjudge a person (acc.) *to anything*,' and translating the use *Ic eom ... wiht on gewin sceapen* 'I am a creature destined to strife.'[40] It is perhaps to be wondered at that those deep in the gloom of Germanic fatalism have not made more of this interpretation: bow and sword or falcon are designated or destined for strife. As for the solution, it is impossible to say which is right: either, the weapon-smith's manufacture or the austringer's training and perhaps seeling (if the Anglo-Saxons engaged in that cruel treatment of hawks); or, the predesignation, preordination even, of weapons or of falcon for deeds of slaughter.

*Riddle 53* has the solution 'battering-ram.' Perhaps there is an heroic moment in lines 8b–11a:

> Nu he fæcnum wæg
> þurh his heafdes mægen   hildegieste
> 10   oþrum rymeð.   Oft hy an yste strudon
> hord ætgædre.

> Now it clears a path by the strength of its head for the guileful one, the other warlike visitant. Often they together pillaged the hoard in violent assault.

In line 10b, MS *an yst* has been much discussed and variously emended. Without much confidence, I follow those editors who interpret *an* as *on* and turn *yst* into a clear dative. The sense of *yst* is perhaps not unlike that of *storm* at *Beowulf* line 3117 'a shower (of missiles)' – perhaps together with a military sense (first recorded much later), as in *to take by storm.*[44] The heroic-sounding compound *hildegiest* is not found elsewhere, though other martial compounds with *-gæst* as second element are found. The plundering of the hoard is reminiscent of *Beowulf* lines 3073b–75 in some of its wording, where we readily emend MS *strade* to *strude* and where no one has as yet attempted to explain the obscure *est* by reference to the more obscure *yst* of the riddle.[42]

*Riddle 55* has had a variety of proposed solutions: a weapon, perhaps a shield; a weapon-holder, perhaps a scabbard or a sword-rack; a gallows, its traditional construction rather like a triangular harp (unlike the models produced to explain the fragments found at Sutton Hoo); or the Cross, in Old English merging with a gallows, perhaps like that in *The Dream of the Rood* seen in several functions.[43] Here I am concerned only with heroic aspects, prominent in this riddle. In lines 1–2 there is what looks like a carousing scene in hall, but may be a scene of divine worship:[44]

> Ic seah in healle, þær hæleð druncon,
> on flet beran   feower cynna ...

> I saw in hall, where men were drinking, four kinds being carried over the floor, ...

An interest in drink is high on the heroic agenda; *wrætlic wudutreow* 'fine wood from the forest'[45] might be a wooden drinking-vessel, but two lines later, it is clearly *rode tacn* 'symbol of the cross.' A simple mind in love with

the long-lost heroic age is soon disappointed in the hope that this is a trowl-
the-bowl riddle, four kinds of drink – the thirsty original audience readily
recreated by such a mind may try to solve this part of the riddle in terms of
wine, mead, beer, and ale – redolent of the Germanic vice of drunkenness so
clearly described by Tacitus in *Germania* 23. As it emerges that this is a
poem of the Holy Eucharist, it provides a prime example, not available to
John Lingard, for his generalization of 1806:[46]

> To judge of the advantage which the Saxons derived from their conversion, he
> [the impartial observer] will fix his eyes on their virtues. *They* were the off-
> spring of the gospel; their vices were the relics of paganism.

Another heroic aspect turns on the subject of the riddle, perhaps a gallows,
more probably the sign of the Cross, warding off[47] attack (lines 12b–14a):

> Þæt oft wæpen abæd
> his mondryhtne,   maðm in healle,
> goldhilted sweord.

That one, a treasure in hall, often warded off a weapon, a gold-hilted sword.[48]

However bright the promise of drink-hail may look in the opening, however
noble the treasure and sword may look near the close, in the sign of the
gallows, *wulfheafedtreo* line 12 (the same perhaps as *rode tacn*), this riddle
reaches out to an Anglo-Saxon servile stratum, an underclass unknown to the
world of Germanic heroic poetry.[49]

*Riddle 71* is so badly damaged at the end that all that can be said of the
solution is that it is a weapon made of iron, probably a sword. The object
belongs to a powerful or rich man,[50] *Ic eom rices æht* 'I am a powerful man's
possession' (line 1a), and *wraþra laf ‖ fyres ond feole* 'that which remains
after the action of those angry ones, fire and file' (lines 3b-4a) is reminiscent
of the kenning *fela laf* for 'sword-edge' (*Beowulf* line 1032).

*Riddle 73*, also badly damaged, has almost certainly 'spear' as its solution,
though Pinsker and Ziegler prefer 'bow and incendiary arrow.' This is not the
place to argue against that solution, except to say that the *eþelfæsten* (line 25)
makes good figurative sense for the body, or within it, the seat of life, entered
by the spear rather than a fortress struck by incendiary arrows. As for the
description in terms of the parts of a human body, with *eaxle* 'shoulders'
(line 16), *swiora smæl* 'narrow neck' (line 18a), and *sidan fealwe* 'pale-
coloured sides' (line 18b), the tall spear or lance seems to fit the comparison
with a man better than a burning arrow would. One thinks of Hero's account
of Beatrice's abuse of men in *Much Ado about Nothing*, III.i, including this

of a tall and, presumably, thin man: 'if tall, a launce ill headed.' Some of the heroic lexical elements in the riddle include *min frea* 'my master' used of a secular lord (line 8), *gif his ellen deag* 'if his courage avails' (line 9), *æfter dome*,[51] perhaps 'in pursuit of glory' or 'in accordance with the command' (line 10), *on fyrd wigeð* 'carries me into battle' (line 21), and *wiga* 'warrior' (line 23). Several other similar elements in the edited text, at least as strikingly heroic, owe that aspect to the editors who have supplied them in their struggle with the lacunae in the text.

Where does this listing of heroic aspects lead us? Some riddles clearly body forth moments set in the world of heroes. *Riddle 80* does so perhaps most fully, showing the varied uses of the horn in an heroic and courtly society. Many other riddles make use of locutions reminiscent of Old English heroic poetry, but their heroic sense goes no deeper than words: aspects are, by definition, superficial. In others of the riddles the heroic element is slight, for the most part read into the poems by Anglo-Saxonists so much in love with Germanic heroic literature that they find it as gallantly as Don Quixote found occasions for his sort of display of chivalry. As far as I am concerned, I enjoy the bookishness of the riddles. If academics do not like bookishness, who will?

Pembroke College, Oxford

## NOTES

1  I use the translation in W.R.M. Lamb, ed., *Plato, Charmides, Alcibiades,* etc., Loeb Classical Library (1927), *Alcibiades*, II, 147 (Loeb edn, 261). For the post-medieval understanding of the Greek, cf M. Ficino, *Omnia Diuini Platonis opera* (Basle: Froben 1546), 47, 'Est enim ipsa natura uniuersa poesis ænigmatum plena.'

   For the etymology of *ainíssomai* (Attic dialect *ainíttomai*) and *aínigma,* see H. Frisk, ed., *Griechisches etymologisches Wörterbuch*, vol. 1 (Heidelberg: Carl Winter 1960), 40–1; P. Chantraine, ed., *Dictionnaire étymologique de la langue grecque*, vol. 1 (Paris: Klincksieck 1968), 36.

2  'Es beherrscht sie ein eigenthümlicher, durchaus nationaler Kunststil.' A. Ebert, *Allgemeine Geschichte der Literatur des Mittelalters im Abendlande,* vol. 3 (Leipzig: F.C.W. Vogel 1887), 42. Ebert had written a good monograph on the Latin riddles of the Anglo-Saxons: *Die Räthselpoesie der Angelsachsen, insbesondere die Aenigmata des Tatwine und Eusebius*, Berichte über die Verhandlungen der Königlich Sächsischen Gesellschaft der Wissenschaften zu Leipzig, Philologisch-historische Classe, vol. 29 (1877),

20–56; summarized and augmented in vol. 1 of his *Allgemeine Geschichte der Literatur des Mittelalters im Abendlande* (2nd edn; Leipzig: F.C.W. Vogel 1889), 603n, 628–31, 651–7. Ebert in his study of 1877 (p. 23) discusses the Latin riddles of the Anglo-Saxons and the transition from them, especially Symphosius, to the vernacular riddles of the Exeter Book.

3  For convenience, I use the numbering of the riddles in what is still the standard edition: G.P. Krapp and E.V.K. Dobbie, eds, *The Exeter Book*, The Anglo-Saxon Poetic Records, vol. 3 (New York: Columbia University Press 1936). In the quotations of Old English texts, including the riddles, I often depart from the editions cited, especially in punctuation.

4  Because closest to the Vulgate, I quote *The Holie Bible Faithfully Translated into English, out of the Authentical Latin*, the Old Testament (Doway: L. Kellam 1609–10); *The New Testament of Iesus Christ Translated Faithfully into English, out of the authentical Latin* (Rhemes: Iohn Fogny 1582).

5  H. Morley, *English Writers: An Attempt towards a History of English Literature*, vol. 2, *From Cædmon to the Conquest* (London: Cassell and Co. 1888), 224–5.

6  Jonathan Swift, *On Poetry: A Rapsody* (Dublin and repr. at London 1733), 8; cf H. Williams, ed., *The Poems of Jonathan Swift* (2nd edn; Oxford: Clarendon Press 1958) 2: 643, lines 103–4.

7  M. Trautmann, 'Cynewulf und die Rätsel,' *Anglia* 6 (1883) Anzeiger: 168 (at least, he rejects, p. 169, the assurance of attribution to Cynewulf); but contradicted by himself in M. Trautmann, ed., *Die altenglischen Rätsel* (Heidelberg: Carl Winter; New York: G.E. Stechert 1915), 139–40. H. Pinsker and W. Ziegler, *Die altenglischen Rätsel des Exeterbuchs*, Anglistische Forschungen 183 (Heidelberg: Carl Winter 1985), 336–7.

8  A.J. Wyatt, ed., *Old English Riddles* (Boston, Mass., and London: D.C. Heath 1912), 122–3. N.F. Barley, 'Structural Aspects of the Anglo-Saxon Riddle,' *Semiotica*, 10 (1974), 174; Barley is greatly influenced by E.K. Maranda (chiefly on Finnish riddles) in 'Structure des énigmes,' *L'Homme*, 9 (1969): 5–48.

9  K. Crossley-Holland, *The Exeter Riddle Book* (London: Folio Society 1978), 139.

10  H. Göbel, ed., *Studien zu den altenglischen Schriftwesenrätseln* (Würzburg: Königshausen und Neumann 1980), 538–606.

11  See R.W. Chambers, M. Förster, and R. Flower, eds, *The Exeter Book of Old English Poetry* (London: P. Lund, Humphries and Co. for the Dean and Chapter of Exeter Cathedral 1933), fol. 130ᵇ.

12  On riddles the editorial unity of which is palaeographically at variance with the manuscript evidence, see C. Williamson, ed., *The Old English Riddles of the* Exeter Book (Chapel Hill: University of North Carolina Press 1977), 353.

13 See M. von Rüden, Wlanc *und Derivate im Alt- und Mittelenglischen. Eine wortgeschichtliche Studie*, Europäische Hochschulschriften, series 14 Angelsächsische Sprache und Literatur, vol. 61 (Frankfurt am Main, Berne, and Las Vegas: P. Lang 1978), 110–13. Cf n50 below.

14 See C. Williamson's discussion, *Old English Riddles*, 179–81; he regards the solution as uncertain.

15 J. Bosworth and T.N. Toller, eds, *An Anglo-Saxon Dictionary* (Oxford: Clarendon Press 1882–98), T.N. Toller, ed., *An Anglo-Saxon Dictionary ... Supplement* (Oxford: Clarendon Press 1908–21), s.v. The text of *Beowulf* used in this paper is F. Klaeber, ed., *Beowulf* (3rd edn; Boston, Mass.: Heath 1936, with supplements 1 and 2, 1941, thereafter Lexington, Mass.: Heath 1950).

16 Cf. J.R.R. Tolkien, 'Beowulf: The Monsters and the Critics,' *Proceedings of the British Academy* 22 (1936): 252–3 (pp 10–11 of separate).

17 Cf D. Whitelock, 'Wulfstan and the Laws of Cnut,' *English Historical Review* 63 (1948): 433–52; and D. Whitelock, *English Historical Documents*, vol. 1 c 500–1042 (2nd edn; London: Eyre Methuen; New York: Oxford University Press 1979), 461 n1. For the text of VIII Æthelred 33, see F. Liebermann, *Die Gesetze der Angelsachsen*, vol. 1 (Halle: Niemeyer 1898–1903), 267; my translation is slightly more literal than the translation given by Whitelock, *English Historical Documents*, vol. 1 at page 451:

> And if a man in holy orders or a foreigner is for any reason defrauded of property or of life, or is bound or beaten or insulted in any way, the king shall then be for him in the place of a kinsman and protector, unless otherwise he has another.

On the other hand, *mundbyrd* is a legal term, with more than one sense.

18 See D. Bethurum, ed., *The Homilies of Wulfstan* (Oxford: Clarendon Press 1957), 253, lines 55–9. I quote from Bethurum's commentary on the homily, 354.

19 See E.H. Sehrt, ed., *Vollständiges Wörterbuch zum Heliand und zur altsächsischen Genesis*, Hesperia 14 (Göttingen: Vandenhoeck und Ruprecht 1925), 400 s.v. *mund-boro*.

20 Cf T. Starck and J.C. Wells, eds, *Althochdeutsches Glossenwörterbuch* (Heidelberg: Carl Winter 1972–90), s.vv. *mundbora, muntboro*; J.D. Pheifer, ed., *Old English Glosses in the Épinal-Erfurt Glossary* (Oxford: Clarendon Press 1974), 49, 934.

21 I follow the construction, but not the wording, of E.T. Donaldson's *Beowulf A New Prose Translation* (London: Longmans 1967), 49–50.

22 See O. Cockayne, ed., *Leechdoms, Wortcunning, and Starcraft of Early England*, Rolls Series, 35, vol. 2 (1865): 216, *Læce Boc*, II, xxv, line 3, and 232, *Læce Boc*, II, xxxi, line 12.

23 Cf the notes in the editions by C. Williamson, *Old English Riddles*, 361–2,

214 Eric Gerald Stanley

and H. Pinsker and W. Ziegier, *Die altenglischen Rätsel*, 314.

24 The solution 'chopping block' was first proposed by M. Trautmann, 'Die Auflösungen der altenglischen Rätsel,' *Anglia Beiblatt* 5 (1894): 49 and is accepted by Pinsker and Ziegler, *Die altenglischen Rätsel*, 155.

25 The suggestion by Pinsker and Ziegler, p. 156, is attractive at first sight: *mid ældum* here is not the usual empty, poetic formula 'among men,' that is, 'on earth,' comparable with *in burgum* 'in the dwellings, on earth,' three lines lower down; but is rather (with long stem vowel) 'among or by means of flames.' There is, however, no parallel in Old English for any plural use of *æled*.

26 It seems not impossible that *laþran* is a comparative absolute, and so I translate it; for other examples, see B. Mitchell, *Old English Syntax* (Oxford: Clarendon Press 1985), §§ 183–6.

27 Dobbie, Anglo-Saxon Poetic Records 3: 325.

28 See the excellent discussion by R. Gleißner, *Die »zweideutigen« altenglischen Rätsel des* Exeter Book *in ihrem zeitgenössischen Kontext*, Sprache und Literatur (Regensburger Arbeiten zur Anglistik und Amerikanistik), 23 (Frankfurt am Main, Berne, New York, Nancy: Peter Lang 1984), 10–16.

29 Cf Williamson's apparatus and notes on no. 76, *Old English Riddles*, at 111 and 359–60.

30 In an elaborate note, Pinsker and Ziegler, *Die altenglischen Rätsel*, 313–14, attempt to justify an emended reading *sal* for manuscript *salo*, wishing to make the horn itself *\*sal*, an unrecorded adjective which they interpret as 'silent'; but apart from the difficulty inherent in that reading, the horn is not silent though, of course, it has to be blown. The darkness of the horn provides the antithesis to the fairness of the lady who touches it nonetheless.

31 Cf Tupper's note on lines 3–5, in F. Tupper, ed., *The Riddles of the Exeter Book* (Boston, New York, Chicago, and London: Ginn 1910), 218.

32 The riddle is fully edited by H. Göbel, *Studien zu den altenglischen Schriftwesenrätseln* (see n10 above), 486–537.

33 M. Trautmann, 'Die Auflösungen der altenglischen Rätsel,' 1894 (see n24 above), 49. See also L.K. Shook's edition of this riddle, 'Old English Riddle No. 20: *Heoruswealwe*,' in J.B. Bessinger and R.P. Creed, eds, *Franciplegius: Medieval and Linguistic Studies in Honor of Francis Peabody Magoun, Jr.* (New York: New York University Press; London: Allen and Unwin 1965), 194–204; and cf Pinsker and Ziegler, *Die altenglischen Rätsel*, 184.

34 Cf E.G. Stanley, 'The Date of *Beowulf:* Some Doubts and No Conclusions,' in E.G. Stanley, *A Collection of Papers with Emphasis on Old English Literature*, Publications of the Dictionary of Old English 3 (Toronto: Pontifical Institute of Medieval Studies 1987), 221–2, and see the references in

n48. There appear to be no illustrations of falconry in manuscripts earlier than the Exeter Book; see T.H. Ohlgren, *Insular and Anglo-Saxon Manuscripts* (New York and London: Garland 1986), 150 (no. 167, 10, MS Cotton Julius A.vi, fol. 7$^v$) and 250 (no. 192, 11, MS Cotton Tiberius B.v, fol. 7$^v$).

35 Cf W.M. Lindsay, ed., *Isidori etymologiae sive origines* (Oxford: Clarendon Press 1911), XII. i. 3; see also R. Maltby, ed., *A Lexicon of Ancient Etymologies* (Leeds: F. Cairns 1991), s.vv. *anima, animal, animalis*. The matter is discussed in the note on *Riddle 20* line 8 by Pinsker and Ziegler, *Die altenglischen Rätsel*, 186–7 (their *Riddle 18*), where *gæst* at *Riddle 9* l. 8 (their *Riddle 7*) is adduced, with a clear reference to the vital principle of the cuckoo, the solution accepted universally.

36 Thus Pinsker and Ziegler's note on line 14a (*Die altenglischen Rätsel*, 187).

37 Cf. E. Sievers, 'Zu Cynewulf,' *Anglia*, 13 (1891); 15; but see also Tupper, *Riddles*, lvii; and Wyatt, ed., *Old English Riddles*, 81.

38 See Shook, 'Old English Riddle No. 20,' 201; 'shaped amid combat' is the translation given by W.S. Mackie, ed., *The Exeter Book Part II*, Early English Text Society, OS 194 (1934), 109 and 113. Shook's 'shaped for conflict' agrees, for example, with P.F. Baum, *Anglo-Saxon Riddles of the Exeter Book* (Durham, N.C.: Duke University Press 1963), 38 and 41 (nos 46 and 51) 'shaped for fighting'; C. Williamson, *A Feast of Creatures. Anglo-Saxon Riddle-Songs* (Philadelphia: University of Pennsylvania Press 1982; London: Scolar Press 1983), 78 and 81 (nos 18 and 21) 'shaped for battle'; Pinsker and Ziegler, *Die altenglischen Rätsel*, 41 and 47 (nos 18 and 21) 'zum Kampf(e) geschaffen.'

39 J.B. Bessinger, Jr, ed., and P.H. Smith, Jr, programmer, *A Concordance to the Anglo-Saxon Poetic Records* (Ithaca and London: Cornell University Press 1978), 467–8, s.vv. *gewin, gewinn, gewinne,* and *gewinnum*.

40 Cf C.W.M. Grein, ed., *Sprachschatz der angelsächsischen Dichter* (rev. edn J.J. Köhler; Heidelberg: Carl Winter 1912–14), s.v. *scyppan*, 2. 'constituere, designare, destinare, decernere'; thus first C.W.M. Grein, ed., *Sprachschatz der angelsächsischen Dichter*, vol. 2 (Cassel and Göttingen: Wigand 1864), 400, s.v. *sceppan*.

41 See *The Oxford English Dictionary*, s.v., 5.; *Middle English Dictionary*, s.v., 2.(a).

42 There is no difficulty in producing some such explanation:

næs he goldhwæte   gearwor hæfde
3075   agendes est   ær gesceawod.

By no means had he beheld sooner, more readily, the (hoard-)owner's gold-active assault.

As in all interpretations, *goldhwæt* 'gold-abounding, active in gold' is difficult. Examples of /y:/ written <e> are rare in *Beowulf*, only *-hedig* line 3165 (to which the tribal name *Fres-*, *Frys-* is sometimes added). It is not a convincing solution of a desperate crux.

43  For a good survey of solutions, see Williamson, ed. *Old English Riddles*, 300–3. For a later refinement of the solution 'the Cross,' see Pinsker and Ziegler, *Die altenglischen Rätsel*, 275–6; and cf E. von Erhardt-Siebold, *Die lateinischen Rätsel der Angelsachsen*, Anglistische Forschungen 61 (Heidelberg: Carl Winter 1925), 107–15, with special reference to Tatwine's *aenigma* IX 'De cruce Xristi,' M. de Marco, ed., with translation by E. von Erhardt-Siebold, *Tatvini opera omnia*, Corpus Christianorum, ser. lat. 133 (1968), 176, from which it seems that the Roman mode of capital punishment for slaves may, by the Anglo-Saxons, have been conflated with Anglo-Saxon hanging for the unfree, as indicated in the Laws. Cf Liebermann, *Gesetze*, 1: at 100, 176–7, and 191: Ine 24 on hanging of a *witeþeow Englisc-mon* 'an Englishman condemned to slavery for a crime'; VI Æthelstan 6,3 on the punishing of slaves including (near the end) hanging; and the Latin III Edmund 4 hanging as a punishment of a slave. This may form the connection between Tatwine's riddle and the *wulfheafedtreo* of *Riddle 55* l. 12, which Tupper, the first to propose the solution 'cross' (*Riddles*, 189) did not find. Cf E.G. Stanley, 'Wolf, My Wolf!' in J.H. Hall, A.N. Doane, and R.N. Ringler, eds, *Old English and New ... in Honor of Frederic G. Cassidy* (New York and London: Garland Publishing 1992), 53 and 57 (n17).

44  Cf the note in Pinsker and Ziegler, *Die altenglischen Rätsel*, 276.

45  Thus Mackie's translation, *Exeter Book*, 147, keeping the ambiguity of the original, unlike Pinsker and Ziegler's translation (*Die altenglischen Rätsel*, 93) 'einen herrlichen Baum,' which explicitly anticipates *rode tacn* of line 5.

46  J. Lingard, *The Antiquities of the Anglo-Saxon Church*, Newcastle: printed by Edward Walker; sold by Keating, Brown, and Keating, London, 1806), 1:48–9. In G. Clark, '*Beowulf*: The Last Word,' in Hall, Doane, and Ringler, eds, *Old English and New*, 16, use is made of this statement of Lingard's to which attention had been drawn by me in *The Search for Anglo-Saxon Paganism* (Cambridge: D.S. Brewer; Totowa, N.J.: Rowman and Littlefield, 1975), 23; Clark not only confuses the editions of Lingard and so gets the date of publication wrong by thirty-nine years, but also fails to notice that I distance myself from Lingard, saying *Search*, 24, 'Yet, surely, Lingard went too far.'

47  Thus Tupper's note on *abæd*, *Riddles*, 192.

48  It is not possible to tell if, as in my translation, *maðm in healle* varies what, without much confidence, I take to be the subject *þæt*. The construction of these lines is obscure.

49  Unless it were in the editorial reading *þeow* at *Beowulf* line 2223, where nothing can be read after the initial *þ*. The editorial reading goes back to

N.F.S. Grundtvig, ed., *Beowulfes Beorh* (Copenhagen: K. Schonberg; London: J. Russell Smith 1861), 167, the note on lines 2223b–24a (his lines 4440–1), where, with reference to Grein's edition only, he rejects the reading *þegn* of Kemble and Grein. The reading has been often discussed, especially in connection with line 2224b *heteswengeas fleah* 'he fled from hateful beatings,' and line 2408a *hæft hygegiomor* 'captive sad in mind,' where 'captive' has been interpreted as 'slave'; see, for example, F. Liebermann, *Die Gesetze der Angelsachsen*, vol. 2, 2 Rechts- und Sachglossar (Halle: Niemeyer 1912), 621 s.v. *Prügel*, specifically 3.a.; J. Hoops, *Kommentar zum Beowulf* (Heidelberg: Carl Winter 1932), 257; the note on the line in Klaeber's third edition, 208; and in E. von Schaubert's edition, part 2 Kommentar (1961), 130; and T. Westphalen, *Beowulf 3150–55* (Munich: W. Fink 1967), 219 n429.

50  The West Saxon Gospels for Luke 1:52 have the following rendering of *potens*: all manuscripts (even those of the twelfth century) *rican* or (Hatton) *rice*. For very late Old English and early Middle English, see *Middle English Dictionary* (part R.6, published 1986) s.v. *riche*, adj., 1 and 6. West Saxon as late as the first half of the eleventh century, has clear evidence of *riclic* for 'powerful' in Lambeth Psalter, Psalm 44:4, where *potentissime* 'oh, most mighty' is glossed *riclice vel stranglice vel riclicost*; cf Regius Psalter and Salisbury Psalter 44:4 *riclicost*. The common *rice* and the rarer *riclic* may well not be coterminous in meaning, but cf Lambeth Psalter, Psalm 85:14, *sinagoga poetentium* glossed *gesamnung ricra vel mihtigra*. Of course, for greater clarity the polyseme *rice* 'rich' and 'powerful' can be replaced by more monosemantic adjectives based on the stem *mæht*, *miht*, e.g. Lindisfarne and Rushworth *mæhtig*. See the important discussion of *wlanc* and *welig* by M. von Rüden, Wlanc *und Derivate*, 43-53. Unless 'in some quarters at least' is clearly defined, the textual evidence does not support M.R. Godden's statement, 'Money, power and morality in late Anglo-Saxon England,'*Anglo-Saxon England*, 19 (1990). Godden writes (52): 'In some quarters at least the old sense ['powerful'] of the word [*rice*] seems no longer to have been recognized.' It is possible that 'rich' was increasingly felt to mean 'moneyed' rather than more generally 'propertied; of the status and power of a person of property' in Anglo-Saxon times, much as it is in Modern English; and writers sensitive to the possibility of misinterpretation may have chosen adjectives less open to it. The Vercelli scribe is not among such writers when he allowed the transmitted reading to stand at *The Dream of the Rood* lines 44b–45a: *Ahof ic ricne cyning* ‖ *heofona Hlaford*; cf Ruthwell Cross [*ahof*] *ic riicnæ kyniŋg heafunæs h[l]afard* 'I raised up a mighty king, lord of heaven.' In that use ambiguity is unlikely; sometimes ambiguity seems impossible, especially when the sense of *rice* is defined by its an-

tonym in a particular use. For example, Iudex 3 (Liebermann, *Gesetze*, vol. 1: 474): *Domas sceolon beon butan ælcere hadarunge: þæt ys, þæt he ne murne naðer ne rycum ne heanum, ne leofum ne laðum folcriht to recceanne* 'Judgements are to be without respect of person: that is, that he [the judge], when deciding a case in *folc-riht*, have regard to neither the mighty nor the humble, neither friend nor foe.' But perhaps money came to buy justice by the time in the twelfth century when this was translated into the Latin of Quadripartitus, and the translator changed the contrast to *diuiti uel egeno* 'rich or indigent.'

51 Cf Klaeber's note on *Beowulf* line 1720.

# Bibliography of C.B. Hieatt

(Short reviews, papers delivered, and students supervised have been omitted.)

'Oaths in the "Friar's Tale."' *Notes and Queries* ns 7 (1960): 5–6.

*The Canterbury Tales* of Geoffrey Chaucer. Adaptation for young readers, with A.K. Hieatt. New York: Golden Press 1961.

*The Canterbury Tales of Geoffrey Chaucer.* Selection edited and translated with A.K. Hieatt. New York: Bantam Books 1964.

'*Pearl* and the Dream Vision Tradition.' *Studia Neophilologica* 37 (1965): 139–45.

'*Winner and Waster* and the *Parliament of the Three Ages.*' *American Notes and Queries* 4 (1966): 100–4.

*Beowulf and Other Old English Poems.* Translation. New York: Odyssey Press 1967. Second edition, New York: Bantam Books 1983.

*The Realism of Dream Visions: The Poetic Exploitation of the Dream Experience in Chaucer and His Contemporaries.* The Hague: Mouton 1967.

*Sir Gawain and the Green Knight.* Adaptation of medieval romance for children. New York and Toronto: T.Y. Crowell and Fitzhenry and Whiteside 1967.

*Essentials of Old English: Readings with Keyed Grammar and Vocabulary.* New York: T.Y. Crowell 1968.

*The Knight of the Lion.* Adaptation of medieval romance for children. New York and Toronto: T.Y. Crowell and Fitzhenry and Whiteside 1968.

'The Mock Debate of the Owl and the Nightingale.' *Studia Neophilologica* 40 (1968): 155–60.

'Roland's Christian Heroism.' *Tradition* 24 (1968): 420–9.

*The Knight of the Cart.* Adaptation of medieval romance for children. New York and Toronto: T.Y. Crowell and Fitzhenry and Whiteside 1969.

'A New Theory of Triple Rhythm in the Hypermetric Lines of Old English Verse.'
  *Modern Philology* 67 (1969): 1–8.
'The Bird with Four Feathers: Numerical Analysis of a Fourteenth Century Poem,'
  With A.K. Hieatt. *Papers on Language and Literature* 6 (1970): 18–38.
'A Case for *Dux Moraud* as a Play of the Miracles of the Virgin.' *Mediaeval
  Studies* 32 (1970): 345–51.
*Edmund Spenser: Selected Poetry.* Edition with A.K. Hieatt. New York: Appleton-
  Century-Crofts 1970.
*The Miller's Tale* of Geoffrey Chaucer. New York: Odyssey Press 1970.
'The Moral of the Nun's Priest's Tale.' *Studia Neophilologica* 42 (1970): 3–8.
*The Joy of the Court.* Adaptation of medieval romance for children. New York and
  Toronto: T.Y. Crowell and Fitzhenry and Whiteside 1971.
'Dream Frame and Verbal Echo in The *Dream of the Rood.*' *Neuphilologische
  Mitteilungen* 72 (1971): 251–63.
'Prosodic Analysis of Old English Poetry: A Suggested Working Approach with
  Sample Applications.' *Revue de l'Université d'Ottawa* 42 (1972): 72–82.
*The Sword and the Grail.* Adaptation of medieval romance for children. New York
  and Toronto: T.Y. Crowell and Fitzhenry and Whiteside 1972.
*The Castle of Ladies.* Adaptation of medieval romance for children. New York and
  Toronto: T.Y. Crowell and Fitzhenry and Whiteside 1973.
'Ogier the Dane in Old Norse.' *Scandinavian Studies* 45 (1973): 27–37.
'Alliterative Patterns in the Hypermetric Lines of Old English Verse.' *Modern
  Philology* 71 (1974): 237–42.
'The Fates of the Apostles: Imagery, Structure, and Meaning.' *Papers on Language
  and Literature* 10 (1974): 115–25.
'*Karlamagnus saga* and the Pseudo-Turpin Chronicle.' *Scandinavian Studies* 46
  (1974): 140–50.
*The Minstrel Knight.* Adaptation of medieval romance for children. New York and
  Toronto: T.Y. Crowell and Fitzhenry and Whiteside 1974.
'The Rhythm of the Alliterative Long Line.' In *Chaucer and Middle English Studies
  in Honour of Rossell Hope Robbins.* Ed. Beryl Rowland. London: George Allen
  and Unwin 1974. 119–30.
'Envelope Patterns and the Structure of *Beowulf.*' *English Studies in Canada* 1
  (1975): 249–65.
*Karlamagnus saga: The Saga of Charlemagne and His Heroes.* Vols 1 and 2.
  Toronto: Pontifical Institute of Mediaeval Studies 1975. Vol. 3. 1980.
'The Harrowing of Mermedonia: Typological Patterns in the Old English *Andreas,*'
  *Neuphilologische Mitteilungen* 77 (1976): 49–62.
*Pleyn Delit: Medieval Cookery for Modern Cooks.* With Sharon Butler. Toronto:
  University of Toronto Press 1976; Rev. ed. 1979: Tr. and adapted into French by

Brenda Thaon (now Hosington) as *Pain, Vin, et Veneison*. Montreal: Editions de l'Aurore 1977.

'The Relationship of *Karlamagnus saga* VII to Its Source.' *Proceedings of the Third International Saga Conference*. Oslo 1976. Unpaged.

'"Eliduc" revisited: John Fowles and Marie de France.' *English Studies in Canada* 3 (1977): 351–8.

'Do-It-Yourself Medieval Feast.' *Ralph: For Medieval-Renaissance Teaching* 5 no. 2 (1978): 1–2.

'Hrut's Voyage to Norway and the Structure of *Njala*.' *Journal of English and Germanic Philology* 77 (1978): 489–94. Repr. in *Sagas of the Icelanders: A Book of Essays*. Ed. John Tucker. New York: Garland 1989. 272–9.

'On teaching *Beowulf*.' *Old English Newsletter* 11 no. 2 (1978): 18–19.

'Some Unidentified or Dubiously Glossed Loanwords in *Karlamagnus saga* and Their Implications for Translators and Source Studies.' *Scandinavian Studies* 50 (1978): 381–8.

'Vilhjalm Korneis in the *Karlamagnus saga*.' *Olifant* 5 (1978): 277–84.

'Charlemagne in Vincent's Mirror: The *Speculum historiale* as a Source of the Old Norse Karlamagnus saga.' *Florilegium* 1 (1979): 186–94.

'Pattern in Part VI of *Karlamagnus saga*: A Comparison of Analogues, Translation, and Revision.' *Proceedings of the Fourth International Saga Conference*. Munich 1979. Unpaged.

'"To boille the chiknes with the marybones": Hodge's Kitchen Revisited.' In *Chaucerian Problems and Perspectives: Essays presented to Paul E. Beichner, C.S.C*. Notre Dame: University of Notre Dame Press 1979. 149–63.

'*Une autre fourme*: Guillaume de Machaut and the Dream Vision Form.' *Chaucer Review* 14 (1980): 97–155.

'Analyzing Enchantment: Fantasy After Bettelheim.' *Canadian Children's Literature* 15/16 (1980): 6–14.

'Divisions: Theme and Structure of *Genesis A*.' *Neuphilologische Mitteilungen* 81 (1980): 243–51.

'*Judith* and the Literary Function of Old English Hypermetric Lines.' *Studia Neophilologica* 52 (1980): 252–6.

'The Roast, or Boiled, Beef of Old English.' *Book Forum* 5 (1980): 294–9.

*Rædellan of Heorðwordhorde mid þa 'Rædellan in Heolstre' of Se Holbytla*. Binghamton, N.Y.: Center for Medieval and Early Renaissance Studies. *Old English Newsletter Subsidia*, Vol. 1981. Annotated translations into Old English.

'The Redactor as Critic: An Analysis of the B-Version of *Karlamagnus saga*.' *Scandinavian Studies* 53 (1981): 302–19.

'The Text of *The Hobbit*: Putting Tolkien's Notes in Order.' *English Studies in Canada* 7 (1981): 212–24.

'"Greensauce": Elderflowers.' *Petits Propos Culinaires* 12 (1982): 68.

'"Ore pur parler del array de une graunt mangerye": The Culture of the "Newe Get", circa 1285.' In *Acts of Interpretation: The Text in its Contexts 700–1600; Essays on Medieval and Renaissance Literature in Honor of E. Talbot Donaldson*. Ed. M.J. Carruthers and E.D. Kirk. Norman, Okla.: Pilgrim Books 1982. 219–33.

'Stooping at a Simile: Some Literary Uses of Falconry.' *Papers on Language and Literature* 19 no. 4 (1983): 339–60.

'Angus Fraser Cameron, 1941–1983.' *Proceedings of the Royal Society of Canada* 22 no. 4 (1984): 65–6.

'The Case of Cinderella.' *Canadian Children's Literature* 33 (1984): 92–6.

'Modþryðo and Heremod: Intertwined Threads in the *Beowulf*-poet's Web of Words.' *Journal of English and Germanic Philology* 83 (1984): 173–82.

'Parallels, Useful Analogues, and Elusive Sources.' In *Approaches to Teaching Beowulf*. Ed. J.B. Bessinger, Jr and R.F. Yeager. New York: Modern Language Association of America 1984. 123–9.

'Caedmon in Context: Transforming the Formula.' *Journal of English and Germanic Philology* 84 (1985): 485–97.

*Curye on Inglysch*. Edition with Sharon Butler. Early English Text Society SS 8. London: Oxford University Press 1985.

'The *Karlamagnus Saga* Version of the *Chanson de Basin*.' In *Les Sagas de Chevaliers: Riddarasogur*. Ed. R. Boyer. Paris: Presses de l'Université de Paris-Sorbonne 1985. 235–47.

'The Mystery of Figgs & Phantoms.' *Canadian Children's Literature* 13 (1985): 128–38.

'Karlamagnus saga.' in *Dictionary of the Middle Ages*. Edited by J.R. Strayer. New York: Scribners 1986. 216–9.

'Recipes from Beinecke MS 163.' *Yale University Library Gazette* 61 (1986): 15–21.

'Two Anglo-Norman Culinary Collections Edited from British Library Manuscript Additional 32085 and Royal 12. C. xii.' With R.F. Jones. *Speculum* 61 (1986): 859–82.

'Reconstructing the Lost *Chanson de Basin*: Was It a *Couronnement de Charlemagne*?' in *The Romance Epic*. Studies in Medieval Culture 24. Kalamazoo: Medieval Institute Publications 1987. 103–14.

'On Envelope Patterns (Ancient and – Relatively – Modern) and Nonce Formulas.' in *Comparative Research on Oral Traditions: A Memorial for Milman Parry*. Ed. John Miles Foley. Columbus, Ohio: 1987. 245–58.

'The Dreams of Troilus, Criseyde, and Chauntecleer: Chaucer's Manipulation of the Categories of Macrobius et al.' *English Studies in Canada* 14 (1988): 400–14.

'Further Notes on *The Forme of Cury* et al.: Additions and Corrections.' *Bulletin of the John Rylands University Library of Manchester* 70 (1988): 45–52.

*An Ordinance of Pottage: An Edition of the Fifteenth Century Culinary Recipes in Yale University's MS Beinecke 163, with a Commentary on the Recipes and Adapted Versions for the Modern Kitchen.* London: Prospect Books 1988.

'The "Poignant" Flavour in Medieval Cooking.' In *Oxford Symposium on Food and Cooking, 1987: Taste. Proceedings.* London: Prospect Books 1988. 103–5.

'A Brief Guide to the Scansion of Old English Poetry.' *Old English Newsletter* 23 (1989): 33–5.

*La Novele Cirurgerie.* Edition with Robin F. Jones. Anglo-Norman Text Society 46. 1990 for 1988.

'Falconry.' *The Spenser Encyclopedia.* Toronto: University of Toronto Press 1990. 298–9.

'Transition in the Exeter Book "Descent Into Hell": The Poetic Use of a "Stille" yet "Geondflowende" River.' *Neuphilologische Mitteilungen* 91 (1990): 431–8.

'Listing and Analyzing the Medieval English Culinary Recipe Collections: A Project and Its Problems.' In *Du manuscrit à la table: Essais sur la Cuisine au Moyen Age et Répertoire des manuscrits médiévaux contenant des recettes culinaires* Ed. Carole Lambert. Montreal: Les Presses de l'Université de Montréal 1992. 16–21.

'Répertoire des manuscrits médiévaux contenant des recettes culinaires.' With Carole Lambert, Bruno Laurioux, and Alix Prentki. In *Du manuscrit à la table.* Ed. Carole Lambert. 315–88.

'Beowulf's Last Words vs. Bothvar Bjarki's: How the Hero Faces His God.' In *Heroic Poetry in the Anglo-Saxon Period: Studies in Honor of Jess B. Bessinger, Jr.* Ed. Helen Damico and John Leyerle. Studies in Medieval Culture 32. Kalamazoo: Medieval Institute Publications 1993. 403–24.

'Problems Posed by the Early Medieval Recipe Collection in Danish and Icelandic: Culinary Confusion Compounded?' *Scandinavian-Canadian Studies* 6 (1993): 15–26.

*The Tale of the Alerion: A Translation of Guillaume de Machaut's 'Dit de l'Alerion.'* With Minnette Grunmann-Gaudet. Medieval Texts and Translations. Toronto: University of Toronto Press 1994.

*Beginning Old English.* With Brian Shaw and O.D. Macrae-Gibson. Old English Newsletter Subsidia. Binghamton: Center for Medieval and Early Renaissance Studies 1994. Computer program with guide.

# List of Contributors

Thomas Cable is Professor in the Department of English at the University of Texas at Austin.

Robert Payson Creed is Professor of English at the University of Massachusetts at Amherst.

John Miles Foley is William Byler Chair in Humanities and Professor of English and Classics at the University of Missouri.

M.S. Griffith is Tutor and Lecturer at New College, University of Oxford.

James Keddie is a graduate student with a SSHRCC Doctoral Fellowship in the Department of English at the University of Western Ontario.

J.R. Lishman is Lecturer in the Department of Computing Science at the University of Aberdeen.

O.D. Macrae-Gibson is Honorary Reader in the Department of English and Honorary Research Fellow in the Department of Computing Science at the University of Aberdeen.

David Megginson is Assistant Professor in the Department of English at the University of Ottawa.

Douglas Moffat is Associate Editor for the *Middle English Dictionary* at Ann Arbor, Michigan.

Geoffrey Russom is Nicholas Brown Professor of Oratory and Belles Lettres, and pro tem Chair of the Department of English at Brown University.

Brian Shaw is Lecturer in the Department of English and the Faculty of Part-Time and Continuing Education at the University of Western Ontario.

T.A. Shippey is Professor in the Department of English at Saint Louis University.

Eric Gerald Stanley is Rawlinson and Bosworth Professor Emeritus of Anglo-Saxon in the University of Oxford and Emeritus Fellow of Pembroke College, Oxford.

M.J. Toswell is Assistant Professor in the Department of English at the University of Western Ontario.